THE BOLLINGEN SERIES VII

HERBERT FRIEDMANN

The Symbolic Goldfinch

ITS HISTORY AND SIGNIFICANCE
IN EUROPEAN DEVOTIONAL ART

157 ILLUSTRATIONS

THE BOLLINGEN SERIES VII

PANTHEON BOOKS

Manufactured in U.S.A.
Printed by S. A. Jacobs, The Golden Eagle Press
Halftones by The Beck Engraving Company

TO
TWO KARENS
AND THE MEMORY
OF A THIRD

Foreword and Acknowledgments

THIS STUDY of the occurrence, symbolism, and art historical significance of the goldfinch in European devotional art began when I first recognized the bird in some dozen or more Italian Renaissance paintings in the Samuel H. Kress Collection, now in the National Gallery of Art, Washington. By force of circumstances the work has had to be done in odd moments and spare time, chiefly evenings and Sundays, and because of this intermittent method, it has taken longer than would otherwise have been necessary. In the past two and a half years, I have combed large segments of the literature for goldfinch material — the major journals, monographs, catalogues of museums and of temporary exhibitions, even of sales; and the various many-volumed encyclopedic histories by authors like Venturi, van Marle, Friedländer, Post, and others. The paintings in the National Gallery of Art, Washington, the Walters Art Gallery, Baltimore, the Museum of Fine Arts, Philadelphia, the Metropolitan Museum and the Bache Collection, New York; the Museum of Fine Arts and the Gardner Museum, Fenway Court, Boston, and the Fogg Museum, Cambridge, have been examined and notes made directly for the present study; the magnificent photo-

[ix]

Foreword and Acknowledgments

graphic resources of the Frick Art Reference Library and the Dumbarton Oaks Research Library, Harvard University (including a set of the Princeton Index of Early Christian Art) and the Richter Archives in the National Gallery of Art, have been generously made available to me. The materials thereby collected do not pretend to be exhaustive but it is felt that they do cover the entire range, in meaning, in time and in geography, of the use of the goldfinch as an accessory element in European devotional art.

The interpretation of this material and the researches into its symbolic meanings have involved countless hours, chiefly evenings, of work in the Library of Congress and the library of the National Collection of Fine Arts.

Many kind friends have helped with suggestions, criticisms, or material. Mr. Charles P. Parkhurst, Jr., and Dr. Hanns Swarzenski, both of the National Gallery of Art, Dr. Richard Offner of New York University, and Dr. Edgar Wind of the University of Chicago, read over most of the manuscript and their comments have been truly helpful and are deeply appreciated. Mr. John Walker, Chief Curator of the National Gallery, has taken a kind interest in the progress of my studies, which has meant a great deal to me, and also has given me the benefit of his advice on specific points brought to him. To Mr. David E. Finley, Director, and Mr. Macgill James, Assistant Director, of the National Gallery, I am indebted for many courtesies and for assistance in procuring some of the illustrations for the present work. Mr. Jeremiah O'Connor, Curator

[x]

Foreword and Acknowledgments

of the Corcoran Art Gallery, has given me access to the library of that institution and has called to my attention a few paintings pertinent to my study. For permission to examine possible goldfinches in paintings in their storage vaults, I am indebted to the officials of the Walters Art Gallery, Baltimore, and to Mr. Henri Marceaux, Curator of the Johnson Collection, Fine Arts Museum, Philadelphia.

Mrs. Leila F. Clark, librarian of the Smithsonian Institution, has "run down" one or two particularly obscure and incomplete references in literature for me, and Mrs. Nathalie Scheffer of the Dumbarton Oaks Research Library has kindly made some translations for me from the Russian literature. Dr. Alexander Pogo, of the History of Science Society and the Carnegie Institution, has kindly looked up certain literary desiderata in the Widener Library at Harvard University, while Dr. W. W. Francis of McGill University has had rare items in the Osler Library photostated for me. Dr. Erwin Panofsky, of the Institute for Advanced Studies, at Princeton University, contributed a number of suggestions and references, which are here gratefully acknowledged. Dr. Henry E. Sigerist of the Institute of the History of Medicine, Johns Hopkins University, has aided me with valued comments on Medieval and Renaissance plague literature which bears somewhat, even though in a negative way, on one aspect of the goldfinch problem. Miss Elizabeth Mongan of the Alverthorpe Gallery, recently appointed to the staff of the National Gallery of Art, has given me suggestive clues and references in her special field of the graphic arts. Dr. Charles de Tolnay of the Institute for Advanced Studies, at Princeton University, has read the final chapter and given me the benefit of his great store of data on Michelangelo. Monsignor John M. Cooper, of the Catholic University of America, has kindly answered some questions bearing on Catholic theological interpretations.

For photographs of works of art pertinent to my studies, I am indebted to private owners of pictures such as Mrs. Richard M. Hurd (through the O'Toole Galleries), Mr. Robert Lehman, Mrs. Harold I. Pratt, and the late Mr. Percy S. Straus, and to a number of the leading dealers among whom may be mentioned Duveen Brothers, M. Knoedler and Company, Lilienfeld Galleries, and Georges Wildenstein. The following public institutions have also permitted me the use of photographs of paintings in their collections: Baltimore — Walters Art Gallery; Boston — Museum of Fine Arts, and the Gardner Museum, Fenway Court; Cambridge — Fogg Museum, Harvard University; Chicago — Art Institute; Detroit — Art Institute; Philadelphia — Johnson Collection, Fine Arts Museum; New Haven — Yale University Art Gallery; New York — Metropolitan Museum of Art, and New York Historical Society; San Diego — Fine Arts Museum; Toledo-Art Museum; Washington — National Gallery of Art; and Worcester — Worcester Art Museum. A special grant to cover the expenses involved in bringing together these and other photographs, some of which had to be made especially for this study, was given me by the American Philosophical Society, Phila-

Foreword and Acknowledgments

delphia, without whose generous support the present report would have been much poorer.

This study would never have been started, let alone brought to its present degree of completion, but for the magnificent collection assembled and given to the American nation by Mr. Samuel H. Kress. It supplied the original impetus as well as a sizable nucleus of the material. If this publication serves to enlarge our understanding of even a small aspect of our artistic heritage, the credit for it belongs in large part to the great benefactors of our public galleries. Less than a lifetime ago, a study of the present sort could not have been made in America. With the chaos existing, and likely to continue for some time, in Europe, it is not impossible that work of this kind may continue to be pursued here more than in the homelands of the art involved. If that should come to pass, the importance of our art collections, brought into being almost wholly by private individuals and subsequently given to the public, will assume ever greater proportions, and our indebtedness to their donors will increase accordingly.

Contents

Contents

[xv]

List of Plates

[xvii]

List of Plates

List of Plates

List of Plates

[xx]

List of Plates

[xxi]

List of Plates

List of Plates

List of Plates

[xxiv]

List of Plates

[XXV]

List of Plates

THE GOLDFINCH IN UMBRIAN ART

UMBRIAN GONFALONES OR PLAGUE BANNERS

THE GOLDFINCH IN BOLOGNESE AND
FERRARESE ART

[xxvi]

List of Plates

[xxvii]

List of Plates

[xxviii]

List of Plates

THE SYMBOLIC GOLDFINCH

Chapter I. Introduction

IN the great number of devotional paintings produced, largely in Italy, but also in Bohemia, Bavaria, the Rhineland, France, England, the Low Countries, Spain, and even Russia, between the latter part of the Middle Ages and the late Baroque, probably few accessory symbols occur with greater frequency than the figure of a small bird. Of the literally hundreds of cases of this sort wherein the birds are definitely identifiable to species, approximately seventy-five to eighty per cent are of one kind, the goldfinch. (This, of course, is not counting the special case of the white dove which stands for the Holy Spirit). The goldfinch, one of the brightest plumaged of the small, common, widely distributed birds of Europe, obviously lent itself readily as a symbol because it was as well known to the town dwellers as to the country folk, for it had long been a favorite household pet. Its role in the household was not exactly that of a common cage bird such as the canary is today, but more of that of an animate plaything for the children. Children were often given a live bird on a long string, and would amuse themselves by letting it fly about, holding firmly to the other end of the tether to prevent its escaping. In his study of "Dante and the Animal Kingdom" (1902, p. 230) Holbrook, quoting from the great poet (*Conv.* iv, xii, 161-167) writes that, ". . . children of Dante's time . . . seem, after attaining to an apple, and just before rising to the wish for fine apparel, to have longed for a little bird." What was true for Italy was true for other lands as well. The birds became tame quite readily and seemed not to mind familiar handling. As a matter of interest it may be noted that a number of portraits of children have come down to us in which the child is playing with a tethered goldfinch. Examples, to mention but a few, are Bronzino's portrait of Don Garcia de' Medici in the Uffizi[1] (plate 1), Titian's group portrait of the children of King Ferdinand I in the collection of Lord Desborough, Panshanger, England, Van Dyke's "Child with a Bird," in the Kaiser Friedrich Museum, Berlin, and Rubens' painting of

[*1*]

his two sons in the Liechtenstein Gallery in Vienna. A similar example with, however, not a goldfinch, but another favorite, but less frequent, pet bird, the greenfinch, is Alessandro Allori's portrait of a young boy, in the National Gallery of Art, Washington (plate 2).

Further evidence of the familiarity and affection with which the goldfinch was regarded is to be found in the literature of French art of the thirteenth and fourteenth centuries. Thus, Martin,[2] in discussing a fifteenth century manuscript illumination, writes that of all birds, the French artists loved to depict especially the goldfinch, the most cherished bird of France during the Middle Ages and the most brilliant of all the avifauna of the country, and that it was always the goldfinch that was intentionally given the place of honor in these paintings. In a later passage (p. 89) in his description of the Missel des Evêques de Paris, begun by Jacques du Châtelier, 1427-1438, which contains many birds, he points out that included among them is a goldfinch, ". . . beloved of the Parisian painters, and always given a place of honor."

As we shall see, later on in this account, the goldfinch was connected in the popular mind with an augur of a supernatural type in connection with disease, and to some extent with that dread scourge of the late Middle Ages and early Renaissance, the plague. This, together with its purely avian attractive qualities, not only possibly served to increase its popularity as a household figure, but also (and this is important for its role as a symbol in art) made it even more widely and favorably known to the people of all the art producing parts of Europe. Therefore it could, when adopted into art, more readily serve to convey its symbolic message than if it were a strange thing needing explanation to be intelligible in itself.[3]

Just when the goldfinch was first introduced into devotional art is difficult to say because in the late Middle Ages sculpture forged ahead earlier than painting and the first small bird symbols were in uncolored sculpture (either originally uncolored, or since divested of their original polychromy) and are therefore not clearly identifiable as to species. Even their size and shape are not too diagnostic as their carvers were not interested in birds as such, but merely in symbols in bird form. Without anticipating too much of the discussion of the mystical content of the goldfinch icon, gone into in detail later in another chapter, it may be said that the aviform figure of the human soul goes back not only to the earliest of Christian catacomb decorations but even to the hieroglyphics of ancient Egypt. But in its application to the devotional art of Christianity this winged "soul" attained fresh transformations, as Vloberg says in his discursive book on the Madonna and Child in French Art,[4] "... nourished by the living water of the unique life, and enervated by the mystic wine. It is especially the glorious dove, mounting in the sky, disengaged from the earth, the pure freedom of the immaterial..."

Early in the fourteenth century, especially in France, carved figures of the Virgin and Child with a small bird were produced in enormous numbers. As Vloberg rightly says, it is not only impossible to count them, but no careful critic could feel that he had not omitted some important examples, either in stone, in marble, in ivory, in embroidery, or in colored glass, no matter how extensive a list he had compiled. This great production of icons was rather sudden but must have sprung from earlier figures of similar nature, which, by virtue of wholly external conditioning factors (such as the plague with its concomitant rise of pietistic art) suddenly became very popular. The motif of the small bird held in the hands of the Christ Child may be traced back at least to the seventh decade of the thirteenth century when it began to appear in French sculpture and in Italian painting. It emerged as a vigorous artistic trend at the end of the century, and spread with great rapidity throughout the art producing countries of Europe. Several lines of evidence, each in itself not wholly conclusive, suggest a French locus of origin. For one thing, the percentage of French devotional images containing the motif was far greater at an earlier date than was the relative percentage of Italian pictures of similar subjects in which the bird was included. Sculpture developed earlier than did painting at the close of the Middle Ages and the latter art borrowed extensively, not only in its style, but also in its iconography from the former, more advanced field. It is significant that the small bird motif does not appear in early, pre-Renaissance Italian sculpture, and it may be inferred that its later extensive use in Italian devotional paintings was based on ideas gathered from French Gothic carvings. Furthermore, the surprising appearance of the motif in a late thirteenth century English manuscript illumination (in this case a wholly identifiable goldfinch) indicates the early spread of the influence of French iconic usage. This particular case, which happens to be the only English usage of the icon found in the course of the present study, is close in feeling and in style to the work of the miniaturists of the school of Paris, which is what we should expect from its iconography.

It has been recorded in literature that considerable numbers of French Gothic sculptures were brought to Italy at a very early date and helped to form the styles that developed in such centers as Pisa, Siena, Lucca, and Florence. The popularity of the "small bird motif," examples of which were probably among the pieces so brought to Italy, thereby spread from northern France to what was destined to become the greatest art producing country in Europe. Later, from these two centers, northern France and central Italy, the use of the icon spread to Spain, to Flanders, to Westphalia, Bavaria, Bohemia, and even to Russia. We must remember, when we say "spread" that there is very little difference in antiquity for the icon in France and in Italy. Actually what difference there is, as far as the use of recognizable goldfinches as the "small birds" is concerned, is on the Italian side. In France the motif was almost entirely confined to small sculptures, and it never became a conspicuous feature of French, as it did of Italian, painting. In Italy the icon was used extensively in sculpture as well as in painting, but far more frequently in the latter. The earliest definitely identifiable goldfinches I have found in devotional pictures are in two Italian paintings and in the East English manuscript illumination already mentioned, the Italian paintings being the oldest of the three. The small birds in the French sculptures are today largely unidentifiable. Some were originally of uncolored stone or alabaster; others that may have had telltale polychromy have long since lost it and have been reduced to undiagnostic monochromy. By far the greatest bulk of the goldfinches (or other small birds) in devotional art are to be found in works produced in Italy. It may be thought that this is merely due to the fact that Italy was the greatest producer of religious art in Europe, but the ratio of Italian to nonItalian "bird-bearing" paintings is entirely out of proportion to the relative artistic output of the countries involved. The Italian pictures outnumber all the rest combined by more than ten to one.

In the present study are amassed data on nearly five hundred (actually 486) devotional paintings containing goldfinches. While by no means exhaustive, this material furnishes a sufficient and representative sampling to give an accurate conception of the range in time and geography of the use of this symbol, and also of the type of paintings (subject matter) in which it occurs. The following facts concerning its distribution and occurrence are presented in advance of an analysis of its symbolic content, and are mere summaries of the material studied.

The devotional pictures in which goldfinches occur are either simple two-figure groups of the Madonna and Child, either of the formal, traditional, enthroned type, or of the more humanized, more intimate, ground-seated type (the so-called "Madonna of Humility") or they are more elaborate multiple figured compositions. These may be repetitions of the two-figured Madonna and Child type with one or more members of the Holy Family or with one or more attendant saints or angels; they may be the rather special three-figured group of the Madonna and Child and Infant St. John; they may be Nativities of any degree of simplicity or complexity; they may be Adorations of the Shepherds or of the Magi; they may be representations of the Mystic Marriage or of the Coronation of St. Catherine, or of the Rest on the Flight into Egypt (a special case of the Holy Family picture). Symbolic goldfinches have not been found in any devotional pictures in which Christ is depicted (or inferred) as older than a small child.[5] Very occasionally goldfinches occur in pictures of the Annunciation, but these are not typical. As a matter of fact, while the theme is one of the most frequently painted in religious art, only three such pictures have been found containing the goldfinch. Two of these are by the same artist — Lazzaro Bastiani (one in Klosterneuburg, Austria, and one in the Museo Civico, Venice), and both have a multiplicity of bird forms in them.[6] The one in Venice contains a guinea fowl as well as a goldfinch; the one at Klosterneuburg contains in addition to a goldfinch, a guinea fowl, and a parrot, as well as a stag and a snake. Bastiani, like so many north Italians, was probably interested in natural history and indulged his fancy in these paintings.[7] The other, also Venetian, and also full of birds, is by Carpaccio (Venice, Cà d'Oro). Aside from all this, it may be noted that goldfinches were inserted occasionally in pictures of individual saints or other personages connected with one or more of the symbolic meanings of the bird.

Of 486 paintings of the types here included, containing goldfinches, over 450 are Madonna and Child groups with or without attendant saints, angels, cherubs, or donors: of these, almost half are of the Madonna and

Child alone, while in a little more than that there are various other person-ages in attendance. In some cases it is difficult to tell whether a picture of the two-figured type may not originally have been a central panel of a polyptych, since dismembered, and may originally have been accompanied by attendant figures. However, the panel, in such a case, is treated as a picture of itself. It is a matter of no great moment at best, as the symbolism of the bird appears, in most cases, to bear no particular relation to the identity of the attendant figures when any such are present.

These 486 devotional pictures containing the goldfinch are attributed to 254 artists,[8] of whom 214 are Italian, 10 are Germanic (includes German, Bohemian, and Austrian), 7 are Flemish, 16 are Spanish, 3 are French, 1 is English, 1 Russian, 1 Dutch and 1 a Portuguese who worked under Italian influence in Italy, Alvaro de Pirez de Evora, a Portuguese who came to Italy at the beginning of the fifteenth century and worked under the influence of Martino di Bartolommeo. None of the seventeenth century Dutchmen seem to have used the goldfinch symbol, although one of them, Karel Fabritius, singled it out for what practically amounts to a bird portrait (The Hague, Mauritshuis).

Before attempting to trace in detail the history and occurrence of the goldfinch motif in the various schools, countries, and centuries of its usage, we may discuss its symbolic content, its allegorical significance, as this is, after all, the reason for its appearance in devotional art. While it seems highly probable that the original thought behind the introduction of the small bird motif was part of the desire to give to representations of the Christ Child some of the attributes of a child, this in itself would not have been enough to permit such an innovation. The fact that the small bird was already a well established icon of suitable symbolic content was what made such an attempt permissable and successful.

Chapter II. The Symbolism of the Goldfinch

THE symbolic meanings of the goldfinch are both of a special and of a more general sort. By the former is meant those significances restricted to the goldfinch; by the latter those connotations shared by it with other birds. It seems that the earliest meanings are those expressable equally by any or all small birds while the more restricted implications were added subsequently and tend to apply to the goldfinch in particular. When it is said that originally all small birds regardless of species, were equally usable in this connection it should be remembered that to some extent this may be a subsequent generalization due to our inability to identify with certainty the early crudely carved or graven avian images.

The early, relatively non-specifically restricted meanings associated with the goldfinch are as follows:

1. The goldfinch (or other small bird) represents the Soul as opposed to the Body, the spiritual in contrast to the earthly part. The soul being the loftier, more aspiring part was early connected with the idea of being winged and came to be pictorialized in the form of a bird, or at least in a form approximating that of a bird. Such icons appear to derive from the oldest of catacomb decorations, and may even go back to Egyptian hieroglyphics. This is the interpretation stressed by several writers, of whom we may mention in particular Yrjö Hirn, who, in his learned book "The Sacred Shrine. A Study of the Poetry and Art of the Catholic Church," 1912, p. 373, so disposes of the motif of the little bird. St. Ambrose explains the two sparrows of the Gospel as signifying the Body and the Soul "for both are lifted up to God by spiritual wings."

2. The goldfinch symbolizes Resurrection. This meaning is perhaps more intimately connected with the barn swallow than with any other single species of bird but is shared in by the goldfinch, the linnet, and

by other forms as well. In the thirteenth and fourteenth centuries when interest in the apocryphal books of the Bible flourished so greatly, artists were quick to seize upon the aesthetic possibilities involved in the various legends thereby made known. One of these, the "Pseudo-Matthew Legend," was that of the Christ Child playing with toy or clay birds which His companions brought to Him, and which He miraculously brought to life.[1] This bringing to life quickly came to stand for the idea of Resurrection. The swallow, long considered as a sign of spring, of the rebirth of the year, was assumed to hibernate in the mud through the winter and then become revitalized with the advent of warm weather. The similarity between the idea of the dormant mud-encrusted swallow and the clay bird is obvious. Its connection with the Resurrection theme (and thereby with Christ) led to its being called in parts of Germany the "Madonna Bird."[2] Next to the goldfinch we find that the barn swallow is the bird most frequently depicted in early paintings of the Madonna and Child. As an example in point we may mention the picture by Banchi in the Kress Collection in the National Gallery of Art, Washington (plate 54). Other artists who represented barn swallows in similar compositions include Sienese masters such as Giovanni di Paolo, Neroccio, and Pietro Lorenzetti, Umbrians like Pinturicchio, Florentines such as Rossello di Jacopo Franchi (in at least 10 pictures!) and even the less mystically inclined Venetians such as Giovanni Bellini. A bit of negative evidence bearing on the Resurrection symbol lies in the fact that the goldfinch (or the barn swallow or other substitute form) does not appear to have been introduced into any paintings of the Resurrection. When the event itself was treated in a wholly obvious fashion it was apparently deemed unnecessary to include a symbolic reference to it as well.[3]

Associated with the theme of Resurrection, after death, but in a minor sense, is the idea of recovery after serious illness, especially the plague. This, however, is a later meaning, almost wholly restricted to the goldfinch, and is treated below in its proper place. Immediately united with the theme of Resurrection, however, is the matter of Redemption, and then that of Immortality, towards which Resurrection is the great first step. The phoenix and the peacock are the birds usually used to symbolize Immortality; the goldfinch, as far as I know, has not been so used, except insofar as the idea is implicit in the Resurrection theme.[4]

3. The goldfinch (and certain other small birds, such as the robin and the bullfinch) symbolizes Sacrifice and especially, the Passion. Apparently the presence of even a spot of red in the plumage was sufficient to serve to connect any small bird with the theme of sacrifice and of martyrdom. This was based on the early legend to the effect that while Christ was carrying the cross on the way to Calvary, a little bird fluttered down to His head and pulled out a thorn that was rankling in His brow. The sacred blood tinged the feathers of the little creature, who has worn the mark ever since.[5]

In his study of the manuscript of the Greek Physiologus in the library at Smyrna, Strzygowski[6] has pointed out that a representation of Christ on the cross appears in four places, one of which is in the chapter on the *charadrius,* a mystical healing bird. The motive for this usage of the illustration is to convey the thought that Christ (and through Him, mankind) would recover on the cross. In an earlier page in the same work, the *charadrius* is interpreted as equivalent to Christ. This refers directly to the Crucifixion, in which the *charadrius* is the symbol of the redemption that the human race thereby achieved from its sins and illnesses. Strzygowski further describes an illustration in the Physiologus (missing in the Smyrna version) of a bed chamber in the style of the high Renaissance, with two beds, in one of which lies a patient, and a *charadrius* which at one time looks at the sufferer and at another time turns its head away. It may be mentioned at this point, as an interesting side light on the use of the bird in art, that although the *charadrius,* or its later transidentification into the goldfinch, is thus intimately connected with the theme of the Crucifixion (also as a symbol of Sacrifice and of Resurrection) it does not occur in any representation of Christ on the cross as far as I have been able to ascertain.

4. The Goldfinch may symbolize Death. We have just seen that the goldfinch is closely linked to the theme of the Crucifixion, which, while a very special case, is nevertheless, a form of Death. The thought that the bird may have a more general Death symbolism derives from the following sources, which are, admittedly, only suggestive. Firstly, we have a bit of evidence in the writings of Leonardo da Vinci. In one passage in his notebooks he writes that it is said of the goldfinch that if its young are imprisoned it will carry spurge to them, preferring to see them dead than alive without liberty. Spurge is a plant with supposedly poisonous juices.

From this it would seem that the bird was connected with the concept of a death bringer. Secondly, inasmuch as the goldfinch seems to have combined in itself the meanings inherent in the other bird symbols held by the Christ Child or by His mother, it may be recalled that in an enamel triptych made in France in the second half of the fifteenth century by the so-called "Master of the Orléans Triptych" (Walters Art Gallery, Baltimore, and in two other versions, one in the Victoria and Albert Museum, London, and one in the Musée des Arts Décoratifs, Paris) the Virgin is holding a completely black bird in her right hand; the Infant Jesus puts His right index finger to its bill. Black is a very widespread and ancient symbol of Death and Mourning; a black bird would then be a Bird of Death — an omen of coming Death. It is something of this sort of symbolic meaning that de Tolnay assumes in his interpretation of the retreat of the Christ Child from the small bird offered Him by the little Baptist in Michelangelo's marble relief (Burlington House, London).[7]

The sophistication of the Renaissance often led to very diverse bipolarity of meanings in one and the same symbol; it may be that we have such a case here where the goldfinch stands for the immortal soul and also for death. It is possible that physical death may have been looked upon as the beginning of the thereby freed soul's immortality.

The later, more specifically restricted connotations of the goldfinch are the following:

1. AS AN AUGUR IN TIME OF DISEASE (and particularly, the Plague).

This particular aspect of the goldfinch problem is of unusual complexity in that the basic legend behind it is by no means definitely or continuously restricted to the goldfinch. As a matter of fact, the legend of a bird with miraculous curative powers was already a well established and respectably hoary part of the superstitions that passed for natural history in medieval Europe before anyone pronounced the bird involved to be a goldfinch. The legend is clearly traceable directly to classical sources, to a bird called KARADRIOS (charadrius). Just when the goldfinch came to be identified with this fabulous bird is not wholly clear but that it was not later than the latter part of the thirteenth century is fairly demonstrable. Because of the involved history of the legend, with its confusing variety of ornithological identifications, it may be simpler to present it in its proper historical chronology, rather than trace it backwards from its Quattrocento or Trecento connotations through the centuries (and identifications) to its classic roots. In other words, the order of presentation is the opposite of that in which the stages were unravelled in the course of the present study.

As far back as the sixth century B. C. the Ionian writer Hipponax[8] expressed the belief (not apparently new with him) that jaundice was transferable to the "yellow" plover (probably the golden plover, *Charadrius apricarius* of ornithologists). In order to rid a jaundiced patient of his illness it was only necessary to have him look at a plover; the illness then went over to the bird, as one could see as the bird closed its eyes. Arndt[9] has stated in this connection as indicative of the widespread knowledge of this legend among the Greeks, that Aristophanes in his play "The Birds" has the bird sellers in the markets of Athens carefully cloak their birds so that prospective buyers might not be cured before the sales were consummated. Unfortunately for this bit of evidence I must admit that careful perusal of two different translations of "The Birds" has failed to reveal any mention of this incident. I can only assume that perhaps it was a touch added by some erudite producer in giving a stage presentation of the play, or that the translations checked by me were incomplete. However, we have an independent but similar piece of corroborative evidence in Gesner.[10] This pioneer among natural history compilers, referring to Euphronius,[11] relates that the plover absorbs the jaundice when looking at, and being looked at by, a sick man and that the effect is so rapid and so potent that the bird dealers hide this bird from their customers until the latter have paid, lest they be cured in advance by the bird's glance. An essentially similar account is given by St. Jerome in his comments on Aelian as related by Aldrovandus.[12]

In his valuable account of the charadrius legend, Eder,[13] quoting Lauchert,[14] cites Aelian, Pliny, and Plutarch as sources from which the legend may have come into medieval European culture. Aelian (Nat. Anim., xvii, 13) mentions the curative effects of looking at, and being looked at by, the charadrius in cases of jaundice. Pliny (xxx, c., 11.94) reports the same of a bird called IKTEROS (also the Greek word for jaundice), or in Latin, Galgulus or Galbulus; Plutarch (Sympos. probl. v. 7, c., 2, 8) notes that the bird does not turn away its eyes from the sick man because of refusal to exercise its powers, but because it cannot endure the sick man's glance. This last seems significant as the starting point of a new meaning infused into the old legend, a matter of judgment of the patient by the bird, which, as we shall see, developed into a moralizing symbol in its Christian application. Thus, Eder writes that, ". . . the charadrius indicates whether the illness of a man to whose bedside he is brought is to be fatal or not. In the first eventuality the bird turns away, but if the patient is going to recover, the bird looks at him and draws out the disease to itself. Thus too did the Savior turn His countenance from the Jews because of their lack of faith, and came to the heathen, took their infirmities upon Himself and bore their diseases, and made them healthy.

"According to this account the charadrius symbolizes Redemption, with special reference to the summoning of the Gentiles. Another interpretation is found in the Waldensian Physiologus, where its characteristics are related to the individual sinner, who is lost when Christ forsakes him, but saved when He looks upon him."

As indicative of the wide geographic spread of the charadrius legend in its "pre-goldfinch" days, it may be pointed out that it is mentioned in a poem by "Freidank," a pseudonymous medieval German bard, and is alluded to in a religious poem, "El Sacrificio de la Misa," by Gonzalo de Berceo, a thirteenth century Spanish poet.[15] Furthermore it may be noted that in his compendium of medieval German troubadour songs, von der Hagen[16] quotes one of Meissner's poems (vol. 3, p. 92 f.) ". . . Like this bird so does Christ: When a sick man is about to die in sin, he is angry with him and turns away his glance, and the man is lost. But if the man wants to be saved, then is God's mercy so great that his suffering is alleviated" (p. 198). Another poem dealing with the charadrius is to be found in this compilation — Boppe (vol. 2, p. 378, l. 5) in one passage relates the story of the charadrius in a rather novel way, mentioning that it bears in its right leg a stone which has healing properties for the eyes (in the Physiologus the healing power is ascribed to its excrement). He wants this stone for the gentry, that they may touch their eyes with it, and with their increased powers of vision may distinguish between those worthy of their gifts and those unworthy, but for himself he wants the bird's glance, so that by turning it from the miserly rich he might bring about their destruction, while bestowing it among the kindly he might ensure the permanence of their good fortune.

In France we find many proofs of the currency of the charadrius legend. To take but a single instance from the thirteenth century; in the Cathedral of Lyons there is a stained glass window representing a rather large bird in the act of absorbing the illness from a patient, with the caption "Cladrius" obviously a variant of Charadrius (plate 5).

Still farther to the west, in England, we have ample traces of the legend, of which we may mention but a couple. In the Pierpont Morgan Library in New York, an illuminated manuscript bestiary made near Lincoln in the second half of the twelfth century (P.M. Library Ms. 8) shows a "Calendar Predicting a Sick Man's Recovery."[17] Furthermore, in his study of the symbolic use of animal forms in English Church architecture,[18] Collins notes that in the bestiaries the charadrius is often drawn like a white thrush or plover but in some instances it is represented as a huge bird with curly feathers and a long neck as in the mutilated bestiary in the British Museum (Vat. D. 1). In the sculpture at Alne (which looks rather like a raven pecking out the eyes of a dead man) the inscription "Caladrius" shows what the interpretation must be. Collins raises the interesting question as to the possible derivation of the Charadrius legend from such Biblical passages as Ezekiel VII 22 and Psalms lxxx 7. These passages are as follows:

Ezekiel VII 22. "My face will I turn also from them, and they shall pollute my secret *place*: for the robbers shall enter into it, and defile it." Psalms lxxx 7. "Turn us again, O God of hosts, and cause thy face to shine and we shall be saved."

These passages have to do, respectively, with pollution and with restoration, sin and redemption. I cannot help but feel that the possible connection with the charadrius is rather remote, and can find no illustration of either in art.

The most important medieval source, because of its ecclesiastical authority is the *Speculum Ecclesiae* of Honorius of Autun. This book of sermons, dating from the first half of the twelfth century, definitely describes the charadrius as a pure white bird (not like the goldfinch in this regard!) but is cited as the first account of the miraculous powers of the goldfinch by Kondakov and other students of Byzantine and early Russian icon painting.[19]

It should be noted in this connection that the legend of the charadrius and the legend of the eagle are the only ones used by Honorius in the sermon written for Ascension Day. The charadrius we are by now familiar with; the eagle legend is interpreted by Honorius as follows: "The eagle is of all creatures that which flies highest, and alone dares to gaze straight into the sun. When teaching his young ones to fly he first flies above them, then takes them up on his widely spread wings. Even so did Christ ascend into Heaven higher up than all the saints to His place on the right hand of the Father. He spreads over us the wings of His Cross, and carries [us] on His shoulders like lost sheep."

At the risk of interrupting the chain of thought followed in these pages it seems worthwhile to point out that in early western medieval works (such as the Lyons window, the Alne sculpture, and some of the English bestiaries) the charadrius is large, not too readily distinguishable from a raven or an eagle as compared with its representation as a smaller bird (goldfinch) in later French, Germanic, and in Italian pictorializations. Yet, in the work of the early Sienese sculptor, Tino da Camaino[20] we find that in two of his figures of the Madonna and Child (one in the Detroit Art Institute, and one in a private collection in Rome) the Child holds a very large, hawk-like bird which struggles and bites at His hands, a motif also present in one of the figures of Virtues on a tomb in Santa Maria Donna Regina. Tino's figures of the birds held by the falconers adorning some of his sepulchral monuments are not very different from those held by the Christ Child. While it does seem that the birds held by the falconers are meant to be merely their trained birds of the chase, and not symbolic creatures like the ones held by the Christ Child, one cannot help but wonder if they may not have some mystical significance even if only of a tenuous and indirect sort. With all his shortcomings Tino was not too poor an artist as not to be able to render more distinctly the differences between fierce birds of prey and the innocuous charadrius. If however, he (or his advisors) followed Honorius in connecting the legends of the eagle and of the charadrius as symbols dealing with the Ascension he might well have reduced both to a more or less common figure. Also it should be remembered that the charadrius itself was thought, as related by Bochart,[21] a seventeenth century French scholar, to be an eagle or falcon.[22] However, this digression concerning Tino leads only to speculation, and is beside our main point. Furthermore, I have seen none of the sculptures involved except in photographs, and there may actually be more difference than I know.

Before passing to those variants of the legend, and especially those documents, literary and artistic, that definitely bring the goldfinch into the picture, and especially because of the not too completely satisfactory chain of evidence linking these earliest goldfinches with what went before, it may be well to recall that the exact identification of the bird involved in the charadrius legend was a perplexing problem to many a writer of the past five centuries. This may help to explain how it was possible, in this state of comparative indecision, for a bird so completely at variance with the accepted description of the charadrius to come to be adopted as a substitute identification. Thus, in Tychsen's edition of the Syrian Physiologus[23] from a manuscript in the Vatican, a considerable part of chapter xv, "Concerning the Charadrius" is devoted to the arguments for and against various identifications of it. Tychsen begins with the mention of the charadrius in the Laws of Purification in Leviticus ". . . which Moses remembered as gleaming white with a most dazzling radiance (Lev. xi, 19, Deut. xiv, 18), nowhere marred by any other defiling color . . . ," and discusses many subsequent interpretations.

Von Hovorka[29] quotes Grimm as identifying the charadrius as the lark (Alauda). Von Hovorka rightly mentions, however, that Eder identifies the charadrius as the "triel," the stone curlew or thick-knees, *Oedicnemus* of ornithologists, and further states that in the Tyrol a belief that the crossbill (a sparrow with crossed tips to the mandible and maxilla; the genus *Loxia* of ornithologists), as an aid against jaundice is still prevalent. Eder (*cit. supra*) notes that Grimm calls the bird not charadrius but "galadrot" citing "galadrius" as a variant reading for charadrius and assumes this to be the calandra or lark.

Thompson[25] suggests that the charadrius is the stork; that in this legend we have to do with eastern tales of the stork. in Hebrew *chasad* (Lev. xi, 19; Deut. xiv, 18) arising from a confusion of names, *chasad* and *charad* being too much alike not to have been confounded.

The identifications proposed by various early writers for the charadrius include a plover, thick-knees or stone curlew, eagle, falcon, egret, stork, cockatoo, lark, dove, thrush, crossbill, and oriole! Surely with so wide a choice it should have been possible for still another bird to assume the mantle of the charadrius, changed as it was from its pagan prototype in the hands of medieval moralizers.

In 1322 Cecco d'Ascoli wrote an encyclopaedic poem in five books (the fifth unfinished) known as "Vita Acerba" or as merely "Acerba."[26] A miniature illustrating a XIVth Century manuscript of this work in the Medicean library in Florence[27] is said (by Kondakov) to show a father bringing a goldfinch to the bedside of his sick child, the mother stands behind, everybody is anxious to see if the bird will heal the child with its own eyes and they are rejoicing because the goldfinch looks at the child.

If true, this seems to be the earliest literary reference in Italy (at least as far as I have been able to ascertain) that definitely identifies the goldfinch (and at the same time the lark —"calandrinus") with the charadrius legend. However, this may not be the original source for this identification even for Italy as a goldfinch occurs in a painting of the Madonna and Child, by Deodato Orlandi (plate 127) signed and dated in 1306,[28] and in a still earlier, Dugento, panel by the so-called "Maestro della Maddalena" (Florence; Acton collection) (plate 33). In the latter work the Child holds a small bird in His left hand, while with His right one He reaches for a flower held by the Madonna. While the bird is not too well rendered, it is definitely a goldfinch, and is the earliest instance of its use in this connection that I know.[29] With regard to the picture, by Orlandi (Mrs. R. M. Hurd collection, New York) it should also be remembered that Deodato, a provincial Lucchesean artist, may not have had the disease augur symbolism in mind when he painted his panel. While Deodato was, by the town of his residence and by his training, a follower of the Berlinghieri, he was not simply this, but to some extent a pseudo-Sienese eclectic as well. This indicates a mental receptivity beyond that of a mere plodding provincial, which is borne out by his very early use of the then new goldfinch motif.

Unfortunately for the continuity of our discussion, I must raise a doubt as to whether the Florentine manuscript of the "Acerba" referred to really mentions the "cardellino" or goldfinch, and whether that was not a touch added, possibly inadvertently, by the Russian author Kondakov, from whose account Mrs. Scheffer's translation was made for me. Otherwise it must be assumed that the various printed editions of Ceccho's once famous and widely known work[30] vary in the illustrations and even in the text.

Thus, the only one that I have been able to consult (printed in 1516 by Marchio Sessa and Piero di Ravani Busono, "revised and amended and freed of many later errors, and transcribed from its ancient source") is in the Osler Medical Library at McGill University at Montreal. Dr. W. W. Francis, the scholarly librarian of this famous collection of books, has kindly had the pertinent parts photostated for me. In this edition the bird is called "chalandrello" (lark) and not "cardellino" (goldfinch) and it is healing a "donna" (woman) and not a child.[31]

Cecco moralizes in a somewhat different manner from Honorius, as the following translation of mine indicates.

Of the nature of the Chalandrello, Cap. xvii, Third Book, leaf 55 verso, last line and leaf 56 recto

> The chalandrello which is
> all white, is borne
> before him who is sick.
> Of what I tell you here
> you should miss none of it.
> If he is to die, he turns to his nest.
> If he is to save himself,
> he looks to the sick one.
> This creature shows its nature such.
> So too does this lady to whom he looks.
> From death to life, and in health
> she turns her gaze upon the soul
> involuntarily looks to see
> if, though she lives, it dies because
> she lives in sin.
> O how many traduce hope in this world
> because of evil deeds,
> forego redemption in this life,
> bearing death everywhere about.

The lark, calandrino or calandrello, seems to have "taken hold" very well in its "charadrius" role in Italy, although it does not figure to any extent in the art of that country. Thus, a century and a half later, Leonardo da Vinci, in his so-called "H" manuscript entitled "Fiore di Virtù," based on Cecco's "Acerba," repeats the legend,[32] but is careful to record it as something "which is related," not which is necessarily true or which Leonardo was willing to sponsor.[33]

An unquestionably identifiable goldfinch in an East-English miniature dating from the late thirteenth century is of interest here. This miniature from the Psalter of Robert de Lisle now in the British Museum (MS Arundel 83, II) shows the Christ Child sitting on His Mother's left knee, holding a goldfinch in His left hand. It is not possible to guess which particular symbolism is involved in this case, but the picture is of importance to our present study as establishing the advent of the goldfinch into extreme west European devotional art not later than the end of the thirteenth or the beginning of the fourteenth century.

On the other hand, a late persistence of the "pre-goldfinch" charadrius is exemplified in a woodcut of the Upper Rhenish school, dating from about 1460 representing the Madonna in a Garden (Lessing J. Rosenwald Collection; National Gallery of Art).

The fact that in the third quarter of the fourteenth century Konrad von Megenberg,[34] writing the earliest German book on natural history, gave wholly separate, in no way even slightly connected accounts of the calader (charadrius) and of the stieglitz (goldfinch) reveals that no transidentification of the former with or into the latter had taken place in Germany up to that time, or that if it had, it was not very generally accepted. This is significant when we consider the absence of the goldfinch icon from true Germanic painting until the following century (not in Bohemian art, however, where the Italian influence was felt much earlier) although the symbol had already great and long standing popularity in Italy.

However, we have already seen that the lark, "calandrello," was early identified with the charadrius. It is of interest to note, and most pertinent to our theme, that Konrad Gesner, in his "Icones Avium," published in Zurich in 1560, gives Alauda (lark) as one of the names for the goldfinch, showing that the connection had been established between these two.

One of the independent lines of evidence supporting the thesis that the goldfinch came to substitute for the charadrius lies in the fact that there are a considerable number of devotional paintings in which the birds held by the Christ Child can only be explained on the basis of this mystical "common denominator." We have already seen that the identifications proposed for the charadrius were very diverse, involving pure white birds such as white thrushes or plovers, spotted "plovers," hoopoes, cockatoos or paroquets, orioles, hawks, etc. Among pictures showing a white bird in the Child's hand we may mention the following:

1. A thirteenth century Florentine painting by a follower of Cimabue, sometimes identified with the so-called "Master of the Rucellai Madonna" (plate 7) in the Parish Church at Mosciano, shows a fairly sizable whitish bird,[35] large enough to be a dove, in the Virgin's left hand, which the Infant Saviour stretches out His hands to reach. The bird has no nimbus, a feature usually present in representations of the Dove of the Holy Spirit. As a matter of fact, I doubt if any early pictures (in their original condition) show the Dove without a nimbus. In other words, I doubt if the identifications of such unhaloed white birds current in literature as doves can be maintained without question. In representations of the Trinity or of the Annunciation, the bird is obviously the Dove of the Holy Spirit, but in early pictures of the Madonna and Child there is no valid reason for assuming this identification. In later pictures, done at a time when symbolism was kept less clearly in mind such vagaries not only were possible but actually were perpetrated.[36]

2. Another, later example is a painting of a Madonna and Child by Pietro de Saliba, (New York, Mrs. Morton H. Meinhard collection), dating from the latter part of the fifteenth century. In this work the Child is holding a small white bird the size of a goldfinch in His left hand. The bird certainly is not a dove and cannot have been intended as such; and may well be a "calandrello"; it has a curiously wrinkled, cloth-like appearance, at least in the reproduction.

3. A fifteenth century Spanish painting by an unknown member of the school of Evila (see p. 49) of the "Madonna and Child with St. Anne" shows a small white bird held on a long string by the Infant Jesus. This work is of interest in giving a greater geographic "spread" to the rendition of the charadrius in art.

4. An English "Madonna and Child" done about 1350, now in the Museum at Bergen, Norway.

Aside from these cases of pure white birds we may mention a few instances of other charadrius identifications.

The "spotted plover" is apparently the basis for the weird, and otherwise inexplicable bird held by the Christ Child in Lippo Vanni's "Madonna and Child with Angels" in the Gallery at Le Mans (plate 8).

The "ikteros" or "galbulus," or golden oriole is convincingly depicted held by the Holy Babe in Carlo Crivelli's triptych in the Brera, Milan (plate 9). From the purely artistic side it is surprising that this beautiful bird of golden yellow with black wings was not utilized more often in devotional art. Perhaps its relative rareness in many parts of Europe kept it from becoming a commonly kept household pet or a frequently used symbol.

The print of the "Madonna and Child in a Garden" done in the Upper Rhineland about 1460 (plate 3) is pertinent here as the bird is colored yellow. It may be a halting, hesitating attempt to use the oriole identification for the charadrius, whose medieval mystical albescence the artist was not able to wholly shake off.

Mention has already been made of instances where the bird held by the Child is a form of paroquet (Pinturicchio, van Eyck, etc.), and also where the bird is definitely hawk-like (Tino da Camaino).

In his historical writings on Russian icon painting Kondakov contributes material of the greatest interest and pertinence. In one place[37] he writes that, ". . . very popular in Florentine art was the representation of the Virgin holding the Christ Child with a goldfinch. This picture represents at the same time the play of the Child and also the preservation from illness because in ancient times the goldfinch was brought to sick children with the belief that the cheerful little bird had a 'lucky eye' and protected the patient from illness."[38]

Kondakov's statements are very definite as to the "widespread belief in the miraculous nature of the goldfinch in the western medieval church" but the evidence for his statements is nowhere produced in anything like the quantity or quality such sweeping assertions require. It is true that we have now traced the charadrius legend to the point where the goldfinch was superimposed onto it, but we have still to learn why the goldfinch should have been the particular bird so chosen more than any other. Kondakov's statements appear to be based on the fact that the goldfinch is the usual substitute for the charadrius in western European Renaissance and late Medieval art, rather than on the reasons why it became so.

To put the matter in a different way, it should be pointed out that if there were really a widespread belief in the miraculous nature of the goldfinch in the western medieval Church, there should be some mention of it in the various aspects of the literature that bear on this field. The fact remains that I have been completely unable to find anything beyond Kondakov's doubtful statement on Cecco d'Ascoli's "Acerba" and Richter's erroneous version of Leonardo's statement, quoted above, that definitely brings the goldfinch into the picture. I cannot help but admire Kondakov's acumen in seizing upon this slender shred of evidence but I also feel that the wording of his conclusion is far too generous for the meager data he had. It is, of course, possible that the Russian literature, which unfortunately is closed to me, offers some further material, but this is doubtful as the legend was supposed to have been chiefly a western European one. In the writings of the Dominican and Franciscan mystics, I have found no mention of the goldfinch. Even the compilation of de Gubernatis[39] includes no trace of any goldfinch legend. Hopf[40] likewise makes no mention of it.

Unfortunately for the conclusiveness of our study we must admit we have nothing in the way of documentary proof as to just where and when the goldfinch was first introduced as a Christianized charadrius substitute, but the following suggestion seems to be in agreement with all the known data, to simplify and to clarify the picture and to be borne out by outside evidence.

We have already had hints to the effect that the icon of a small bird in the Christ Child's hand entered Christian art very early, possibly first in northern France and spread thence to Italy.[41] The actual birds in these early French statuettes are not identifiable as they are in sculpture which was either uncolored to begin with, or has since lost its polychromy. That the idea of including a small bird in "Madonna and Child" paintings was taken over from its use in earlier and contemporary sculpture is in accord with the usual tendency for the less developed art to borrow in its infancy from its more advanced sister.

The Italians of the late Middle Ages and of the early Renaissance, to say nothing of their neighbors in other parts of Europe, were greatly addicted to playing with words. Puns and anagrams were looked upon as something not merely accidental but actually suggestive of kindred qualities in the objects represented by the words involved. Behind this tendency was a long and honored tradition. Did not the Church itself make use of anagrammatic symbols? The lark was called "calandria," "chalandrello" or "calandrino"; the goldfinch "cardellino," "cardino" or "cardarello." Surely "calandrello" and "cardellino" were too similar not to have frequently tempted the punsters and came to be ever more intimately connected in the popular mind with each such attempt.

Still another play on words may be pertinent. In early devotional images done under the influence of the Byzantine tradition, before the advent of the small bird motif, the Christ Child was frequently depicted as holding a scroll case in His hand. The goldfinch is therefore, to some extent, a replacement of the scroll, and to that degree may have some partial symbolic identification with it. The scroll contained a message; the small bird, too, in its symbolic usage, was the bearer of a message. The scroll, in Italian is *cartellino*, the goldfinch *cardellino*. While I have found no definite allusion to this similarity in Italian writings of the period, it would be very surprising if it had been allowed to pass unnoticed.

Not only do we have ample parallel usages of anagrams as a basis for transidentification of objects, but also, in this particular case, the fact that the anagram or the pun is in the Italian language helps to explain the fact that the goldfinch symbol in art is overwhelmingly an Italian one. Naturally puns and anagrams do not retain the essence of their character when translated and it follows that their suggestive effect is correspondingly lessened, if not destroyed, by such a process.

Lest we be accused of pushing one idea too far, we may now turn to other data bearing on our icon. Writers on manuscript illuminations and other miniatures of the thirteenth century stress the fact that the goldfinch was the most cherished bird, especially in France, during the Middle Ages, the one most frequently depicted by artists (not necessarily in religious themes) and the one always given the place of honor when several birds were introduced in the same illustration.[42] Aside from its great popularity as a pretty, brightly colored, easily tamed, companionable bird, it had the distinction of being of all birds the one most addicted to feeding on the seeds of the thistle. Its French name "chardonneret," its Italian name "cardellino," its German name "distelfink," are all of great antiquity and all attest to its connection in the popular mind with the thistle. The importance of this for our present iconographic problem lies in the fact that in France (and to a lesser extent elsewhere) there was an old belief dating at least from Carolingian times that the thistle, when properly prepared, had great medical properties in the treatment of many diseases. This belief gave rise to some of the forms of this otherwise lowly plant being called "Blessed Thistle," (*Carduus benedictus*), "Holy Thistle," even "Our Lady's Thistle" (*Carduus marianus*). In the XIVth Century the Order of the Thistle was founded in France (at Moulins, January 1, 1370) in honor of the Virgin[43] by Louis II (The Good) Duke of Bourbon on the occasion of the marriage of his daughter Anne.

In a sense parallel to this Order of the Thistle, at least from the standpoint of our present study, is the fact that towards the close of the Middle Ages there was founded the Order of the Calander Brothers (calander being the then current version of charadrius) whose duty it was not to let any member die without means for obtaining the grace of the Church, *i. e.*, to die without all means for redemption (obviously a reading of the legend of the calander, kaladrius, or charadrius). Until about a century ago the Kalanderhof in the Kalandergasse in Berlin remained as mute evidence of this former interest.[44]

Here then, on the one hand, was a familiar, beloved, friendly bird already well connected in the lay mind with the thistle, concerning which there was a widely known and popular therapeutic belief,[45] and on the other a not unrelated legend in need of a unifying, generally understandable and readily acceptable symbol. In the absence of definite proof I can only submit this as a possible contributing factor for the entry of the goldfinch into the charadrius legend. Whether this be tentatively accepted or not, it is only right to point out that our one definite fact about the appearance of the medieval charadrius is its pure white color, and this is certainly disregarded in the substitution of the goldfinch.

It should be remembered, however, that the lark, calandrello, is pale in color, but that two of the classical variants, IKTEROS and GALGULUS were golden yellow birds — probably the European oriole and that the original CHARADRIUS was the "yellow plover." The original classical version probably became known again to scholars with the humanistic revival of interest in the ancient classics.

On the other hand it may be recalled that in Oldenburg, according to Frazer[46] the goldfinch and turtle dove (a very pale, whitish dove) are interchangeable symbols to this day in the treatment of consumptive patients.[47] Another tangential but very pertinent bit of evidence is afforded by a fourteenth century painting by Simone Martini in the sacristy of San Agostino in Siena (plate 74). This work has to do with Beato Agostino Novello, with scenes from his legend. In the central panel the blessed Agostino is standing with a book in his hand and a small angel whispers in his ear. On either side are small trees, and on the trees on either side of him are two goldfinches (on the trees on his right there may even be a third goldfinch, but the photograph seen was not sufficiently clear to tell with certainty). Why all these goldfinches swarming about the figure of Agostino? Why the symbol and why its multiplicity? The answer obviously lies in the character and deeds of the man who is here being honored. Beato Agostino Novello was a Spaniard who came to Siena where he established hospitals for the care of victims of the plague.

With the advent of the epidemics of the bubonic plague, all other illnesses became secondary in importance, and there was a tendency to apply to the greater disease the amulets and portents previously used in connection with minor ailments wherever the symptoms showed the slightest or even no similarity in any of their details.[48]

Another bit of evidence helping to indicate the path by which the goldfinch came into the picture lies in the following fact. I am informed that the Hebrew tongue does not distinguish very clearly between thorns and thistles. This seems to connect, and in the medieval mind, may possibly have served to identify allegorically the thorns on the brow of Christ and the thistle. We have already seen that the goldfinch, among other birds, symbolized the Passion because of its red marks, supposedly from the blood of Christ from Whose brow it extracted a thorn.

There is still another fragment, purely suggestive in nature, to add to this discussion as to how the goldfinch came to "take on" the role of the mystical charadrius. The latter bird, although identified at times (as by Honorius of Autun) even with Christ Himself, had had no connection with devotional art until the ravages of the plague tended to bring the charadrius legend into the conceptual orbit of the artists working on devotional icons. The imminent danger of death during the epidemics, the hope for Divine aid against the dread disease, and, more fatalistically, the conviction that the next world was the only one in which safety was not only important but even still possible, all tended to bring pietistic art more and more intimately into the daily lives of the people. The introduction of the charadrius would not have been thinkable in the Middle Ages when the Church was wholly authoritarian and dogmatic, but became possible in the fourteenth century because of the changes brought by the attempts of the Franciscans to make religion appealing emotionally and of the Dominicans to make it intellectually convincing. The resulting tendency to humanize churchly concepts affected not only the religious atmosphere but also the art forms associated with it. Representations of sacred personages had to be naturalistically rendered; still symbolic iconic figures no longer satisfied the masses.

In the latter half of the thirteenth century religious art had already been humanized enough for artists to attempt to give a child's attributes to the representation of the Christ Child. Among these was the little aviform plaything. Thus, when the legend of the charadrius, bound up so closely as it was with one of the chief contemporary factors in the sudden expansion of devotional art, became included in the mass of guiding concepts bearing on the production of these icons, the artists found themselves faced with the fact that the Christ Child was already commonly depicted holding another bird — the goldfinch. To represent Him holding two birds was not only artistically unhappy, but also might have created the possibility of difficulty in determining the relative positions and importance of the two, and of confusion to the lay spectators not too well versed in their birds. It created a problem. It seems, looking back as best we can, that there would be a distinct advantage to be gained if the two could be merged. This, I believe (but cannot prove) caused a desire, even if not a wholly conscious one, to find a symbolic union whereby the already established pictorial element could serve both its original purpose and also that of the mystical disease augur.

Lest it seem far fetched to assume a mental bent or willingness to transpose and reidentify meanings with symbols, we may recall that the ". . . medieval man thought and felt in symbols, and the sequence of his thought moved as frequently from symbol to symbol as from fact to fact. . . ." [49] As Taylor has put it, there was a ". . . ceaseless sweep of allegory through men's minds. They felt and thought and dreamed in allegories; and also spent their dry ingenuity on allegorical constructions . . . the Middle Ages did not demand that allegory should have its feet planted on the earth, so long as its head nodded high among the clouds, or its sentiments wandered sweetly in fancy's gardens. . . ."

In a painting by Francesco di Antonio da Viterbo, the goldfinch is flying directly from the Child's hands to a kneeling donor. The Infant Saviour points towards the latter with both hands, indicating a directness and intentness of connection quite unusual in devotional pictures. There can hardly be any doubt that the bird is here the disease augur, the bird of healing, as otherwise there would be little reason for this intensity of direction.

Not infrequently in religious art we find artists using two symbols of similar import, each apparently intended to clarify and to support the other, in the event either one were not readily understandable by itself. In this connection it may be noted that in a number of pictures in which the Christ Child is holding a goldfinch He is also wearing a red coral amulet about His neck. The triptych (plate 112) by Allegretto Nuzi and The Master of The Fabriano Altarpiece (National Gallery of Art, Washington) is such an instance, and may serve to typify the others of like content. The red coral, it is true, was an amulet, not particularly against the plague, but against the Evil Eye. However, the contagious nature of the plague made it one of the most available misfortunes to be transmitted by the possessor of the Evil Eye, and the two became connected in the popular mind.

Another, and highly peculiar, example of this "reinforced" symbolism is afforded by Carlo Crivelli's exquisite little "Madonna and Child" in the Bache collection, New York. Here the Child holds a goldfinch in both hands, eyeing it somewhat furtively, while below to the Child's right on a balustrade at the bottom of the picture is a fly. The fly is a symbol of Beelzebub, the god of the Philistine city of Ekron. According to Wardle[50] the name Baal (or Beel) is a common title for a Semitic deity, particularly a local one, and is often compounded as a prefix with the name of the city where the particular deity was worshipped. Zebub appears in the Bible as a noun meaning flies (Isaiah VII, 18; Eccles. X, 1), from which it follows that the whole name Baalzebub or Beelzebub means "God of Flies," *i. e.*, the god who can bring or send away flies. "Pliny records in his "Natural History" that the inhabitants of Elis, in time of pestilence, cried to the "Disperser of Flies" and that as soon as sacrifice was offered to the deity the flies perished and the pestilence ceased. The epithet "Disperser of Flies" is attached in Greek literature to the names of Zeus and Hercules. Flies, like mice, were recognized in ancient times as bringers of disease, and it seems quite likely that a god who was able to drive away flies should be regarded as one who had power over disease. . . . As a god of healing Baalzebub may well have been supposed to have power over demons, since in Semitic thought diseases were regarded as inflicted by demons. . . ." As though to convey still further the disease repelling symbolism of the juxtaposition of the goldfinch and the fly, Crivelli has strung along the top of the picture some apples, symbol of death, and a gourd, the antidote for the apple, symbol of recovery and redemption.

In spite of the suggestive value of the material presented above, it is necessary to use great caution in attributing to the goldfinch too great an anti-plague symbolism. So many meanings are involved in the icon that we must ever be on guard against simplifying any given instances of its use. It is certainly significant, and not at all corroborative of its too extensive use as a symbolic plague augur, that the goldfinch seems to have had no particular connection in art with the figures of the two main patron saints of victims of the plague — Saint Sebastian and Saint Roch. It is true that the latter occurs relatively infrequently in Sienese, Florentine, and Umbrian painting, being more commonly depicted by artists of the Venetian and other northern Italian schools.

Being a personage of the latter part of the fourteenth and early part of the fifteenth centuries, St. Roch could not, of course, be expected to figure in the earlier and even the contemporary art of Italy.[51] By the time of his death and canonization, Sienese, Florentine, and Umbrian art were probably far too fixed in their content and usages of saintly figures to utilize an additional one to any great extent. This, however, does not hold in the case of Saint Sebastian. The explanation for the lack of any pictorial tradition connecting the goldfinch with this most frequently painted saint, lies, I think, not in the fact that the two were not compatible and related symbolically, but in the fact that Sebastian was already a customary, traditional figure in devotional art before the goldfinch came into the picture.[52]

The use of the goldfinch seems to have been given its first impetus with the attempt to humanize the hieratic Madonna and Child icon, developed under the influence of the Byzantine tradition. This was in keeping with the general Trecento tendency to give to the Christ Child a child's attributes instead of representing Him merely as a small grown-up. Subsequently, in spite of the fact that the little bird came to have, among its other meanings, that of a protection against the plague, it was so closely connected with the figure of the Christ Child (because of its symbolizing also the themes of the Soul and of the Resurrection) that it remained separate from the usage of the Sebastian figure. Quite similarly there appears to be no connection in its artistic usage between the goldfinch and the figures of Saints Cosmas and Damian, the patron saints of those who cure the sick, *i. e.*, of the doctors.[53]

2. As a Symbol of Fertility

The goldfinch also symbolizes Fertility. Just when this meaning came to be connected with the goldfinch is unknown, but it was probably at the time of the great reawakening of interest in the classics. Pliny may well have been a primary source, and through him, the older sources. There was an old legend, which Pliny relates, of a small bird called AKANTHIS, or acanthis, which laid great numbers of eggs. Pliny remarks that,[54] "... all animals, the larger they are in bulk, are proportionately less prolific: the elephant, the camel, and the horse produce but one, while the acanthis, a very small bird, produces twelve. ..." That the goldfinch was identified with the acanthis is proved by two wholly independent bits of evidence. In his famous work on "Iconologia" first issued in the sixteenth century, Cesare Ripa gives the following under the title Fecondità (fruitfulness) — "A young woman crowned with juniper leaves, holding close to her bosom a goldfinch's nest with young ones; little rabbits playing near her and new hatched chickens.

"The juniper denotes fecundity, because from a small seed, it becomes so great that birds perch on it. The birds, rabbits, hen and chickens all denote fruitfulness, which is the greatest blessing a married lady can have."[55]

This allusion to a nest of goldfinches is undoubtedly to be connected with the legend in the Protevangelium (The Apocryphal History of James Concerning the Birth of Mary) where we find that St. Anne sees a nest of small birds (sparrows? or goldfinches?), at the sight of which she bewails her barren condition, when there suddenly appears before her the angel announcing the coming birth of Mary. This incident, rarely used in art, is, however, shown in a fifteenth century painting in the cathedral at Burgo de Osma, painted by an unknown Spaniard, probably a member of the workshop or close circle of Nicolau and Marzal de Sas[56] (plate 10). As elsewhere pointed out, a bird frequently substituted as a fertility symbol is the titmouse, usually one particular species — the coal tit. It is of interest in this connection to recall that in Filippino Lippi's "Madonna and Child with Saints Jerome and Dominic," in the National Gallery, London, there is a carefully delineated coal tit bringing food to a nest full of young. The nest is shown exposed like a finch's, whereas, in fact, the tit actually nests in a hole in a tree (which would render it impossible for the artist to show it).

The other piece of evidence lies in the fact that as early as the seventh century, Bishop Isidorus of Seville, in his "Etymologiae" used the name Acanthis for the goldfinch. His work was widely copied by monastic scribes and formed one of the main sources of natural history lore in the Middle Ages. Much later, in the eighteenth century, when scientific nomenclature was first established in biology, the generic name *Acanthis* was applied to the goldfinch and its close relative, the linnet, by men whose interests were primarily not in iconography, but in natural history, indicating the degree to which the identification of the goldfinch with the fabulous acanthis had become both widespread and accepted.[57]

It would seem, at least in part, that the great predilection for the goldfinch in Madonna and Child pictures was that thereby they were endowed with the power to insure offspring for the family for whom they were painted. The importance of this question for the better families, especially in Italy in which each town had its rival families striving for power, and which was not unified under one royal house, is obvious.[58] A lack of interest in such worldly matters as fertility or the plague on the part of such a mystical ascetic as Fra Angelico may well account for the absence of the goldfinch in his numerous Madonna pictures.[59] Conversely, it is highly probable, to say the least, that the fertility meaning was definitely behind the use of the bird by Raphael in his "Madonna del Cardellino" (Uffizi Gallery, Florence) (plate 117). This picture was painted as a wedding present from the artist to his friend Lorenzo Nasi and the bird in it could hardly have been a plague augur. (Even though it is true that Raphael assiduously avoided matrimony all his life, it would take a most hardened cynic to assume that he considered it similar to the plague.) It should, of course, be remembered, that even when the bird was used as a symbol of Fertility, it remained at the same time also a symbol of the Soul and of Resurrection. It so happens in the case of Raphael's "Madonna del Cardellino" that the genesis of the picture is known. Thus, Muntz[60] writes of this work as follows. "There is no trace of effort in this picture and yet the artist must have bestowed much thought upon the grouping, which seems so elegant and so unstudied. Four drawings . . . preserved at Oxford and at Vienna, and another in the Wicar collection, not to mention those which have been lost, show us the phases through which the composition passed before reaching its pictorial stage. In the first study (Albertina, Vienna) the Virgin in a sitting position, is intent upon a book she has in her right hand, while her left is carelessly rested upon the body of her Child, who is standing up and trying to reach the book as if to divert her attention. The infant St. John is wanting, but in the second study (Oxford) the artist takes a step forward as there are three figures in the composition. But the main idea of the scene is different again, for the Virgin is reading a book, both the divine infant and St. John listening attentively. . . . In the interval Raphael made up his mind to work into this scene a motive which he had treated before; that of St. John presenting to his companion the bird he has just caught.[61] Each of the succeeding designs marks a further advance, viz. the substitution of the goldfinch for the book, which is transferred to the Virgin's left hand, a change in the part taken by St. John, who instead of being a mere spectator, becomes an important actor in the scene. . . ."

It seems wholly plausible and indeed, probable, that the artist, painting a picture as a wedding present for his friend should wish him a fruitful marriage blessed by offspring.

The composition of the Madonna with the Christ Child and the young St. John may in itself be, to some extent, a fertility picture — a plea for fruitfulness. Richardson[62] shows Fecundity represented, ". . . by the figure of a matron of a pleasant countenance, resting on a couch; with one hand she is caressing two children; the other . . . she holds a cornucopia (here changed to a book). . . . The attribute of caressing two children expresses one of the greatest consolations of the married state, and indicates the happiness and delight that mankind enjoys in rearing up their beloved offspring. . . ." A derivation from as far back as Horace is suggested.[63] [64]

Another item bearing on the Fertility symbolism, merely suggestive in nature, unfortunately not at all conclusive, is the fact that in all the hundreds of pictures examined, I have found none in which both the goldfinch and St. Thomas occur together. The Apostle Thomas was the great preacher of asceticism; he berated and belittled marriage and the having of offspring; he argued that men should devote their lives directly to God and not to Mankind. Obviously, a goldfinch connoting Fertility would be ill placed in his company.

While there is no proveable certainty, there is another factor that may conceivably have made the goldfinch the symbol of Fertility in a special sense. When we recall that Pliny definitely states the acanthis to produce twelve offspring, and when we recall that the goldfinch became the substitute for the charadrius, which in turn was identified by the religious mystics of the Middle Ages with Christ Himself, a parallel between the twelve offspring of the bird and the twelve disciples of Christ becomes possible. What better kind of fruitfulness than to have disciples to continue one's efforts and to spread one's qualities? In connection with this connotation of "disciple" in the idea of "offspring" we may further recall that Pliny himself sings the praises of the goldfinch, ". . . which is the very smallest bird of any, will do what it is bid, not only with the voice but with the feet as well and with the beak, which serves it instead of hands." [65] In other words the bird is pictured as a faithful instrument of its master's will, carrying out its instructions as completely as it can, and not giving what may be an early attempt to express our modern colloquialism, mere "lip service."

It may be pointed out at this time that another crumb of evidence bearing on the fertility symbolism of the goldfinch lies in the fact that the bird has patches of bright yellow in its wings. This color was a symbol of fruitfulness, among other things.[66] [67]

This leads us to still another line of reasoning concerning the introduction of the goldfinch as a plague augur. As we have now seen, the little bird was widely used as a symbol of fertility, a plea for progeny on the part of the donors of the pictures in which it appears. The ravages of the plague made this matter of fecundity all the more important and urgent; if there were enough children there would be a greater chance of some of them surviving and carrying on the family names and fortunes. There were two ways of besting the bubonic scourge. The individuals might escape it and themselves serve to continue their line (if affected, they might even recover, but this was more doubtful), or having sufficiently great numbers of offspring the families would survive. The concepts of fertility and survival were brought into unusually urgent and close relationship by the tremendous death toll of the plague. It has been estimated that during the more serious epidemics of the disease in the fourteenth century alone over a quarter of the people of Europe died from it, while in some localities the mortality reached as high as sixty-five percent; whole communities were practically wiped out; others partly so. The plea for progeny became so intertwined with the plea for protection from the plague that the one symbol came to stand for both together and for each separately. The urgency of this dual plea is reflected in the fact that in paintings done during the worst plague periods, such as for example, the fourteenth century, the symbolic goldfinch is usually more closely connected with the Christ Child, being either held by Him or offered to Him, while in later times, such as the latter part of the fifteenth and the first half of the sixteenth centuries, it is not infrequently merely inserted as an accessory not particularly associated compositionally with any of the divine personages represented.

These, then, are the chief meanings involved in the use of the goldfinch motif. It seems to me that the very number and diversity of these connotations probably served to increase the frequency with which the figure was used for each of its major meanings. Thus, if an artist wished to include a symbol of the Soul he could have used any suitable bird but the chances of his choosing a goldfinch for this purpose were increased by virtue of the fact that it also served other desirable, even if not at the moment, specifically desired, purposes. The pomegranate, to take another example, was co-equal with the goldfinch as a symbol of Fertility and of Immortality, but its significance in Christian art practically stopped there, while the goldfinch carried other implications as well, which led to its being used as a Fertility symbol more frequently than the pomegranate. (Occasionally both were introduced together — a double plea for fertility, each helping to fortify and to clarify the other, as in the tondo by Fra Bartolommeo and Albertinelli in the National Gallery of Art, Washington). (Plates 70 and 70a).

A few minor elements in the mystic significance of the goldfinch deserve brief mention. It cannot be proved that they actually enter into its use in art, but are of interest in revealing other facets of the composite mentality in the European approach to the goldfinch. The little bird was, to some extent, considered symbolic of the Church; in Brittany it is still called "Pabor," that is, "Pape d'or" because of the likeness of its crimson head patch to the papal tiara, and also from the golden yellow color of parts of its plumage. In its role as a household pet, the goldfinch was widely taught to draw up little buckets of water on a type of "endless chain" device in its cage, and may thus have been vaguely connected with the motif of Baptism. This habit has been recorded of the captive goldfinch in many parts of Europe, and in Holland the common name of the goldfinch to this day is "putter," meaning drawer-of-water.[68]

Another, even though slight, connection with the idea of the bird as a "drawer of water" is to be found in the legend of the robin noted in a previous connection, where we found the bird was said to bring a drop of water each day to cool the tongues of those parched with thirst in Hell. That the robin and the goldfinch are to some extent interchangeable symbols is evidenced by their inclusion together in numerous devotional paintings. To take but a single example, we may mention Bonifazio Veronese's "Coronation of St. Catherine" (Washington, National Gallery of Art.)

The painting by Fra Bartolommeo and Albertinelli (plates 70 and 70a), referred to above, is of interest here as well. In it the goldfinch is depicted as drinking from the baptismal cup, which, together with St. John's cross, is lying on the ground in the lower front of the picture. It seems not improbable that here the goldfinch serves to symbolize Baptism as well as Resurrection; indeed the two are not unrelated themes.

Another, and probably inconsequential, item bearing on the goldfinch may be related. Junghaus, a German naturalist, traveling in Italy around 1890,[69] saw many dead goldfinches for sale in the markets in Rome. Turning to his Italian comrade he said, "How can one kill such pretty birds to eat them?" The Italian replied that it was not right to kill goldfinches because they were the beloved bird of Jesus ("Lieblingsvogel des Herrn Jesus"). Junghaus connects this with the occurrence of goldfinches in old Italian Madonna pictures, but states that he knows no legend behind this usage.

Stimulated by Junghaus's paper, Leverkühn,[70] the learned librarian of King Ferdinand of Bulgaria, a few months later, in the same journal presented a poem by Fr. Kind, from Th. Echtermeyer's "Auswahl deutscher Gedichte," 1872, No. 92, p. 120, in which he suggests may be found the legend behind the concept of the goldfinch as the "beloved bird of Jesus." However, the poem is quite whimsical and certainly not to be looked upon as seriously intended. Its point is that after God had colored all the other birds the goldfinch alone was left plain ashy gray. The little bird then begins to ask for a speck of red, a dash of white, etc., eventually asking for most of the pigments, while the Creator in a mood of amused tolerance daubs its feathers with the various colors. The moral seems to be that no matter how unimportant an individual may be, he is assured of spiritual raiment if he only holds fast to his piety and takes his troubles to God.

In this connection it may be noted that Auber,[71] in writing of the use of the small bird symbol, states that the dove connotes, through the significance of the beautiful colors of its feathers the favors and gifts of Providence to the soul. "La colombe est indiquée, dans le psaume LXVII, comme signifiant par les belles couleurs de ses plumes, les faveurs de la Providence sur les âmes qui se conduisent comme la colombe fait ici. Les vertus, et surtout la constance dans les périls et les vicissitudes de la vie, *inter medios cleros*, sont pour le fidèle autant d'ornements véritables, comme sont pour l'oiseau ses plumes argentées, dont le reflet se mêle admirablement à l'or des belles plumes de sa queue. . . ." This is essentially similar to the meaning implicit in Kind's poem and the two may be based on a common tradition. There are, thus, some slight suggestive data to the effect that just as the goldfinch came to substitute for the charadrius, it also came to replace the dove to some degree.

It may be pointed out that inasmuch as the goldfinch came to be a substitute identification for the charadrius and inasmuch as the charadrius was at times identified with Christ Himself, the goldfinch would also have this meaning. This in itself would account for the frequency with which it was used in Madonna pictures, and would also account for its lingering in popular tradition as the "beloved bird of Jesus."

Still another fragment concerning this approach to the meanings inherent in the goldfinch deserves mention here. Konrad von Megenberg, writing in the third quarter of the fourteenth century in Germany,[72] notes that the goldfinch sings beautifully although it feeds on the sharp spines of the thistle. This he considers a "great wonder" and goes on to say that the bird is therefore a symbol of the Good Preacher on Earth, who has to endure greatly and, although living among the thorns of this world, cheerfully serves God.[73] A still further bit of evidence linking this bird with God in the popular mind is afforded by a mid-eighteenth century German naturalist, Jacob Theodor Klein,[74] who calls the bird "Fringilla Jovis" without further explanation.

Chapter III. The Types of Pictures in which the Symbolic Goldfinch Occurs

INASMUCH as over ninety percent of the devotional pictures containing goldfinches are Madonna and Child groups, we may first briefly discuss the relatively small number of cases of other types of paintings and then come back to the main body of the goldfinch material. Such pictures as St. Francis preaching to the birds, the Noah story, and scenes of Paradise, where, among other birds, the goldfinch also occurs, are not considered in this study. In these pictures the birds are birds, not symbols in bird form. Only nine Nativities have been found to contain goldfinches, three of them by Florentine painters (one from the shop of the Master of San Miniato, now in the Museum of Fine Arts, Boston (plate 68), one by a follower of Filippo Lippi, now in the Louvre, Paris, and one by Piero di Lorenzo (Louvre), one by an Umbrian, or more properly an Umbro-Florentine, Piero della Francesca (National Gallery, London) (plate 119 and 119a), one by a Sienese, Taddeo di Bartolo (Servi Church, Siena) (plate 80), one by a Bolognese, Francia (Royal Gallery, Bologna); two by German painters (one by Friedrich Herlin, now in the Städtisches Museum, Nördlingen, and one by Michael Wolgemut, in the Marien-kirche, at Zwickau) and one by the French painter Jacques Daret (Thys-sen collection, Lugano) (plate 22). The frequently painted theme of Adoration, either of the Shepherds or of the Magi, is curiously free of goldfinches, only six cases (five Italian and one Dutch) being known to me. Domenico Ghirlandajo included a goldfinch in the foreground of his panel of the Adoration of the Magi (now in the Uffizi) as did some genera-tions earlier his fellow Florentine, Andrea da Firenze (Worcester, Mass., Art Museum), (plate 39); while a little known Marchigian painter, Fol-chetto da Sanginesio, introduced no fewer than three goldfinches in a little panel of the Adoration of the Shepherds (Johnson collection, Phila-delphia Art Museum) (plate 136). In Sassetta's "Journey of the Kings"

(Metropolitan Museum, New York) (plate 90) two goldfinches are to be found in the lower left corner, one on the ground and one on the wing about to pick a bit of food off a plant. This picture is part of a larger one depicting an Adoration and is therefore included at this point. The fifth one is by the Sienese, Girolamo de Benvenuto (Montepulciano Gallery). In a Dutch work, an "Adoration of the Kings" by Geertgen van Haarlem, there is a perfectly identifiable goldfinch. In a painting of the Adoration of the Magi by the German painter Hans von Kulmbach (Kaiser Friedrich Museum, Berlin) there are three birds in the background, but while the photograph seen is not too good, it is doubtful if any of them is intended to be a goldfinch.

The "Rest on the Flight into Egypt" apparently is a theme that has little connection with the use of the goldfinch. I have seen but one Italian and one German painting of this subject that include a goldfinch. The former, in the Kunsthistorisches Museum, Vienna, was once attributed to Raphael, but is not so considered today. I know this picture only from a small black and white reproduction. A goldfinch, in the lower right corner, stands on the ground with its back to the spectator; its head turned slightly to the right; it has no intimate bearing on the action or the characters in the picture. The German picture, by Hans Baldung Grien (Germanisches Museum, Nürnberg) reveals a goldfinch and another dark bird of similar size on a tree in the upper background above the figure of the Mother and Child (plate 28).

The St. Catherine legend, either her Mystic Marriage with the Christ Child or her Coronation, was too far removed from the usual devotional icon and too specialized in its own sense to have much need of the goldfinch as an accessory symbol. Nevertheless this little bird occurs in at least four paintings of the Mystic Marriage and in one of the Coronation of St. Catherine, in all of which the Christ Child is the active, and St. Catherine the passive, character. The four pictures of the Mystic Marriage are as follows: one by "School of Orcagna" (Louvre, Paris); one by Francescuccio Ghissi of Fabriano (Picture Gallery, Vatican), one by his contemporary and fellow townsman, Allegretto Nuzi (formerly Art Market, Berlin[1]), and one by an eclectic follower of Nuzi (Offida, Sta. Maria della Grazia). The panel by Ghissi I know only by description; I really cannot vouch for the accuracy of the identification of the bird as a goldfinch, although it is referred to as a "cardellino" in the guide book to the Vatican's picture gallery. The one pertinent painting of the Christ Child crowning St. Catherine is by Bonifazio Veronese (National Gallery of Art, Washington). The goldfinch is perched on a fragment of the saint's wheel of martyrdom lying on the ground at her feet.

Two frequently painted episodes in the story of the Infant Jesus, the "Presentation in the Temple" and the "Circumcision" apparently never have goldfinches included in their pictorialization.

We now come back to the pictures of the Madonna and Child, with no elaborate theme of action (such as "Adoration," "Journey to Egypt," etc.). As we have already seen, over ninety percent of the goldfinches occur in pictures of this type. At the outset it may be emphasized that there seems to be no essential difference, with regard to the symbolic use of the goldfinch, whether or not the two main personages are alone or are attended by other saintly figures, angels, cherubs, or even donors. The list of saints that have been identified in these paintings includes most of those most frequently depicted, and as far as I can see there is nothing common to those that do occur in "goldfinched" pictures by which they differ as a group from those I have not yet found so associated. Among those that do figure in these pictures are Agatha, Agnes, Andrew, Anne, Anthony Abbot, Anthony of Egypt, Anthony of Padua, Apollonia, Ansanus, Augustine, Barbara, Bartholomew, Benedict, Bernardino of Siena, Bonaventura, Catherine of Alexandria, Catherine of Siena, Celia, Christopher, Clara, Dominic, Dorothy, Elizabeth, Francis, George, Hubert, Jacob, James, Jerome, John the Baptist, John the Evangelist, Joseph, Julian, Lawrence, Leonard, Liberatus, Lorentino, Louis, Lucy, Luke, Margaret, Mark, Martin, Mary Magdalene, Matthew, Michael, Monica, Nicholas of Bari, Nicholas of Myra, Nicholas of Tolentino, Onuphrius, Paul, Pergentino, Peter, Peter Martyr, Philip, Reparata, Roch, Rosalie, Sebastian, Stephen, Thomas Aquinas, Ursula, Venantius, Zacharias, and Zenobius.[2]

Aside from this variation in the personnel of attendant figures, or the total lack of any, there are only two groups of "Madonna and Child" pictures that call for special comment as embodying a distinctly different theme from the rest. One is the special and relatively late one of the "Madonna and Child and Infant St. John." It was not until the rigid formality of the traditional, hieratic, enthroned Virgin and Child icon had undergone the humanizing influence of the Franciscan and Dominican breezes in the atmosphere of the early Renaissance that so charming a playful interlude could have been utilized in devotional art. The theme derives from the Pseudo-Matthew legend, one of the tales in the apocryphal books of the Gospel, of the Christ Child's play with his companions. Among these was one to the effect that as His playmates brought Him their toy clay birds He miraculously brought them to life. As already shown in an earlier chapter, this lent itself readily to a most pleasing symbolism of the Resurrection. By no means all of the pictures of the Madonna, Christ Child, and young St. John represent this specific theme. As a matter of fact many of them have no bird involved in them; they are merely extensions of the "Madonna of Humility" pictures. When I first began this study, I anticipated that the chief occurrence of the goldfinch would prove to be in pictures of this type, but, as I quickly realized, this is far from the truth.

As stated above, goldfinches have been found in some 19 paintings of this type, all but one of them by Italian artists; the exception being by the Spaniard Zurbaran (plate 21). One closely allied picture, the "Madonna of the Siskin," by the great German, Dürer, utilizes another species of bird, the siskin, whose symbolic meaning is, however, nearly the same as the goldfinch's, and shows that the idea of this particular composition had spread northward into Germany by the late fifteenth century. The Italian paintings here pertinent to our topic are Florentine (or under Florentine influence), Umbrian, Sienese, Bolognese, or Venetian. It is in keeping with the conservative character of Sienese art that I have been able to find but one such attempt at instilling a lighter vein into devotional painting by one of its painters (Fungai). The relative absence of the Bolognese school from my list is, I think, due to lack of available photographic material rather than to the actual non-existence of more such pictures. Francia painted pictures of the Madonna, Christ Child, and Infant St. John on many occasions but none that I have seen happen to have goldfinches in them, although in at least seven other panels of the ordinary "Madonna and Child" type he did introduce the bird. The lone Bolognese work of this type that I have found containing a goldfinch is Antonio da Crevalcore's "Holy Family with the Infant St. John."

The bulk of the pictures of this particular composition are Florentine;

not very surprising when we recall that St. John was the patron saint of that city. The artists involved are Bugiardini (in the Borghese Gallery, Rome); "Tomasso," a temporary name used by Berenson for an artistic personality close to Lorenzo di Credi (in the Musée Napoléon III at Angers); Pesellino (plate 63), (in the Harold I. Pratt collection, New York; this picture has also two attendant angels); school of Filippino Lippi (Florence, Ferroni Museum); Pier Francesco Fiorentino (Fogg Museum, Cambridge, Massachusetts); Piero di Cosimo (2 works; 1 in Rijksmuseum, Amsterdam; 1 in private hands); school of Verrocchio (Louvre, Paris; illustrated in van Marle, vol. xi, p. 569); school of Baldovinetti (Lee collection, Richmond); and one painting by Raphael in his Florentine period (the Madonna del Cardellino of the Uffizi, Florence) (plate 117). Another painting done under Florentine influence, but probably of Milanese workmanship, now in the Uffizi, Florence, is by a follower of Leonardo da Vinci. It has been attributed by some crtics to Bernardino Luini, by others to Cesare da Sesto. In any event, its inspiration derives from Leonardo, and it is therefore mentioned at this point.[3]

By Umbrian painters other than Raphael, who is discussed above in connection with the Florentines, this idyllic icon seems to have been used but little. Pinturicchio painted a picture of this type with a goldfinch (Fogg Museum, Cambridge, Massachusetts), and an unknown follower of Perugino made another (Cantiano, at Cagli, Collegiata).

A strange composition by another Umbrian, Bernardino di Mariotto, may be mentioned here. This picture, now in the Galleria Comunale at Perugia, combines the old enthroned type of Madonna with the freer, ground-seated Virgin with the playing Children. The Madonna, Christ Child and Infant St. John are all three grouped as in a "Madonna of Humility" but are placed on the top of a high throne, below and beside which are Saints Francis and Benedict. The young St. John offers flowers to the Christ Child. A goldfinch is perched in left profile on the front edge of the raised throne, just above the steps leading up to it. A picture of this sort, combining two opposite tendencies seems more an effort for largeness and impressiveness of composition than of meaning, and its application of an accessory minor symbol such as the goldfinch appears likewise dictated by its decorative value rather than by its possible significance.

The two Venetian versions of this composition are both by Antonio

Solario (one in the National Gallery, London, and one in the Walters Gallery, Baltimore). In neither is the theme of the play of the two Children suggested any too well. In the London version, the goldfinch, on a long string the end of which is in the Christ Child's left hand, is walking on a balustrade; in the Baltimore picture the bird is held in the Child's left hand. In the latter version there is a second female figure identified as Elizabeth by Berenson,[4] but called the Magdalene in the Walters Gallery label (plate 105).

The lone Spanish painting of this group, by Zurbaran (plate 21), however, is hardly in accord with the gist of the apocryphal story. This panel, now in the Fine Arts Museum, San Diego, California, shows the young St. John offering a goldfinch in his right hand to the Christ Child, who is seated on His Mother's lap; and who half turns towards His Mother away from the bird.

I have purposely refrained from alluding to instances in sculpture where a small bird is involved in a Madonna and Child composition because of the impossibility of being certain of its identification as a goldfinch. However, inasmuch as the great bulk of the small birds so used in devotional paintings are goldfinches, it seems probable that the same form was probably intended in the majority of the comparable sculptures as well. Inasmuch as the field of sculpture offers one highly unusual example of this three-figured composition of the Virgin, Christ Child, and young St. John with a small bird, I include it here, and shall discuss its symbolical importance more fully later on in this study. This work is the marble tondo made for Taddeo Taddei by Michelanglo, now in Burlington House, London (plate 139). Here, alone not only in Italian, but in all representations of the theme either in sculpture or painting, the Christ Child retreats from the bird that is offered Him by the little St. John. He is obviously frightened by it and the Virgin, understanding this, gently tries to hold off the impetuous St. John with her right hand. Incidentally, this work is unique in another respect; by virtue of the unfinished state of the carving of the bird, which is probably intentional on the master's part (being a technique he frequently employed), the bird is given a nervous agitation, a flurry of movement, an excited activity, equal to that of the Christ Child who leaps over His Mother's outstretched leg in his wild scramble to the safety of her embrace.

In this connection it may be pointed out that Tolnay[5] actually calls the bird a goldfinch. This is, of course, merely an assumption based on the prevalence of this bird in earlier and contemporary Florentine painting (Tolnay refers to a goldfinch by Bernardo Daddi in his description of the tondo). Without anticipating unduly our subsequent discussion of this work, it may be noted that here surely we do not have to do with a literal application of the apocryphal story, as the bird is very much alive before the Christ Child has been given it. Keeping in mind the fact that the unfinished, actually only roughly indicated, carving of the bird renders its identification mere guess work, it may be noted that its size, insofar as this may be estimated from its blurred outline, is rather large for a naturalistic goldfinch, and too small for a dove. The blurred movement does, of course, make for a larger mass than would a quietly static pose of the bird. Nevertheless, I think Tolnay is reasonably justified in connecting this bird with the goldfinch motif.

Another type of the Madonna and Child painting that calls for comment is the representation of the Virgin nursing the Child, the "Madonna lactans." While this icon has far greater antiquity than the preceding one of the three-figured group, it enters into the present story to a smaller extent. The icon itself derives from catacomb art of the third century,[6] and, while used by artists all through the period from then on to the Baroque, it never attained a numerical abundance comparable with that of the more ordinary composition of the Madonna and Child.

Recently Meiss[7] has shown that the representation of the Virgin suckling the Child had a particular significance in the thought and consequently in the art of the late Middle Ages. It showed the one situation wherein the Virgin was most concretely and most intimately the Mother of Christ, and set forth that character and attribute of the Virgin which arose from her motherhood, her role as "Maria Mediatrix," the motherly, compassionate intercessor for mankind before the more impartial, paternal justice of Christ or God the Father. As we have seen, the goldfinch, aside from being the usual bird symbol of "soul" was also a symbol of special favors (fertility, protection from disease, etc.). We may well ask whether, its scarcity in pictures of the "Madonna lactans" type may not be, to some extent, a reflection of the thought that in the presence of the supreme general intercessor, a symbol for special favors was considered superfluous and therefore not inserted as a rule.

Paintings of the nursing Madonna and Child containing goldfinches, by the following artists may be noted in this connection. A picture attributed to the fourteenth century Sienese master, Barna (R. M. Hurd collection, New York), shows the Child nursing at His Mother's left breast, as he toys with His left foot and holds a goldfinch in His right hand. Aside from bringing the goldfinch into a picture of this sort, the artist here gives an early attempt to enliven the panel by activating the Child as in the "Bambino Vispo" type.[8] Giovanni di Camuseto (S. Giovanni dei Campi, near Piobesi Torinese) painted a Madonna nursing the Child, attended by saints and angels. This work was painted in 1359. Masaccio (Oratory, Montemarciano) painted the Child sitting on the Virgin's left knee, nursing at her left breast, and holding a goldfinch in His left hand. The bird is too damaged to render its identification certain, but it appears to have been intended to be a goldfinch, and was restored as such[9] (plate 45, 46).

Leonardo da Vinci (Hermitage Gallery, Leningrad) included a goldfinch in his "Madonna Litta"[10] (plate 71). The Christ Child is shown nursing at His Mother's right breast; a goldfinch is held in His left hand which is almost hidden by his body so that the bird seems, at first glance, to be perching on His left groin. In the photograph seen, it is very dark, only the head being clearly decipherable. The bird's head is seen in right profile, its bill turned away from the Child's body. There are at least three old and rather free versions of this painting; one by Bernardino de' Conti (Poldo Pezzoli collection, Milan) and two by Boltraffio (one in Museo Civico, Milan, and one in an unknown private collection). All these have retained the motif of the goldfinch in the shadows in the Child's hand as in Leonardo's original, although varying the details of the pose of the Madonna's head and torso (which might well be looked upon as giving more of a challenge to the copyist to show his originality than would a minor detail such as the bird). In Siena there is a picture by "Maestro Gregorio," known to me only from a very poor outline reproduction,[11] in which the Child holds a small bird in His left hand while nursing at His Mother's breast. The Child's pose is activated, somewhat reminiscent of the one in the picture attributed to Barna.

Of interest in this connection, but not strictly identifiable as a goldfinch, is an alabaster work, dating from the sixth decade of the fourteenth century, by a master of the Rhenish school (Luitpold Museum, Würzburg).[12] The Child, supported on His Mother's left hand, holds His left hand to His mouth, and in His right hand He holds a small bird fairly close to His Mother's breast. It is well known that the Virgin's two breasts were long symbolic of the two Testaments, from which flows the Milk of Doctrine. In this case it would almost appear that the Christ Child deliberately cuts himself off from this nourishment so that the little bird may have it instead, although the bird is not depicted as actually receiving any. The meaning of this work becomes clearer if we recall that in his description of "Fertility" Ripa describes it as a lady ". . . holding close to her bosom a goldfinch's nest with young. . . ." We have here a variant of the fertility symbol.[13]

A Spanish "Virgen de la leche" by a member of the circle of the "Master of the Solsona Last Supper," an Aragonese, middle fifteenth century picture (Plandiura collection, Barcelona) may be mentioned here even though the bird held by the nursing Babe is unidentifiable.

The "Madonna of Mercy" or, as it is often called "Misericordia Madonna" is usually not depicted holding the Infant Jesus, and therefore pictures of this type are not apt to be connected with the use of the goldfinch motif. However there is one such picture, by Parri Spinelli (Arezzo, Pinacoteca) in which the Madonna is holding her Babe, and He, in turn, is holding a goldfinch (plate 58).

Chapter IV. The Goldfinch in Spanish, French, English, Flemish, Dutch, Germanic, and Russian Art

WE may now turn to the "ordinary" Madonna and Child pictures, which form the great bulk of the goldfinch material — over 400 of the nearly 500 paintings discussed in this work. Students of early eastern Christian art have attempted to classify these pictures into categories based on minor characteristics of pose; thus, figures of the Virgin supporting the Child on her left arm and holding His right hand before her breast are referred to as of the "Hodegetria" type; others in which she holds Him with both her hands as the "Blacherniotissa" type; others in which the attitude of the Child is more playful, the "Eleousa" type, etc., etc. I cannot find any correlation between these various compositional types and the frequency of occurrence or the apparent symbolism of the goldfinch in them. It is true that some of them are more abundant than others and so figure more largely in our lists, but beyond that they do not help us in attempting to "break down" this vast material for study. Similarly, attempts have been made to classify each of these paintings according to whether the Madonna is of a sibylline or of a maternal type; *i. e.*, if her relation to the Child is treated as essentially prophetic or as wholly emotional. However, the number of pictures that can be so categorized is relatively small; for one thing, the distinction is to a large extent subjective; and for another, in many cases the rendition is either inadequate to force us into one or the other of these judgments or the artist has striven for an image that partly satisfies both. In the absence, then, of any set schematic framework against which to view them, we may turn to the pictures themselves, and inasmuch as they form by far our chief mass of data, we may simultaneously discuss the occurrence and use of the goldfinch in the art of the various countries and schools involved.

As we have already noted, the bulk of these paintings are by Italians. We may begin by taking up the non-Italian works to clear the way for the main task ahead.

SPAIN

Nineteen of the pictures are by Spanish artists, ranging from the middle of the fourteenth to the middle of the seventeenth century. As we may readily see from this relatively small number of instances, gathered from rich illustrative sources,[1] the goldfinch or, for that matter, any small bird, plays a very minor role indeed in Spanish religious art.[2] This is all the more remarkable when we recall the early presence in Spain of such Italian masters as the Florentines, Starnina and Dello Delli, and the activity at Avignon, in not too far off southern France, of such Sienese painters as Simone Martini and Matteo da Viterbo and their assistants. As Post[3] has put it, ". . . the Italianization of Gothic painting of the fourteenth century was more pronounced in Spain than anywhere else in Europe. In general, the models were, as in other countries, Sienese; but in Castile the presence of Starnina seems to have been sufficient to turn the interest rather to Florence."

The first echoes of Italian precept and influence in Spanish painting are to be found in works produced in the middle decades of the fourteenth century in such widely separated parts of the Iberian peninsula as Catalonia and Seville. This implies that, to have encompassed such a spread, the influence must have begun somewhat earlier. It is understandable to find it appearing early in Catalonia (the province most adjacent to southern France) where we see it in the work of Ferrer Bassa, whose paintings in the Franciscan convent of Pedralbes reveal both Florentine and Sienese influences.[4] That these influences did help to bring into Spain the use of the little bird symbol is demonstrated in Bassa's work. In his wall decoration of the Virgin and Child with Angels, in the Chapel of San Miguel in the convent of Pedralbes, the Christ Child is shown holding a small bird in His right hand. The painting is unfortunately badly damaged and the bird's head is gone, rendering definite identification impossible. This work is said to date from 1346 (Simone Martini was at Avignon from 1339 until his death in 1344). A slightly later picture, from the third quarter of the same century, by an unknown Catalonian painter (now in the Walters Art Gallery, Baltimore) contains, however, a completely identifiable goldfinch. In the central panel of this triptych is a seated Madonna and Child with two Angels; the Child holds a goldfinch in His left hand, the string from the bird's leg being held in His right hand. The bird's body is rather elongated, as in works by Bernardo Daddi and his followers, but has more details of plumage pattern than is customary in Daddiesque paintings. The goldfinch is represented with its wings partly raised, and is apparently pecking at the thumb of the hand that holds it (plate 18).

The mid-Trecento examples at Seville are three frescoed, standing figures of the Madonna holding the Child, all larger than life in size. They are the "Virgen de la Antigua" in the cathedral (plate 12); the "Virgen de Rocamador" in the Church of San Lorenzo (plate 13); and the "Virgen del Coral" in the Church of San Ildefonso. In all three the Child holds a bird. Through the kindness of Professor Post new and excellent photographs of these three paintings have been made available to me. While the birds are poorly rendered in all three, it is not a matter of overinterpretation of inadequate evidence to say that all three are intended to be goldfinches. All have some trace of the dusky loreal and frontal markings and of the occipital and postauricular dark crescent so characteristic of this species. On the other hand, all are apparently much too white in their general coloration for naturalistic goldfinches. Post's remarks on these three pictures are important and pertinent to our theme and may be repeated here[5] ". . . In their present condition they are certainly works of the Trecento, but several stylistic as well as historical considerations suggest that they may be substitutions for, or even repaintings of, earlier icons. . . .

"Critics have broken lances on the question whether the existing style of these frescoes is of French or Italian derivation, but the subsequent repainting even over the fourteenth century foundation is so ruthless that there is little basis for valid judgment. If we reject the hypothesis that the standing posture of the Virgin holding the Child lingered on from more primitive representations, we must acknowledge that it does not belong to Italian painting of the Trecento and that it suggests those carved Madonnas which were so characteristic a product of France in this century and thence probably were popularized as devotional objects throughout

European art, even in Italian sculpture. The invocation of one of the
Virgins under the title with which she was honored at Rocamadour in
southern France might be conceived as having led its author to seek in
that country also his artistic model; but this is not the only instance of
this cult in the Iberian peninsula, as is witnessed by the existence of other
Spanish and Portuguese images of the same title, by the frequent mention
of the French shrine, as a place of pilgrimage, in the *Cantigas* of Alfonso
the Wise in the fourteenth or beginning of the fifteenth century, in the
Cronica rimada del Cid. The *déhanchement* of the Madonna's body, which
is not very pronounced in any of the three examples, is a trait of the French
sculptured Virgins; but from France it had penetrated into the art of all
Europe in the fourteenth century and might, therefore, have reached
Seville via Siena . . . even if the standing posture be French in origin, the
execution, as far as it is not blurred by restoration, reveals at least a partial
knowledge of Italian methods. . . ."

Beginning with these works dating from the middle of the fourteenth
century, we find the use of the goldfinch motif in Spanish painting distributed chronologically as follows. Four of the nineteen paintings are
from the end of the second quarter of the fourteenth century, one each
is from the third and fourth quarters of that century and two from the
first quarter of the fifteenth. I have found no painting done in the second
quarter of the fifteenth century containing a goldfinch, two in the third,
and one in the final quarter of that century. In the sixteenth century we
have three from the first quarter, none from the second, one from the
third and none from the fourth. With a single example from the first,
and two from the second quarter of the seventeenth century our record
of Spanish usage of the symbol ends. In other words, as far as we may
draw conclusions from this not too abundant material, it seems that the
goldfinch symbol was utilized chiefly in the middle of the fourteenth,
and again around the close of the fifteenth and opening years of the sixteenth centuries. These were times of strong extraneous influence in the
history of Spanish art; the first period being dominated by Franco-Italian,
and the second by Flemish (Tournai) inspiration and authority. This
certainly suggests that that motif was not one in which Iberian artists
showed much interest, and that they used it chiefly when imitating, consciously or otherwise, foreign systems of design and iconography.

The Symbolic Goldfinch

The complete list of pertinent Spanish paintings in which I have found the symbol utilized is given in the appendix (see p. 138-139).

Aside from these it should be mentioned that a number of similar devotional panels have been found containing small birds other than goldfinches. In some cases (photographs only seen) the birds are not certainly identifiable. In two pictures the bird appears to be a swallow,[6] while in a third the bird is not certainly identifiable, but is of interest here. It is a small flying whitish bird from whose leg dangles a string the other end of which is held by the Christ Child. The bird seems to have been intended to be the mystical "charadrius" (see pp. 18-20 for a detailed discussion of this symbolism). Aside from this the picture merits passing notice because it is one of only three, not only in Spanish, but in all European art in which I have found the small bird motif in a composition involving the Child being held by His Mother, who, in turn, is sitting on the lap of her mother, St. Anne, the type of picture for which the German art historians have coined the term "Anna Selbdritt." This picture, by an unknown member of the school of Avila, dating from the second half of the fifteenth century, is now in the cathedral at Avila. The only other Spanish "Anna Selbdritt" composition I know of in which a small bird is offered to or held by the Infant Jesus is by Rodrigo de Osona, the Younger (Zurich, Galerie Neupert). This is a later work, dating from the first quarter of the sixteenth century. The third case is a German work by Wolgemut.

A very strange composition depicting "The Child Jesus Learning to Walk," in the Chapter Room of the Cathedral at Barcelona, painted in early fifteenth century Catalonia shows an angel assisting the Infant Jesus to walk (plate 14). He is semi-standing in a go-cart supporting His body on the rail of the cart. Another angel is urging a little bird (clearly, but not expertly, intended to be a goldfinch) towards Him, while a third angel with the enthroned Virgin is apparently cutting the Child's little smock before sewing it together. The whole thing is astonishingly free from any ceremoniousness or churchly authority in so treating of sacred personages in a truly genre fashion; particularly so when we consider the time it was painted. I have found no other instance of this kind, with a bird, in the art of any other country, and only two others with a go-cart.[7] It seems almost too genre in its treatment to be considered a devotional painting, but yet in subject matter and mode of treatment it is definitely pertinent to our theme. Just as the icon of the Child holding the bird was derived in part from contemporaneous genre reality, so too was this scene in all probability. A child in a household would not always have had the bird in hand; the bird would have stood about on the ground at times, and it is not at all unlikely that it would have been used, as a toy is now, to beckon a toddler to make his first steps towards it. The puzzling feature is its wide variance from symbolic iconographic usage, a feature that makes its possible meaning so subordinate to its mere pictorialization that any message it might have been intended to carry to the spectator might well have been lost in the interest in the little play that goes on before his eyes.

There is no need to linger over most of the pictures in the list. While no two are alike, the differences between them are of no great moment as far as the goldfinch is concerned. We may briefly mention, as concluding examples, three of the relatively late works. The earliest of the three is a panel (now in the Johnson collection, Philadelphia Art Museum) by Juan de Juanes (1523-1579), of the "Virgin and Child with Saints," (plate 19). The Child holds a goldfinch in His right hand, and the bird although very poorly colored is nevertheless definitely identifiable. The next work is a picture by Zurbaran (1598-1662) of the "Virgin and Child with the Infant St. John" (plate 21), already referred to in the discussion of this special three-figured composition. The bird is fairly well drawn (the legs are short) and correctly colored in this work. In the latest picture, Murillo's "Holy Family with a Bird" (Prado, Madrid) the Infant Jesus is holding the goldfinch away from the reach of a little dog!

What is true of Spanish painting also holds for Spanish sculpture. Perez y Pando[8] describes and figures approximately 150 statues and figurines of the Madonna and Child made in Spain from the late fourteenth to the seventeenth centuries, and of these only two contain a bird. This is certainly in striking contrast with the great abundance of this icon in French sculpture of the same period, and is even more striking when we recall the obvious transference of ideas from this source to the three frescoes of standing figures of the Madonna and Child done at Seville not later than the middle of the Trecento. Both of the statues are by unknown artists and both are considered as productions of the sixteenth century. In one, "Nuestra Señora del Pilar de Zaragoza," the bird held by the Child's left hand is large enough to be a dove, but appears to be dark in color.

In the other, a Madonna and Child, in the Cathedral in Oviedo, the bird held in the Child's right hand is much smaller and may well have been intended to be a goldfinch. A third, and earlier, pertinent Spanish sculpture, is a fourteenth century painted limestone statue of the Madonna holding the Child, now in the Metropolitan Museum of Art (The Cloisters branch), New York. The Virgin holds the Infant on her left arm and has a large dove in her right hand.

Bird forms were used as decorative symbolic motifs in medieval Spanish architecture, chiefly as parts of ornamental capitals, but the forms involved, so far as they are identifiable, are not especially pertinent to our present theme. In his discussion of these figures, Ramiro de Pinedo[9] mentions nothing that even remotely connects them with the birds held by the Christ Child.

Although not by a Spanish artist, nor a work produced in Spain, a picture of the "Madonna and Child with attendant Angels," by Alvaro de Pirez de Evora, may be mentioned here. This artist was a Portuguese who worked in Italy under the influence of Martino di Bartolommeo. This picture, now in the church of Santa Croce a Fossabanda at Pisa, shows two of the angels making offerings to the Child. One offers Him a goldfinch, the complementary figure on the other side offers Him a flower.

FRANCE

Turning now to paintings by Frenchmen, we find surprisingly few goldfinches. When we recall the great frequency with which French sculptors turned out little figures of the Madonna and Child with a small bird during the fourteenth and fifteenth centuries, and the fact that the French manuscript illuminators loved to depict the goldfinch, this absence is puzzling indeed.[10] On the other hand it should be remembered that devotional paintings of the early "international" Gothic style were never produced in France in such great abundance as in other countries. Stained glass windows rather than painted panels or frescoed walls answered the need for pictorial rendition of sacred themes in the great French Gothic cathedrals, and glass was too formal and unyielding a medium and too much a part of the architecture of the buildings to encourage genre tendencies in religious art. Also it seems that an unusually large part of what paintings were produced has been lost.

We have already mentioned the presence of a goldfinch in a fifteenth century French painting of the Nativity, by Jacques Daret (plate 22), (last known to be in the Thyssen collection, Lugano). In this picture the little bird is perching on the roof of the ruined shed in front of which the action of the picture is placed. From about the same time dates a work by an unknown member of the school of Amiens, of a full length standing Madonna holding the Christ Child on her arm, Who, in turn, holds a goldfinch, (plate 23). The figures are placed in front of a Gothic niche, and the picture is a capital example of a sculptor's design taken over by a painter. This work, now in the Art Institute, Chicago, is, in this respect, reminiscent of the three Spanish frescoes done at Seville in the preceding century, but is far more delicately drawn and is a more attractive painting.

The third and last of the early French paintings wholly pertinent to our theme is by an unknown artist and is said to date from about 1515. It represents the Virgin and Child with two Angels and Saint Margaret and Louis XII of France (Weld Blundell collection). The Child, sitting on His mother's right knee, holds a goldfinch upside down with both hands. As we shall see later this inverted pose of the bird is an Italian motif (chiefly Florentine in origin), and we may therefore look upon this work as not wholly native to France in its conception.

A work, less completely in keeping with our preoccupation with the goldfinch, but nevertheless bearing on it, is a triptych done, not in paint, but in enamel, by the Master of the Orléans Triptych. This work, dating from the second half of the fifteenth century (now in the Walters Art Gallery, Baltimore) has for the theme of its central panel, a Madonna holding the Child in one arm, and in the other a fairly large black bird, to whose bill the Infant Jesus puts His right index finger. Without repeating too much of what the symbolism here involves (see p. 9-10) it may be stated that the black bird has to do with the idea of death, and that one of the meanings inherent in the goldfinch is also connected with death — the Crucifixion. That this particular composition was not without some popularity is indicated by the fact that there are at least two other versions of it extant, one in the Victoria and Albert Museum, London (Salting bequest) and one in the Musée des Arts Décoratifs, Paris.

Some centuries later, when all religious feeling had gone out of French art and only a mild tradition that it was acceptable persisted, we find an artist like Fragonard painting diaphanous "Holy Family" pictures, in one of which the Child is depicted as playing with a white dove.[11] This is probably based on the same lack of understanding as an earlier work by Rubens, mentioned a little later in this chapter, in which a white dove likewise occurs.

ENGLAND

The sole example of English usage of the goldfinch known to me could almost be considered French as much as Anglican as it is close in style and feeling to the school of manuscript illuminators of Paris. It is a work of great interest historically as it is one of the earliest usages I have found; it is a miniature manuscript illumination in the Psalter of Robert de Lisle (MS. Arundel 83, II, British Museum) (plate 24), said to date from the last years of the thirteenth century, and represents the Madonna holding the Infant Jesus who is holding an unmistakable goldfinch. Aside from being the only English work in which I have found the goldfinch motif employed, it suggests the identity of the goldfinch with the small uncolored birds of French Gothic sculptures even at that early date. That the use of the goldfinch in this role is not English, but an importation from across the Channel, is further indicated by the fact there is no legend of the gold-finch in English literature. Shakespeare was exceedingly well versed in the nature lore of his country and made extensive use of this knowledge in his plays and poems, but nowhere does he even mention the goldfinch, although he frequently alludes to most of the other common birds of the countryside. In his study of the ornithology of Shakespeare, Harting[12] makes no comment on the absence of the goldfinch, a further indication that there was no legend about it in England (although it was a common enough bird in that country), and hence no reason to expect its inclusion. Chaucer, to take an earlier author, one more nearly contemporaneous with the production of the miniature, likewise makes no mention of the gold-finch, although he gives considerable space in his "Romaunt of the Rose" to the "calander" or "charadrius," for which mystical bird the goldfinch came to be a substitute identification on the Continent.[13]

[*53*]

It is entirely in keeping with the English knowledge of the charadrius legend to find that this fabulous bird was utilized in early English art. A "Madonna and Child" said to date from about 1350, formerly part of an altar at Odda, Norway, and now in the Bergen Museum, shows a white bird, apparently intended to be a charadrius, perched on a branch to the right of the Virgin, who looks at the Child, who is gesticulating towards the bird. Lest it be thought that the bird is the white dove, so frequent in religious painting, it may be noted that it has no nimbus, whereas the doves of the Holy Spirit in fourteenth century English art (especially in "Annunciations") are so decorated.[14]

THE LOW COUNTRIES

a. Flanders

The painters of the Flemish school similarly used the goldfinch but seldom. I have noted only eight devotional paintings with goldfinches by any of them. These range from the 15th century (Hugo van der Goes and Miguel Sithium) through the 16th (Ysenbrandt, van Orley, the Master of the Mansi Magdalen, and an unknown Flemish painter working apparently under the influence of the German, Dürer), to the latter years of the first quarter of the 17th (Jordaens). When one considers that the artists of the old Flemish school produced devotional paintings in great numbers this paucity of goldfinches becomes all the more striking. It is worth mentioning that birds other than the goldfinch were occasionally introduced in "Madonna and Child" panels by early Flemings, but not more so than in other art producing countries. Jan van Eyck placed a paroquet in the Christ Child's hand in one of his pictures,[15] as did also Adriaan Ysenbrandt in two of his.[16] The exact meaning of the paroquet is conjectural but the following suggestion may be helpful (at least until it is replaced by a better one). The Flemings were essentially naturalistic even to details to an extent generally unknown in Italian art, and a parrot of any sort was to them a token of the East and thereby helped to suggest the locale of the sacred story in which it was depicted. Furthermore, one of the attempts, even though a relatively unsuccessful one, to identify the mystical charadrius, ended in the bird being called a parrot. Also, it may be pointed out, that even in Italian devotional art where the goldfinch was very widely used as an accessory symbol, it was occasionally replaced by a parrot (ex. Pinturicchio's "Madonna and Child," National Gallery of Art, Washington) or occurred in a picture together with a parrot (Bastiani's "Annunciation," Klosterneuburg, Austria).

For a list of Flemish paintings containing the goldfinch symbol see Appendix, p. 139-140.

In the painting by Hugo van der Goes (Royal Gallery, Brussels) (plate 31), the Child holds the goldfinch more tightly than in any other picture I can recall. His left hand firmly clutches the little bird's neck, while His right hand has an equally firm and encircling grasp of its wing tips and tail. It is as if there were urgent need to guard against the possibility of the bird escaping. No such problem is raised by Sithium's panel (Kaiser Friederich Museum, Berlin) in which the Child holds the bird in His right hand much as in the average Italian painting. In the "Madonna and Child with Angels" by Ysenbrandt, the goldfinch is standing free on a railing in front of the Virgin and Child, while in the picture attributed to van Orley (ex A. Wertheimer coll., London) the Child holds an apple in His right hand and a tethered goldfinch on His left.[17] I mention these details inasmuch as they show the whole range of intensity of connection between the bird and the Christ Child (if different schools or even different artists were limited to one stage of this range it would be a matter of considerable interest iconographically).

The picture by Jordaens is quite different from the others, as might be expected from a rather coarse and fleshy Baroque artist. In his composition the young Baptist holds a wicker bird cage; a goldfinch with a string dangling from its leg towards the Christ Child, who is held in His mother's arms. The bird is rather heavy bodied for a goldfinch but has the diagnostic cephalic markings. It is not entirely clear from the action of the picture if the bird has flown out of the cage held by St. John, but this would seem to be implied. This is probably purely a genre touch, but it may be recalled that the wholly unrelated and iconographically completely dissimilar Venetian, Carlo Crivelli, introduced bird cages in at least two paintings of the "Annunciation." Inasmuch as a bird in a cage was an old symbol of the soul imprisoned in the body, it is possible that there is intended here some such meaning as that the coming of Christ presaged the salvation of souls from their physically mortal habiliments.

b. Holland

Dutch painting as it is generally known to gallery-goers is a Protestant art, very largely secular in its subject matter, and is correspondingly unconcerned with the religious symbolism of the Catholic church. Even the earlier native painters hardly antedate the Reformation and their work is also a poor hunting ground for the seeker after goldfinches.

Hugo van der Goes, although born a Hollander, has already been considered in our discussion of the Flemish school with which his work is generally considered closely integrated. This leaves us but a single Dutch work pertinent to our theme, — a late fifteenth century "Adoration of the Kings" by Geertgen van Haarlem (often called Geertgen tot Sint Jans), now in the Rijksmuseum, Amsterdam. On the ruins in the right background are several birds among which is one that appears (in a photograph) to be a goldfinch. The birds have no close compositional or inferential association with any of the persons in the composition, and their possible symbolic significance is therefore open to question. The inclusion of these birds may be merely a reflection of extraneous Italian influence, and not anything native to Holland. On the other hand, as already pointed out (p. 6), the fact that the seventeenth century Dutchman, Karel Fabritius, cared enough about the goldfinch to paint a portrait picture of one shows that the bird itself was popular with Hollanders as with the peoples of other parts of Europe.

Inasmuch as Dutch painting provides us with so little material, mention may be made of a "Madonna and Child" by an unknown Hollander, painted about 1520, now in the Kaufmann collection, Berlin, in which the Child holds a paroquet. This is an iconographic usage which we have already seen in early Flemish religious art. The symbolic connection, if any, of the paroquet and the goldfinch is through the fact that both were substitute identifications for the mystical charadrius.

GERMANY

Use of the goldfinch in Germanic devotional painting ranges in time from the second quarter of the fourteenth to the first decades of the sixteenth century, and in this interval appears more frequently than in the art of France, England, Flanders or Holland. All in all, I have found fourteen Germanic paintings containing goldfinches, of which eleven are of the simple Madonna and Child type.[18] The four earliest of these are all by unknown Bohemian artists of the fourteenth century, indicating that the use of the goldfinch motif reached this southeastern part of Germanic Europe earlier than it did Germany proper, where its earliest appearance known to me is from the beginning of the following century. It also suggests an Italian source of influence. In sculpture, however, the motif of a small bird in Madonna and Child figures is known at least as early as the sixth decade of the fourteenth century in the Rhineland. This certainly implies that the influence of contemporary French sculpture made its appearance in western Germany almost as early as did that of Italian painting in Bohemia, but the former seems not to have exerted much effect on Rhenish painting.

One of the earliest of these Bohemian panels is a Madonna and Child in the royal collections, Buckingham Palace, London. The bird is here a painfully crude affair; the artist evidently did not know how to dispose of its feet which are left merely sticking out stiffly as in some of the less successful pictures done at Siena a century later by Sano di Pietro.[19]

In striking contrast to this one in drawing, in pose, and in details of plumage are two goldfinches in similar but slightly later works (plates 25 and 26), both in Prague, one at Strahowkloster and one in the Rudolphinum Gallery.[20] Here the goldfinch, held by the back (Rudolphinum picture) or by the left wing (Strahowkloster panel), has its wings partly spread, and has turned its head around to peck at the hand that holds it. The former picture is interesting as a bit of material for speculation. In it the goldfinch is unusually large, its length from the top of its turned and somewhat bent head to the tip of its tail being greater than the height from chin to crown of the Christ Child's face. The drawing of the bird as a whole and of its parts in detail is of sufficient accuracy to make me think that the artist could hardly have gone so far wrong in its total size unintentionally. If this be so, then it follows therefrom that he deliberately increased its bulk to give it greater prominence and importance in his painting. It is one of the largest goldfinches I have found, and yet is based on closer observation of the actual bird than in any Italian work of the same period.

Another early Bohemian goldfinch deserves mention because of its unusual pose. This is in a half length Madonna and Child in the Capuchin church in Brussels. The Child, holding the bird in His right hand, seems to be caressing it with His lips and lower right cheek; the most intensely emotional pose I have found in any such painting.[21] Usually the bird is held, looked at, or at most lightly stroked or petted as in Raphael's "Madonna del Cardellino."

The existence of these Bohemian examples earlier than the second half of the fourteenth century indicates that the goldfinch motif was known in that country prior to the sojourn there of Tomasso da Modena (1368-1379 approximately); the apparent absence of further examples later than the end of that century may be due to a diminution of local production of devotional art because of the perplexed and unsettled religious atmosphere brought about by the Hussite movement.

In the pictorial art of Germany proper goldfinches have been found in five fifteenth century and in three early sixteenth century paintings of the Madonna and Child. The earliest of these, by an unknown master of the Upper Rhenish school, dated ca. 1430, of "Mary and the Christ Child amongst the Strawberries," now in the Städtisches Museum, Solothurn, shows a goldfinch, among other birds, on a trellis in the background. Similar in spirit and in general subject matter is Schongauer's "Madonna in a Rose Garden," dated 1473 (St. Martin's Church, Kolmar) (plate 27). In it likewise there are several birds, among them a goldfinch, on a rose-covered trellis in the background. We have already mentioned two "Nativities" by Herlin and by Wolgemut, respectively, both done in the latter part of the century. A goldfinch is to be seen on a parapet in the left background in Wolgemut's "Madonna and Child with St. Anne and Donors" in the Germanisches Museum at Nürnberg. In a simple two-figured composition by an undetermined follower of Pacher (now in Germanisches Museum, Nürnberg) is a bird that is probably a goldfinch, perched on the Child's left hand. In the early years of the sixteenth century we find

Hans Burgkmair (plate 29), introducing a goldfinch in a simple Madonna and Child painting (Germanisches Museum, Nürnberg), dated 1509, just a few years after Dürer's "Madonna of the Siskin" and about the same time the elder Holbein painted three small birds, at least one of which appears to be a goldfinch, in a picture of the "Madonna and Child and Angels" (Germanisches Museum, Nürnberg). From about this time also dates Hans Baldung Grien's "Rest on the Flight into Egypt" (plate 28), already mentioned as one of the few renditions of the theme including a goldfinch.[22] In an altarpiece, dating from ca. 1520, Sebastian Schel painted a goldfinch among other birds on a trellis in the background (Chicago Art Institute), (plate 30).

Devotional art in Germany quickly decreased, and, in fact, subsided, with the advent of the Reformation. The goldfinch appears to have been one of the numerous innocent casualties of the new movement.

In Germany, unlike most of the art producing countries of Europe, the graphic arts — engraving, woodcut, etching, etc., have a history about as old as does the development of modern painting. It is of interest therefore to see what, if any, use the goldfinch icon was put to in these media. One of the earliest pertinent works is a "Madonna and Child in a Garden" by an unknown artist of the Upper Rhineland, ca. 1460, (plate 3). The bird, held in the Child's left hand, is not a goldfinch, but a "charadrius" one of the sources of the composite symbolism of the goldfinch. This print, known only from one copy, is in the Lessing J. Rosenwald collection, National Gallery of Art. The small bird motif was included in pictures of similar subjects by numerous German print makers, among whom may be mentioned "Der Meister der Marter der Zehntausend," the "Meister E. S.," and a pupil of the "Meister der Spielkarten," all dating from the fifteenth century. The identification of the birds is, however, uncertain, but the prints are evidence for the spread of the iconographical pattern paralleling that afforded by painting. In the Rhineland the "taking over" of this theme from Gothic sculpture is reflected in prints somewhat earlier than in painting; in eastern Germanic countries the opposite is true as might be expected where the source was not French statuary but Italian paintings.

The Symbolic Goldfinch

RUSSIA

Goldfinches occur in Russian icons, but are usually so altered as to be quite unrecognizable. In fact, were it not for Kondakov's studies, we would not be able to connect the white, dove-like bird in many of these paintings with the goldfinch. In discussing a famous icon of the Virgin called "Konevskaia" or "Golubitskaia" with the Christ Child holding a bird (plate 32), Kondakov writes as follows.[23]

"A third type is represented in the history of Russian icon-painting by the well known miraculous Virgin honoured at Konevets . . . an island monastery in Lake Ladoga. . . . It shows Our Lady with the Child on her left arm playing with a white bird (much too small for a dove) on His left hand; His right hand holds a string to keep the bird from escaping. This motive of the Child playing with a bird is so well known in Italian painting of the fourteenth century that I have used it as a capital instance of the transmission of iconic types and artistic influence from Italy to Greece (first by way of the Italo-Cretan school) and thence to Russia. The fact is that this particular theme arose and first established itself in the art of northern France . . . and from there spread to Italy. It presents the Christ Child playing, as was the custom in those days, with a goldfinch flying on a string; another element in it is a medieval superstitution that the goldfinch is endowed with a peculiar sensitiveness to disease; if a goldfinch is brought to the bedside of a sick child it feels whether he will recover and looks towards him or away from him accordingly; it was even believed that the goldfinch had a miraculous power of sucking the peccant humors out of a sick child. It is not only in the subject that we can see the connection; the drawing of the child's figure also takes us back to Italian originals of the second half of the fourteenth century (e. g. Spinello Aretino in the Accademia at Florence, 1391) and so through Italy to the prototype in French sculpture; we see the Child pulling at the string with His right hand so as to draw back the bird which is trying to fly off His left. The dates confirm this, as the Konevets icon was brought there in 1393. . . .

"An ancient Panagiarion came to light in 1913 and, by the striking agreement of an independent variant, confirmed the descent of the Russian type from the realistic Italian subject. On this, Mary, holding the Child on her right arm, watches Him; He has taken the bird on His right hand and is looking closely at it, pressing Himself up to His Mother; His other hand is stretching the string attached to the bird and has caught the white veil that shows under her cloak. The goldfinch has its natural dark plumage. . . .

"Purely Russian icons of this theme show a white goldfinch or some sort of white bird instead of a finch."

It would seem from this that the charadrius that flourished in mediaeval mysticism as a pure white bird, became transformed in western minds into a brightly colored goldfinch only to resume its pristine albescence in the hands of the Russian icon painters because of a lack of understanding of the reasons for its western alteration.

Chapter V. The Goldfinch in Italian Art

Introduction

THE overwhelming majority of devotional pictures containing gold-finches are of Italian origin. As already intimated, the preponderance is far greater than the relative output of religious art of Italy as compared with the rest of the art producing countries of Europe; the Italian works including this bird number more than ten to every one produced elsewhere. The earliest picture containing a recognizable goldfinch is is an Italian one, made in the second half of the thirteenth century in Florence by the so-called "Maestro della Maddalena" (plate 33). In this panel the bird, while poorly constructed, is definitely a goldfinch, and is the forerunner of hundreds of others that extend the span of its occurrence in Italian religious art over the next five hundred years to its final, and by then, symbolically empty, inclusion in an eighteenth century "Madonna and Child" by Tiepolo (plate 110).

In these five centuries the motif was adopted, used, and dropped by most of the Italian schools of painting. More explicitly, artists of the following schools have been found to have utilized this icon: The Bolognese, Cremonese, Ferrarese, Florentine, Lucchese, Marchigian, Milanese, Modenese, Neapolitan, Paduan, Parmese, Piemontese, Pisan, Roman, Sardinian, Sicilian, Sienese, Umbrian, Venetian, Veronese, Vicentian, and Viterbian. I have not found goldfinches in what I have seen of the works of the schools of Bergamo, Brescia, Mantua, Rimini, and Vercelli, but all of these were small and are relatively poorly published schools. As a matter of fact, that of Mantua was hardly even a distinct school at all; while Bergamo and Brescia were relatively realistic schools running largely to portraiture rather than to symbolism.[1]

Just as there is a chronological difference in the beginnings of the various schools and in their duration, so we find similar differences in the time of first appearance of the goldfinch icon in the works produced in each of them. For our present purpose, it may suffice to point out that the motif must have spread very rapidly, as we find it very early not only in the large important cities such as Florence and Siena, but also in lesser centers like Lucca, and even in minor provincial towns like Piobesi Torinese in Piedmont.

While the chronological extremes of its occurrence in Italian art are five centuries apart, the goldfinch was not actively used as an accessory symbol during all of this long period. As a matter of fact, if we were to omit Tiepolo's "Madonna of the Goldfinch" and consider it as an atavistic work, and a very few 17th Century Bolognese eclectic works, the real span of the goldfinch symbol extends from the second half of the thirteenth century into the third quarter of the sixteenth. Two hundred years elapsed between the end of the real, active use of the icon, and Tiepolo's meaningless reinstatement of it.

In the following more detailed account of the various Italian schools, there are mentioned and discussed some 440 devotional paintings containing goldfinches by 217 artists as well as a few that are not, strictly speaking, of a devotional nature. The chronology of these works is best treated separately for each school but the following brief statement may be included here. The earliest appearance of the goldfinch is in Florentine art, in the third quarter of the thirteenth century; we find it as early as the first quarter of the fourteenth century in Lucca and Siena and Pisa; in the third quarter, in that of Modena, Milan, Piemonte, Umbria, and Venice; in the last quarter in that of Verona; in the first quarter of the fifteenth century it appears in paintings done in Sicily, Viterbo, and Liguria; in the second quarter in Naples; in the third quarter, in Vicenza and Ferrara; in the fourth quarter, in Padua, Bologna, Sardinia, and the Marche; and in the first quarter of the sixteenth century in Cremona.

The use of the goldfinch symbol appears to have died out everywhere in Italy by the end of the second quarter of the sixteenth century, except in the works of the late Bolognese eclectics of the early part of the seventeenth century and for a lone atavistic reappearance in Venice in the middle of the eighteenth, in a picture by Tiepolo.

The relative importance of the various Italian schools in the present study may be sensed from the number of pertinent works we here record from each. Of the 440 paintings, no fewer than 195 are Florentine in origin, 85 are Sienese, 51 are Venetian, 31 are Umbrian, 16 are Ferrarese, 14 are Bolognese, 13 are Milanese, 11 are Pisan, 8 are Veronese, 4 are Marchigian, 3 each are Sicilian, Ligurian, Vicenzan, and Paduan, 2 each are Cremonese, Piemontese, and Parmese, while single examples are from the other schools.

The 217 artists involved, grouped by schools, are as follows: Florentine 78, Sienese 34; Venetian 26; Umbrian 20; Ferrarese 10; Pisan 9; Milanese 8; Veronese 7; Bolognese 6; Sicilian 3; Piemontese, Neapolitan, Marchigian, and Vicentian 2 each; and the rest 1 each.

Devotional subjects were painted by the artists of Italy almost wholly in portable easel pictures, but were occasionally introduced into frescoes along with the historico-religious subjects for which that technique was chiefly employed. However, of the very great number of devotional paintings that have been found to contain the goldfinch motif, less than five percent are frescoes,[2] all the others being done either in tempera or in oil on wooden panels, with or without gesso bases, or on canvas (later works). A few of the examples in fresco are as follows. One is by a little known Piemontese painter, Giovanni da Camusetto, painted in 1359, on the west exterior of the Church of Giovanni dei Campi near Piobesi Torinese. It represents the Madonna nursing the Child who holds the bird, while on either side is an attendant angel, with St. John the Baptist on one side, balanced by St. Christopher on the other.[3] It must be admitted that the identification of the bird is not entirely satisfactory but, judging from rather small photographs of an original in not too good condition, the bird seems to have been intended to be a goldfinch. Another pertinent fresco is by Ottaviano Nelli in the Lower Church of San Francisco, Assisi, and represents the Madonna and Child with three Saints. The bird in it is definitely a goldfinch. A third, a "Madonna and Child" attributed to Maso di Banco, is now detached from the wall on which it was painted. Allowing these three to suffice for our present purposes, we may now turn to the discussion of the individual schools and their pertinent productions.

Chapter VI. The Florentine School

O F all the Italian schools that of Florence gives us not only the greatest number of devotional paintings containing goldfinches, but also the longest list of artists in whose work this motif appears. There are here assembled data on some 195 such pictures by 78 Florentine painters. The earliest, ca. 1270 (?), is by an artist known only by the descriptive name of "Maestro della Maddalena" of a Madonna and Child enthroned with two Saints and two Angels (Acton Collection, Florence) (plate 33). The Child holds the bird in His left hand; His right one reaches for a flower. The next oldest picture is by an unknown member of Cimabue's "school," ca. 1300 (Sterbini collection, Rome), a diptych in the left half of which is a Madonna and Child with St. Joseph[1] (plate 34). The goldfinch is being handed by Joseph to the Christ Child; it is perched on Joseph's right hand. Strangely enough, I know of no other painting in which the bird is so placed; it is the one instance of direct connection between the bird and Joseph. Inasmuch as it is far too early a picture to be interpreted as merely reflecting pictorial tradition without special symbolic meaning (as in some late works where one often gets the feeling that the artist may have felt that he ought to put in a goldfinch because so many others had done so before him) we cannot pass it by without comment. The action of the picture precludes the possibility of its being based on the Pseudo-Matthew legend of the Child's playful bringing to life the toy birds given Him. Furthermore, the supposed date of the painting[2] may allow us to rule out the humanizing tendencies of later Trecento and Quattrocento art. Of all the symbolic meanings crowded into the figure of the goldfinch, which one or ones have we to do with here? The fact that this work is cast largely in the mould and, even if to a lesser extent, in the spirit of the Italian version of the Byzantine tradition, should remind us that it is definitely of that group of Madonna and Child compositions

[65]

that may be classed as sibylline or prophetic rather than maternal or emotional. Bearing this in mind, it would seem that Joseph is handing to the
Infant the goldfinch as a symbol of the Resurrection that is to come. (The
ideas of Sacrifice and of the Soul are of course also present in connection
with the Resurrection theme.) Just what thoughts were in that nameless
mind whose hand constructed this picture we can never know with certainty but it seems not unreasonable to consider Resurrection as the most
likely theme in this case. Joseph would hardly have been chosen to handle
the symbol of Fertility, and the date of the picture puts it rather early
for the probability of the bird being a plague augur, as the very severe
epidemics which had such great effect on art and iconography came later.

Beginning with these two panels, we find that the 195 Florentine paintings under consideration show the following chronological distribution.
From the second half of the thirteenth century we have 1; from the first
quarter of the fourteenth century we have 10, from the second quarter 61,
from the third quarter 14, and from the last 23; from the first quarter
of the fifteenth century 19, from the second 21, from the third 14, and
from the last 21. In the first quarter of the sixteenth century were produced 11 of our pictures, and with them the production record ceases,
the latest works being done around 1520, from approximately which date
comes Bugiardini's "Madonna and Child with the Infant St. John" now in
the Borghese Gallery, Rome, and a similar composition in the Musée
Napoléon III at Angers, attributed by Berenson to "Tomasso," an artistic
personality parallel with Lorenzo di Credi but at times close to Piero di
Cosimo.

The greatest single production peak of these pictures coincides roughly
with the time of the Black Death fairly late in the second quarter of the
fourteenth century. This quarter century witnessed the creation of more
such works than all the rest of that century and nearly as many as were
produced in the whole of the fifteenth century. On the other hand, early
termination of the use of the motif in the latter part of the first quarter
of the sixteenth century is somewhat surprising, as devotional paintings
continued to be made until considerably later by many Florentine artists.[3]

The fourteenth century is here credited with 108 pictures containing
goldfinches, to the fifteenth century's 75.

For the sake of the factual record and to enable the reader to see exactly what material is behind my remarks and to enable him to add to it, there is given in the Appendix, pp. 141-151, an alphabetical list of the Florentine painters with their works in which I have found goldfinches.

It is obvious from this list that the use of the goldfinch motif was very widespread among the painters of Florence. There were, however, a number of them who apparently never made use of this icon, although they painted suitable pictures in which it might well have been included.[4] Among them are some such as Fra Angelico, Baldovinetti, Botticelli, Filippino and Filippo Lippi, and Giotto, who had followers who did make use of the goldfinch, but whether this implies an acquiescence towards, if not an actual use of, the icon by the masters is not clear. On the other hand we have other non-users of the goldfinch such as Andrea del Sarto and Domenico Veneziano whose work seems entirely apart from the goldfinch motif. Painters like Bronzino,[5] Castagno, the Pollaiuoli, and Pontormo, made relatively few devotional pictures and the absence of goldfinches in them may not reflect a personal reaction to the motif. Even the most prolific goldfinch painters made many devotional pictures without the bird. Some well known artists are entirely omitted here. This does not mean that they did or did not make use of the goldfinch icon, but merely that I have not been able to check the whole of their output and that in the pictures I have seen there were no goldfinches. Masolino, Raffaellino del Garbo, and Lorenzo di Credi are such cases.

In any discussion of the frequency with which a given painter introduced the goldfinch into his work we must remember that some artists, like Giotto, were primarily painters of frescoes and not of easel pictures. The subject matter in fresco art is largely concerned with historico-religious topics and not with devotional subjects. Naturally goldfinches play no symbolic role in them and are therefore not introduced. On the other hand, Giotto's pupils Taddeo Gaddi, Bernardo Daddi, and Jacopo del Casentino, and their followers, were the painters who produced far more pictures pertinent to our study than any others. Being so dominated by the precept and influence of their illustrious master, they would hardly have made such very extensive use of the icon if there had been any definite unwillingness to use it on Giotto's part. We cannot therefore assume that the icon or its symbolism was antagonistic or even foreign to Giotto's iconographic system. He merely had little opportunity to include it in his works. This is definitely not the case with such dissimilar artists as Fra Angelico, Botticelli, the two Lippis, and Andrea del Sarto. As pointed out elsewhere in this study, the goldfinch as a symbol of Fertility and as an Augur in Disease was of no great interest to an ascetic, mystic, despiser of the flesh like Fra Angelico and this may account for its absence in his work. The one picture, sometimes attributed to him, but as often given to his "school," (now in the Schaeffer collection, Frankfort) that does have a goldfinch in it, has the bird almost entirely hidden in the Child's right hand, only its head showing above His closed fingers.

The case of Botticelli is somewhat harder to understand as he had no such overwhelming religious mysticism and asceticism as the friar of Fiesole, but was deeply interested in the humanistic movement of the time and frequently worked on themes from pagan and classical sources. He may be here considered together with his teacher Filippo Lippi, and his pupil Filippino Lippi, both of whom likewise painted many devotional pictures but seemingly never introduced a goldfinch in any of them. We have here a continuous three-generation line of painters of devotional pictures, disinterested in, if not actually opposed to, the use of this motif, plying their trade in a community in which the icon had a great and continuing popularity. It can hardly be mere accidental coincidence that the goldfinch was absent from the works of all three. In order to discover the reasons for this absence we may step back, as it were, from our close scrutiny of the detail of the goldfinch, and see the icon in its proper historical perspective in the development of painting in Florence.

In the nearly one hundred years between Giotto and Masaccio when Florentine painting produced no masters of the first rank (except the, from our present standpoint, rather special cases of Fra Angelico, Orcagna, and Uccello[6]), but was content with copying the manner and diluting the content of what Giotto had left, we find that many of the lesser men, the imitators and followers, the popularizers and distorters of Giotto, and of Orcagna, having relatively less of their own to give, and having a less subtle clientele to deal with, appear almost to have brought to their work the aid of symbols such as the goldfinch, to help assure the appeal and to lower to the general public level of understanding the meaning of what they were depicting. Aside from the very important conditioning factor that their period was that of the greatest plague epidemics with its concomitant demand for more and ever more devotional pictures with a new stress on such matters as Fertility and Protection from Disease, the artists themselves being less able to make the figures in their works convey their messages by purely artistic means, were forced by the demands of an unsubtle public, to rely more and more on obvious symbols. If it were not for the fact that some of the greatest artists did occasionally introduce the goldfinch into their works, one might almost be tempted to conclude that the presence of the symbol was an indication of some lack of intellectual or artistic ability on the part of the painter, or (and this seems more likely) of unusually urgent demands for its inclusion on the part of those ordering the pictures.

Masaccio[7] used the goldfinch once — in an early work, if one may use the term in connection with one who died so young, the "Virgin and Child with St. Michael and St. John the Baptist" in the Oratory at Montemarciano, (plate 45 and 46). Aside from containing the earliest use of the symbol by one of the truly great masters of Florence, this picture is one of the relatively few paintings of the "Madonna lactans" type that includes a goldfinch. Inasmuch as Masaccio never returned to the use of this icon although he painted a number of pictures that gave him ample opportunity to do so, the question may be raised (but unfortunately not answered) as to whether he considered it a trivial thing not on the same plane as the rest of the subject matter in his more mature works.

After Masaccio's untimely death, the course of Florentine painting was left in five main pairs of hands — the developers of the tendencies known as naturalism and expressionism, as well as the continuers of what went before. It is worthy of note, even at the expense of partial repetition, that not one of these leaders — Fra Angelico, Castagno, Uccello, Filippo Lippi,[8] and Domenico Veneziano, made use of the goldfinch motif. Continuing our historical survey we find that the next generation's leaders, the men in it who really gave new ideas, new form, new impetus to painting, men like Botticelli, Antonio Pollaiuolo, and Verrocchio, similarly, for one reason or another, refrained from utilizing the goldfinch symbol. Inasmuch as his influence was so potently and constantly behind much of early Florentine painting, it is only right to mention that Donatello nowhere in all the extent of his *oeuvre* ever introduced this motif.[9]

By the time we come to the next generation we find a gradual but definite change in the situation. By now the main avenues of artistic expression had been explored; what remained was to perfect them, and to pursue them to their highest pinnacles of achievement. Consequently, we find less difference in the use of accessory symbols between artists of unequal talent. These men were, as individuals, following similar or dissimilar paths of art, but were no longer, with only two important exceptions, engaged in an effort to modify the forms and styles and contents and methods of art as they found it. These two were Leonardo da Vinci, who added the academically studied effects of contrapposto and chiaroscuro, and Michelangelo, who in his stormy elemental passion discarded many symbols, expressing through the human form his feelings and thoughts in a more powerful and more immediately realizable manner. An innovator pushing a new method or concept forward in spite of the inertia of the old and the long accepted, is apt to look upon time-honored symbols as part of the residue of earlier inspirational fires and as a cluttering mass of impedimenta to be disregarded if not actually discarded. When, however, the main effort is to perfect and improve the legacy of former generations of artists, the tendency is to keep intact that heritage and to use all of it to the best advantage. Furthermore, the longer any item included in that art heritage, such as the topic of our concern here — the goldfinch, had been in popular use, the more ingrained in tradition it became and the more difficult it was, even for the very freest of artists, to discard it. Thus, at this stage of Florentine painting, we find artists as dissimilar and unequal as Leonardo da Vinci, Domenico Ghirlandajo, Cosimo Rosselli, and Jacopo del Sellaio, meeting on common ground in their symbolic iconography.

Florentine painting continued to have this quality-transcending unity of iconographical harmony until early in the sixteenth century when its course first began to be upset by the dynamic force of Michelangelo, who was destined to alter it more and more as the century progressed.

This, in general, is the historical pattern against which we may view the individual occurrences and the various usages of the goldfinch. Like all general statements, it is oversimplified. It does not follow with any real precision that during the Trecento and the first half of the Quattrocento no important artist was ever guilty of painting a goldfinch in any of his pictures, or that after 1450 all painters, good or bad, used it equally. There are exceptions, but they do not seem to be sufficiently serious to alter the

general truth of the sketchy account just presented. Filippino Lippi is such
an exception; Andrea del Sarto is another. In the case of the former it
may be that influence of his teacher, Botticelli, of whom he was not only
the pupil, and in upbringing almost the son, but also the devoted follower,
may have been responsible to some extent. It seems to me that the absence
of the goldfinch in the two dozen or more Madonna and Child pictures
by Filippino suggests the blindness of his continuance of his master's pictorial usages. The case of Andrea del Sarto is probably to be explained, at
least in part, by his definite leaning towards physical reality as opposed to
the symbolic and the spiritual aspects of religious art. This lack of the
subtler and loftier elements is obvious in his Madonnas regardless of the
presence or absence of accessory symbols.

Aside from the painters who never made use of the goldfinch motif,
there were others who used it but seldom, indicating that it probably did
not strike the same responsive chord in them (or their patrons) that it did
in those who included it in their pictures more frequently. Thus, among
artists who made a considerable number of paintings suitable for the inclusion of the icon, the following appear to have used it but once — Leonardo
da Vinci, and Masaccio. There are many others, such as Albertinelli, Fra
Bartolommeo, Domenico Ghirlandajo, Neri di Bicci, and Cosimo Rosselli,
in only one of each of whose pictures I have found goldfinches. However, I
have not been able to examine all the works of these artists and so cannot
say that they did not use the motif more frequently. It may be pointed
out in passing that the relative absence of the icon from the *oeuvre* of
Ghirlandajo is not wholly in keeping with the severely disparaging opin-
ions of him current in literature. If he were merely the talented but uninspired manipulator of the stock fixtures and of the acquired knowledge
and skill of the art tradition of his city we might expect him to rely on
symbols more often where the subjects painted permitted. However, as
far as I have been able to ascertain, he painted the goldfinch but once and
then as a minor, rather disconnected pictorial element, — in his "Adoration
of the Magi," in which the bird is placed in the bottom center of the picture
and is actually cut off just below its middle by the edge of the painting.[10]
It is merely standing there quite detached from any of the figures and
from the action of the picture.

Turning our attention now to the Florentine painters who used the goldfinch motif most frequently, we find that the immediate pupils of Giotto and of Orcagna and their close followers were unquestionably the most prolific. Over a hundred devotional pictures containing goldfinches are attributable to this group, divided among some thirty-five artists. It must be remembered that it was these painters who lived through the severest plague period when there was an unprecedented demand for portable devotional paintings. Bernardo Daddi and his immediate followers were responsible for thirty-four of these pictures; Taddeo and Agnolo Gaddi for sixteen; and Jacopo del Casentino and his assistants for seven, (plates 41-56). As shown in a later part of this study (p. 110-113), the way in which these "Giotteschi" utilized the icon reflects greatly to the credit of Taddeo Gaddi who is revealed, in this particular, as a greater artistic mentality than either Daddi or Jacopo del Casentino.

Coming to later painters, we find the goldfinch used by Pesellino and his assistants in at least six pictures (plate 66-67), by Pseudo Pier Francesco Fiorentino in seven; by Niccolo di Pietro Gerini in six pictures, by Lorenzo di Niccolo, the Master of the Bambino Vispo, and by the Master of San Miniato in five each; by Piero di Cosimo; Pier Francesco Fiorentino, and by Spinello Aretino in at least four each. The exact number is relatively immaterial; the fact that so many artists made multiple uses of the bird symbol indicates that it met with their approval as painters of pictures and with needs and desires of the art-buying, or rather, the art-ordering public as well.

At the risk of seeming to extend the subject of the goldfinch beyond its proper limits it may be pointed out that there are some devotional pictures that might almost be titled "Madonna and Child not yet with a Goldfinch." In the works of Pseudo Pier Francesco Fiorentino, and of his lesser shadow, Pier Francesco Fiorentino, we find several paintings in which the Child's hands are cupped as if holding some object, such as a goldfinch or pomegranate or other commonly used symbol. Yet the hands are empty and devoid of any possible meaning in their present vacuity. A pertinent example is the panel by Pier Francesco in the Widener collection, National Gallery of Art, Washington, (plate 67). Another very similar one is in the Kaiser Friedrich Museum in Berlin. How are we to understand these works? The answer, it seems to me, lies in the fact that Pseudo Pier Francesco Fiorentino (to say nothing of his shadow) was an uninspired and unoriginal picture maker who took his compositions largely from the works of his abler contemporaries, especially from Pesellino. Like other painters of his day, he probably kept a shop or *bottega*, and it is my guess that he had numbers of such pictures ready in stock, and added to them the symbolic object requested by the purchaser, according to his specifications at the time of the sale. Such a commercial and completely inartistic method seems not incompatible with what little we know of the artist and would explain these otherwise unintelligible pictures. If this explanation be found acceptable, then Pseudo Pier Francesco is to be relegated to the bottom of the pile of goldfinch painters just as deservedly as Masaccio and Leonardo and Raphael are on the top.

An unusual use of the goldfinch occurs in Jacopo del Sellaio's "St. John the Baptist" in the National Gallery of Art, Washington. The Baptist is represented as a youth of 12 or 13 years, standing in a landscape with a view of Florence in the background; at a little pool at his feet a goldfinch is standing as if drinking, (plate 69 and 69a). There is nothing to indicate whether this picture is a fragment of a larger one or a part of a polyptych or not, but taken as it is, by itself, the goldfinch appears to be concerned here with the theme of Baptism.

Chapter VII. The Sienese School

NEXT in importance, for our study, to the school of Florence is that of Siena. The whole course of Sienese painting was somewhat briefer, the number of its artists fewer, and consequently the quantity of its artistic results smaller than was the case in Florence. The use of the goldfinch by the masters of Siena was far more restricted to the "ordinary" Madonna and Child composition than it was in the hands of the Florentines. As a matter of fact, while I have found the bird in some 85 pictures by 34 Sienese painters, only two of these paintings are of other subjects. One is the winsome little panel by Sassetta (in the Metropolitan Museum, Maitland F. Griggs collection, New York) (plate 90), which is actually a fragment of the background of a larger "Adoration of the Magi." The other is a triptych dealing with Beato Agostino Novello with four scenes from his legend, by Simone Martini, in the sacristy of San Agostino in Siena, (plate 74).

The earliest Sienese picture included in this study is by a follower of Duccio, dated ca. 1290, a "Madonna and Child," now in the collection of the Detroit Institute of Arts, (plate 72). It shows the Christ Child holding a very poorly drawn bird which appears to have been intended to be a goldfinch. The little bird is brown with a broad golden stripe across the wings and a red crown, but otherwise it is much too dark and is very poorly formed. Its shape is almost as much that of a swallow as a goldfinch. The next earliest picture is also by a follower of Duccio (Paris, a private collection; illustrated in Perkins, Diana, vol. 8, 1933, p. 115, f. pl. 1-2) and is said to have been painted around the first years of the fourteenth century. The bird in it is too far gone to tell with certainty what species it was intended to look like.

Another panel dating from the same time may be mentioned in passing although the bird in it is definitely not a goldfinch but a swallow — a

Madonna and Child attributed to Segna di Bonaventura (Mrs. R. M. Hurd collection, New York). My reason for mentioning this work is that it offers some suggestive evidence as to the basic significance of the goldfinch in Sienese art.

Sienese painting, until the advent of such extraneous eclectics as Sodoma and Beccafumi, was far more conservative than was any other major school in Italy. It continued, with refinements both of art and of sentiment, the Italianized Byzantine and Gothic traditions, and only to a limited extent did it attempt to instill into its devotional images the naturalism of form and the expression of emotion so sought after in Florence and elsewhere. It follows from this that its use of accessory symbols, such as the goldfinch, was also more traditionalized, less prone to take on new meanings, and especially less prone to do so with meanings so tied to the flesh and so removed from the spirit as Fertility, and as Augury in case of Disease. In other words, the chief connotations inherent in the goldfinch in the hands of Sienese painters are those of the Soul and Resurrection. It is therefore not without significance that we find one of the earliest identifiable usages of a small bird by a Sienese artist to represent a swallow, the bird most intimately bound up with the theme of Resurrection.[1] It does not follow that the devastations of the plague made no mark on Sienese art; the output of devotional pictures reached a fairly high peak in Siena as in Florence (but not to the same degree) during the worst plague period, but the appeal made through art had to do less with the protection of the individual or the family than with the themes of the Soul and the Resurrection, themes bound up with the future life, made suddenly so dangerously imminent by the earthly ravages of the bubonic scourge. That the goldfinch was also symbolically linked to the plague theme in Siena is demonstrated in Simone Martini's inclusion of not one, but four, of these birds around his figure of Beato Agostino Novello, a man whose claim to honor and fame rested largely on his helping victims of the plague, (plate 74).

Unlike the history of Florentine art, which is liberally interspersed with artists of great stature from its beginnings in Giotto to its culmination in Michelangelo, the story of painting in Siena begins with its greatest figures and descends from them to lesser men, never again even approaching its earlier heights. The "founder" and greatest figure of the school, Duccio di Buoninsegna, a slightly older contemporary of Giotto, never included the goldfinch in any of his known pictures although he had ample opportunity to do so had he wanted to, for unlike his great Florentine colleague, Duccio worked on easel pictures and not in the medium of fresco-painting. Therefore we cannot assume a reason for the absence of the goldfinch in Duccio's work similar to that which holds for Giotto. Duccio's predecessors, men like Guido da Siena and Margaritone of Arezzo, seem never to have used the goldfinch either. If we look upon Duccio as the "last great artist of antiquity," compared with Giotto as the "first of the moderns," this absence of the goldfinch motif is merely what we should expect to find in his work. In other words, Duccio presents no problem from the standpoint of the present inquiry; he antedates the goldfinch symbol in Sienese art. The fact that he does so is, however, due to the very conservative nature of his city and its culture, for the motif had already made its appearance in religious painting in not too far away Florence, and had reached the relatively outlying provincial town of Lucca by not later than the first years of the fourteenth century.

Duccio's immediate pupils, Simone Martini, Pietro Lorenzetti and Segna de Bonaventura were certainly not greatly given to using the goldfinch symbol. I have found no goldfinches in any devotional picture by Simone Martini, although, as already mentioned, he did make use of it in his triptych of Beato Agostino Novello and his legend, (plate 74). Similarly, none of Pietro Lorenzetti's numerous Madonna and Child compositions that I have seen contain a goldfinch. The bird does occur in a picture in the Pinacoteca in Siena, labelled "manner of Pietro Lorenzetti" and in another in the same gallery, attributed to his school. The goldfinch in the latter picture I cannot be wholly certain of as the reproduction seen was too poor for more than probable identification. To Segna di Bonaventura in addition to the "Madonna and Child with a Swallow," in the R. M. Hurd collection, New York, already discussed, is attributed another comparable panel in the Pinacoteca, Siena (attributed to either Segna himself or to Francesco di Segna di Bonaventura) in which the Christ Child holds a recognizable goldfinch in His left hand. Another close follower of Duccio, Ugolino da Siena, of whose works I have seen only a part, yielded no goldfinches to my quest, but the so-called "Ugolino Lorenzetti" an artistic personality combining traits of his two namesakes, painted a goldfinch in the Christ Child's left hand in a "Madonna and Child" picture in the Robert Lehman collection, New York, and another, probable, but not certainly identifiable, goldfinch in another similar work in the Wallraf-Richartz Museum, Cologne.

As in Florentine painting, we find in Siena too that the artists most given to the use of the goldfinch motif were the lesser men, ranging from the higher level of such painters as Neroccio, Lippo Memmi, Barna, Taddeo di Bartolo, Luca di Tommé, Andrea Vanni, Benvenuto di Giovanni, Girolamo di Benvenuto, and Fungai, to the lower one of such rather monotonous picture makers as Sano di Pietro, Cozzarelli, Francesco di Vannuccio, and Gualtieri di Giovanni. Artists of greater originality and higher gifts, such as Giovanni di Paolo, and, except for one attempt apiece, Matteo di Giovanni and Sassetta, appear to have shown no inclination to include the goldfinch symbol in their works.

The chronological distribution of the goldfinch icon in Sienese art is as follows — from the last quarter of the thirteenth century we have 1; from the first quarter of the fourteenth century we have 2; from the second quarter 14; from the third 6, and from the last quarter 9; from the first quarter of the fifteenth century we have 12; from the second quarter 4; from the third 7; and from the last quarter 11; from the first quarter of the sixteenth century we have 18, and from the second quarter 1. The second quarter of the fourteenth century, the period of greatest production in Florence, here runs slightly behind the first quarter of the sixteenth century and only slightly ahead of the first and last quarters of the fifteenth. This difference from what we found in the record of Florentine usage of the goldfinch symbol may be, to some extent, a reflection of the fact that, unlike the painters of Florence, the artists of Siena throughout the history of their school, worked chiefly on easel pictures and correspondingly less on frescoes. This gave to the Sienese a more even and equable chronological distribution of opportunities to create devotional paintings. Such wall decorations as the "Good and Bad Government" or the "Guidoriccio da Fogliano" are the exceptions and not the rule in Sienese painting, whereas the role of the fresco in Florence was dominant to the extent of forming the core of an art of which the innumerable easel pictures, important though they be, are, in some ways, only the periphery. Early in the fifteenth century Florentine artists like Masaccio, Fra Angelico, and Castagno, to mention but a few, were largely occupied with storying the walls of their churches with biblical episodes, and consequently fewer pictures suitable for goldfinches were produced.

The Sienese painters and their works in which I found goldfinches are listed in the Appendix (p. 151-155). The ample illustration, in literature, of Sienese pictures is a relatively recent development as compared with that of Florentine works, and the list, compiled as it is largely from such sources, is therefore probably less complete than is that of the pictures done in the latter city.

Two relatively minor Sienese painters call for special comment in the present connection — Luca di Tommé and Taddeo di Bartolo. Inasmuch as the goldfinch was definitely a minor accessory symbol the artist was, on the whole, even in conservative Siena, relatively free to pose it as he wished, in other words to use it as an opportunity for the expression of his growing mastery over the problems of representational art. No Sienese artists made greater use of this chance than did these two. In their works we find the bird posed in very varying positions, as if the artists were constantly experimenting with it. Thus, in a painting now in the Fitzwilliam Museum, Cambridge (plate 89), Luca di Tommé has placed the goldfinch with its tail towards the spectator, its wings raised, and its head thereby hidden from view![2] When we consider how much easier it is to recognize the goldfinch from its cephalic markings than from its wings, back, or tail, this pose can be interpreted only as a bit of artistic dexterity. In another picture (Siena, Chiesa Contrada del Bruco) the bird, held in the Child's left hand, is in left profile, but unlike most such bird profiles, it has its wings partly raised. Luca was no expert bird illustrator; his goldfinches are creatures more of his memory than of his observation but he constantly experimented with the figure of the bird causing it to be viewed from various sides and angles. Taddeo di Bartolo, similarly, appears to have been much interested in giving animation to the motif, and with results naturalistically more correct. In his "Madonna and Child" in the National Gallery of Art, Washington (plate 77), he places the bird not in the Child's hand, but perched on His left shoulder, in a lively pose with its wings partly arched; its bill open, matching in its restlessness the active pose of the Child Himself, who is here definitely a "Bambino Vispo" type. In another painting (Perugia, Provincial Gallery) the bird, although held in the Child's left hand, has its wings spread, its bill open, and is full of action, quite different from still another usage of the icon by the same artist (Cambridge, Mass., Fogg Museum) where it is held in a quiet, restful position, (plate 78).

We may recall that in our discussion of the three-figured composition of the Madonna, Christ Child, and Infant St. John, we found but a single example of this type of picture, containing a goldfinch, attributed to a Sienese painter, and this one a late work of Bernardino Fungai, done under the extraneous influence of the Umbrian Pinturicchio. The theme was too playful for the tastes and conservatism of the Sienese, and in Fungai's one attempt the goldfinch is placed not near the center of the action of the picture as it was by so many Florentines, but on the ground at the bottom of the painting, standing by an open book.

Iconographically peculiar is Fungai's "Holy Family" in the National Gallery, London. In it the goldfinch is pecking at a plum, which it steadies with one foot.

It remains only to add that a goldfinch occurs in a painting by Sodoma of "Leda and the Swan" (Rome, Borghese Gallery). Inasmuch as the Leda story is not a part of devotional art, I have not included this work in the list of pictures, but I mention it here chiefly because I cannot explain the presence of the bird in it on symbolic grounds, unless it be a fertility symbol, bearing on the fruitful union of Leda and the Swan.[3]

Chapter VIII. The Venetian School

COMPARED with their colleagues in Florence and Siena, the painters of Venice, considering their numbers and their productivity, showed relatively less interest in the goldfinch motif. For one thing, Venetian art was more worldly, more inclined to the magnificent and the sumptuous, and less concerned with spiritual values; it was also relatively more influenced by a devotion to the State as opposed to the glorification or the well-being of the family or person for whom the individual paintings were made than was the case in other Italian art centers. Furthermore, the rise of a distinctive school of painting got a later start in Venice than in many other cities, and that delayed beginning was under the influence of neither a Florentine nor a Sienese, but an itinerant Umbrian, Gentile da Fabriano, and a Veronese, Pisanello. As is indicated in the discussion of that school, the painters of Umbria were not particularly given to the use of the goldfinch motif.[1] The influence of Pisanello was short-lived, as he worked in fresco, which medium proved unsuited to Venetian climate. When, later in its history, the trend of Venetian painting came under the cold, classical influence of Mantegna, this new tendency brought with it no goldfinches. That the goldfinch motif was previously inherent in Venetian painting is proved, however, by its use by such an early artist as Lorenzo Veneziano (ca. 1375) and somewhat later by Donato Bragadin, (plates 91 and 92). Its relative scarcity in the art of the region of the lagoons is indisputable, however, and is reflected by its similar rarity in the works of the adjoining and relatively stationary early school of Murano, which is here treated as a part of the school of Venice. All in all, I have found goldfinches in some 51 pictures by 26 Venetian artists.

The chronological distribution of these paintings is quite different from what we found in Florentine and in Sienese art.[2] From the third quarter of the fourteenth century we have one; then comes a gap of two generations to another lone example produced in the second quarter of the fifteenth century; the third quarter of this century is represented in our list by 6 pictures; the fourth quarter of the fifteenth century by 19; the first quarter of the sixteenth century by 19; the second quarter by 3; the third by 1. This actually ends the meaningful usage of the icon, but surprisingly enough, two centuries later, in the fourth decade of the eighteenth century Tiepolo reintroduced it in his "Madonna of the Goldfinch" (plate 110), (Washington, National Gallery of Art). The time of most active use of the goldfinch by the painters of Venice is largely restricted to the fifty years from about 1475 to about 1525 during which time 41 of the 51 pictures listed were produced.

In considering the record of the goldfinch in Venetian painting we should remember that of all the major Italian schools of painting, that of Venice had the shortest active history accompanied by the most rapid development. The life span of the two generations of the Bellini family practically encompasses the most important developments in Venetian art. Even the works of Giovanni Bellini alone give a surprising epitome of the changes from the early, fairly traditionalized manner to the later, full and free and sumptuous style.

The list of Venetian paintings in which the goldfinch symbol has been noted is given in the Appendix, p. 156-158. Even the most casual glance at this list will reveal the absence of names that to most of us represent much of the best in Venetian painting. Thus, we find no mention of Titian, or Tintoretto, or Giorgione, or Palma. Andrea Mantegna, who came to be so intimately bound up with the development of Venetian art, is likewise absent. Surprisingly few pictures are listed by such prolific painters as Giovanni Bellini, Vittore Carpaccio, and Paolo Veronese. In fact, the only Venetian artists that appear to have made fairly frequent use of the goldfinch symbol were the two Crivellis, Carlo and Vittorio, Solario, and Bastiani. Gentile Bellini and Bartolommeo Vivarini are other names absent from the list; likewise Lotto, Catena, Cariani, and Paris Bordone. It must be understood in connection with these last names that I have not been able to examine the entire output of these artists and it is possible that some of them may have included a goldfinch in a picture not seen by me.

The two Crivellis may be considered together. Those of their paintings here involved that were not done by Carlo are at least reflections of his art from the feebler hands of his brother Vittorio. Carlo Crivelli was off the main line of the development of Venetian painting. In a way he may be said to have looked backward and not forward and became fixed as a sort of anachronistic artistic personality in the midst of an onrushing, surging flood of artistic activity and development. His fondness for accessory symbols (all his works are full of them — vegetables, fruits, flowers, flies, birds) derives from this tradition-loving archaizing tendency, and, I think, explains his inclination to include the goldfinch in his paintings. Vittorio merely aped his brother. In the work of Vittorio the motif is handled in a rather haphazard meaningless manner. Thus, in his "Madonna and Child" (plate 98), (in the Museum of Fine Arts, Philadelphia) the goldfinch is perched high up in the picture on a curtain rod from which is suspended a brocaded curtain hanging down behind the throne on which the Madonna and Child are sitting. In Vittorio's picture in the Vatican, the Child holds a little mirror, and a goldfinch tethered on a string.[3] Carlo himself at least once included the goldfinch without apparent symbolic reason; in his painting of the "Vision Appearing to the Beato Gabriele Ferretti"[4] the bird, very small and inconspicuous because in the middle background, is perched facing away from the spectator, on a horizontal narrow branch of a tree directly over the kneeling figure of the friar Ferretti. It seems quite unconnected with the action of the picture and gives the impression of a merely pictorial and very minor detail. In spite of the great differences in the pictures and the artists one cannot help but recall Luca di Tommé's "Madonna and Child with Angels" in the Fitzwilliam Museum, Cambridge (plate 89), in which the bird also is turned away from the spectator. In Crivelli's painting the bird is turned away from the main personage in the picture as well, and is apparently unaware of the apparition of the Madonna and Child in the mandorla in the sky. This painting seems to suggest that Crivelli was not necessarily using the goldfinch only as a symbol; it also pleased him to include it merely for its pictorial qualities.

Turning now to Bastiani it may be pointed out that not only have we found four of his paintings to contain goldfinches, but two others, here listed as by Giovanni Bellini (Venice, Cà d'Oro, and London, National Gallery) have been attributed as often to Bastiani as to Bellini. That Bastiani had a decided predilection for the goldfinch motif is evidenced, as noted elsewhere in this study, by his inclusion of it in two paintings of the Annunciation, among the very few representations of this theme to contain the bird as far as I have been able to discover. The multiplicity of animal forms in these two works suggests an interest in natural history, a tendency towards faunal embellishment of the stage setting in his pictures that brings Bastiani together with such otherwise completely dissimilar artists as the Marchigian, Folchetto da Sanginesio, and the Veronese, Pisanello, from whose works, indeed, he may have first gotten the idea. Yet in his other works, here of immediate concern to us, his "Madonna and Child" (plate 108) pictures, Bastiani includes no other form of animal life than the goldfinch.

If we were to follow those critics who give to Bastiani the two pictures just as often (and here also, after Berenson) given to Giovanni Bellini, we find that the latter, one of the most prolific producers of devotional art suitable for the inclusion of the goldfinch, is left with but a single case to his credit. This picture (plate 96), (New York, P. S. Straus collection) is one of those unfortunate ones in which the identity of the bird is not wholly certain. I know this work only from a photograph and I include it here as probably a goldfinch. It may be noted, in passing that in another "Madonna and Child" in New York (Bache collection) Bellini has given the Christ Child a swallow to hold.

Carpaccio's use of the goldfinch leaves us in some doubt as to whether he had much idea as to what it symbolized. In his "Saint Ursula Taking Leave of Her Parents" a goldfinch is standing on a parapet in front of the scene. While it may have been intended as a symbol of Sacrifice and of Resurrection and may therefore be prophetic of the saint's martyrdom and of her subsequent bliss in Heaven, it is only by a rather far-fetched assumption on our part that it can be so interpreted. The legend of St. Ursula would hardly have been considered a vehicle for a Fertility symbol, and not a very likely one for a disease augur.

In his "Annunciation" Carpaccio included a number of birds: three white doves on a horizontal rod over the Virgin; behind the announcing angel, on the garden ground are a pheasant, a goldfinch, and two unidentified birds in the far background. Again it is doubtful if the master had any particular symbolism in mind.

In Carpaccio's magnificent "Meditation on the Passion," in the Metropolitan Museum of Art, a goldfinch is to be seen perched on the ruins of the right side of the back of a marble throne on which the dead body of the Saviour is relaxed. Another small bird, possibly intended to be a titmouse, or, perhaps a small bunting, is flying off into the background behind and above the throne. This is the only painting in which I have found the goldfinch in which Christ is shown as older than a small child, but I doubt if the bird has any particular symbolic meaning here. The picture literally teems with zoological specimens; aside from the goldfinch and the titmouse there are a red parrot, two rabbits, a lion (of St. Jerome), a horse and a fox or a wolf, while leopards appear in two places and deer in three. Carpaccio, like so many Venetians, and especially as one of the most genre-minded of Venetian painters, seemed to have a great interest in natural history and frequently introduced animal forms in his pictures without any symbolic significance. In this he was the forerunner of such an artist as Paolo Veronese, who actually ran into difficulties with the Church authorities because of this tendency.

The use of the goldfinch in at least one devotional picture by Paolo Veronese (plate 95) is difficult to discuss as we have no assurance that it necessarily meant anything symbolically to him. It is known that he was in none too good standing with the Inquisition because of his tendency to include irrelevant and even distracting figures and episodes in his religious paintings, and all we can say of his goldfinch is that he was on safe ground in including it.

As pointed out elsewhere in this paper, Tiepolo's use of the goldfinch (plate 110) seems to be a case of atavism, quite devoid of symbolic significance.

Of interest because of its unusual treatment of the goldfinch is Rondinelli's "Madonna and Child" in the Doria Palace, Rome (plate 111). The bird is shown flying off into the background; its departure is watched by both the Virgin and the Child with rather sad prophetic expressions. This suggests that the goldfinch here stands for the coming Crucifixion and the Passion. A work of almost exactly the same composition, by an assistant of Giovanni Bellini shows, not a goldfinch but another, unidentified bird in the same position.[5]

A painting, not included in the list because of its non-devotional nature, but that deserves passing mention because of a goldfinch in it, is an early sixteenth century picture of St. Jerome by Philippus Veronensis.[6] The saint is shown sitting with his lion at his side. In the lower foreground is a stump on which a goldfinch is perched; a piece of paper bearing the artist's signature is attached to the same stump. The juxtaposition of the bird and the signature reveals the symbolic emptiness of the former; it seems included because of tradition and for its pictorial qualities.

Another non-devotional, sixteenth century, Venetian painting that may be mentioned here is Francesco Vecellio's "St. Augustine Expounding the Rules to Three Monks" (in the Church of San Salvatore, Venice). In the lower part of the picture are two monks kneeling and one standing with a book, before St. Augustine who is talking to them. Far up at the top of this tall vertical picture is a break in the wall from which hang some vines and on which sits a goldfinch. Lower down on the cornice of an arch is a white dove. Both birds are far too big for the proper demands of perspective.

Chapter IX. The Umbrian School
(Perugia, Urbino, Fabriano, etc.)

THROUGHOUT their history as a school, the painters of Umbria
seem to be less self contained, more receptive to outside influences
than were those of any other major art center in Italy. Consequently their
history, insofar as it concerns us here as a background against which to
examine their use of the goldfinch motif, is less a continuous unfolding
than a series of relatively disconnected extraneous influences and their
respective results. By and large, it may be said that the Umbrian painters
were not especially interested in the goldfinch symbol, and that when they
made any extensive use of it they were either not trained in Umbria or
had come away from there or were working under the influence of Florentine or Sienese exemplars.

I have found goldfinches in 31 pictures by 20 Umbrian painters, distributed chronologically as follows: the earliest works, 7 in number, date
from the third quarter of the fourteenth century, and are all almost as
much of Florentine as of Umbrian origin, being all by Alegretto Nuzi
(plate 112, 113), or "The Master of the Fabriano Altarpiece." That this
introduction of the goldfinch icon from Florence failed to "take hold" in
Umbria is evidenced by the fact that in the next generation no pictures
with goldfinches were produced there;[1] in the first quarter of the fifteenth
century we have but two; further but three cases dating from the second
and two from the third quarter of that century, and then no more until
the final quarter when at least 6 such pictures were produced; we have 9
from the first quarter of the sixteenth century, and finally 2 from the second
quarter of that century, after which date we find no more. In other words,
in the third quarter of the fourteenth century two Umbrian artists with
Florentine training or leanings produced a group of pictures containing
goldfinches; from the next century but 7 such works are here listed, two

by Ottaviano Nelli; one by Giovanni Boccati, one by Bartolommeo Caporali, one by Ceccolo di Giovanni, one by an eclectic follower of Nuzi,
and one by Bartolommeo di Tomasso da Foligno (plates 112-116). Then,
in the last quarter of the fifteenth century and the first half of the sixteenth, the goldfinch was included in some 17 pictures. Of the 17, 4 were
by Raphael (plates 117, 118), or his followers and are again almost as
much Florentine as Umbrian, 1 is by Piero della Francesca (plate 119)
who is also to a large extent Florentine, and another by a follower of his,
while the others are more completely Umbrian.

The list of the artists of Umbria and their goldfinch-bearing paintings
may be found in the Appendix, p. 159-161.

The list, as in the case of Florence or Siena, is notable for the names
it omits. Among Umbrian painters of note missing here are Gentile da
Fabriano, Melozzo da Forli, Signorelli, and Perugino, while others less
prominent, but also absent, are Lorenzo da Viterbo, Bonfigli, Timoteo
Viti, and Giovanni Santi. The sojourn in Umbria of Benozzo Gozzoli
failed to introduce the goldfinch motif although it was definitely part
of his stock in trade.

The earliest Umbrian goldfinches, those in the works of Alegretto Nuzi
and the "Master of the Fabriano Altarpiece" (plates 112-113) are apparently intended somewhat as anti-plague symbols (Augur plus Fertility),
as is evidenced in the work by the latter artist in the National Gallery of
Art, Washington, in which the Child has a red coral amulet about His neck
as well as the goldfinch augur in His left hand. The question of the identity
of this picture's anonymous painter to whom Offner has given the descriptive name here used is beside our main inquiry, but the following testimony
of the goldfinch as a stylistic detail may be here mentioned. If numbers
3 and 4 of our list of Nuzi's pictures are accepted as by him (as they have
been by Berenson whose attributions are followed here), the goldfinch
in the Washington picture must also be by him, or else the "Master of
the Fabriano Altarpiece" and Alegretto Nuzi learned how to draw goldfinches from each other. The construction is highly peculiar — the ex-
tremely elongated tail and wings and the very unnatural relative length
of the primary wing feathers, which increase in length from the first (outer-
most) to the third or fourth by great jumps, are unmatched in the goldfinches of any other painters.

The absence of a symbol such as the goldfinch from the work of a sublime, impersonal, and impassive artist like Piero della Francesca is to be expected. As a matter of fact it is surprising that he included it even once. In this work, the London "Nativity" (plate 119), some goldfinches, now rather faded and indistinct, flutter about some thistles, on the left side of the picture. The birds are quite small, are in the middle distance, and have to be looked for to be seen. From what is known of the artist and of his works we can say that Piero was not one to indulge in prettiness of landscape; his backgrounds are usually severe and devoid of anything that might dwarf their scale and grandeur. Therefore, the presence of these details of goldfinches and thistles calls for an explanation since they cannot be looked upon as included merely for their pictorial effect. Howe[2] writes that the, ". . . neighborhood of the ass and the goldfinch in this picture reminds us of Pliny's attribute to the *bonhomie* of this pretty bird. The acanthis, he tells us, has no grudge against any living creature, with one exception, the donkey which eats up the thistles from whose seeds he expected to get a meal." The main point is, however, that the birds and the thistles are treated as minor details of the setting and not in such a way as to detract the attention of the spectator from the main action of the picture even momentarily.

In pictures where the goldfinch is inserted in a relatively inconspicuous place or position it seems that it may be reasonably assumed that it was included for one or more of four reasons: firstly, because of tradition or usage; secondly, in a minor symbolic capacity; thirdly, for its pictorial value in filling a spot in a picture; and fourthly, as an easy way for the artist to make more certain that nothing of possible desirability had been left out (the bird had many symbolic meanings and some of them, while desirable, may not have been expressly desired at the moment by the person ordering the picture). In this case we can readily dismiss the first because it was not traditional in Umbria to include the goldfinch; we can also dismiss the third and fourth from what we know of the character of the artist and of his total *oeuvre*. This leaves us only the second possibility — that the birds were included in a minor symbolic capacity. It is my guess that the goldfinches and the thistles are here as iconographic harmonizing elements, bringing into the background some slight reflection of the meaning of the principal characters and action of the picture. This statement requires further elucidation and this, in turn involves a slight digression into the nature of the Umbrian reaction to the ravages of the plague.

In Umbria more than in other parts of Italy the devout populace was in the habit of making solemn processions behind plague banners or *gonfalones* on which were painted representations of the Virgin or some special saint, such as Sebastian, as a protector of the community, in the compositional manner of the Misericordia Madonnas. Painters such as Bonfigli and Caporali (plates 120, 121), made many such banners, and in some of these Bonfigli gives us a clue as to a rather novel and, apparently local,[3] interpretation of the nature of the plague. Thus, in one such banner, in the Chiesa del Gonfalone, Perugia, the Virgin is shown protecting her devotees under the shelter of her spreading cape from plague shafts hurled by none other than Christ Himself. As has been pointed out by Coulton[4] the, "... many mediaeval writers who suggest causes for the Black Death are unanimous ... in attributing it to God's vengeance for an accumulation of past sins in Church and State." What we find in these Umbrian plague banners, especially if we recall how different is the Florentine *gonfalone* by Parri Spinelli (plate 58), is that the Umbrian reaction was essentially that the plague was a punishment to be suffered, with possible supplication, not directly to Christ or to God, but indirectly through the Virgin, whereas in Florence and other centers the reaction was rather to petition Christ directly for relief from this dread punishment. If we accept this suggestion, the relative absence of the symbolic goldfinch from much of Umbrian painting becomes understandable. There was no occasion for its introduction if direct supplication to the Saviour, with Whom the bird was identified, was considered uncalled for and, in a sense, improper.[5]

To repeat, the goldfinch was among other things, an augur in time of illness. In a community, such as Umbria,[6] where the plague was looked upon, even if only to some extent, as a dispensation from Christ as well as from God Himself, the augur could hardly be held by or offered to the Source of that against which it was supposed to function. This may explain why the goldfinch is so largely absent from pure Umbrian devotional art, such as that of Perugino. Is is also significant in connection with Piero della Francesca's picture, to our discussion of which we may return. It seems that the "Nativity" is one of the artist's relatively early works, showing as it does the influence of his Florentine teacher, Domenico Veneziano. Although the latter apparently did not make use of the goldfinch motif himself, and was probably not interested in it, there is every reason to believe that Piero must have met with it during his stay in Florence, as it was so commonly included in devotional paintings there. Coming back to his native Umbria, he carried it with him, but found the motif had little local tradition or understanding. After one attempt, in the "Nativity," he never used it again, and in this picture he disconnected it from the sacred personages and relegated it to the background with a somewhat altered meaning. The goldfinches and the thistles in the background, naturalistically treated though they be, may possibly have served to connote physical man's reliance against the plague — fertility, and medication,[7] just as the main action of the picture depicts spiritual man's hope of life through the birth of Him through Whom redemption and salvation were made possible.[8]

The only other painting known to me in which the treatment of the goldfinch is similar to that in Piero's "Nativity" is Sassetta's "Journey of the Kings," (Maitland Griggs collection, Metropolitan Museum, New York) (plate 90), a fragment of an "Adoration of the Magi." The similarity in the treatment of the motif is further paralleled by the fact that each picture is the only one by its painter that includes the goldfinch symbol. In Sassetta's case this further absence of the motif is more remarkable in that the Sienese painters, unlike their Umbrian neighbors, were much given to its use.

One other Umbrian painting requires special comment. Fiorenzo di Lorenzo's "Madonna and Child" (Jacquemart André Museum, Paris) reveals a goldfinch standing on a parapet; it has a string attached to its leg, the other end being held by the Infant Jesus. This in itself calls for no comment, but according to van Marle this picture was directly inspired by a Florentine work attributed to Verrocchio (Berlin, Kaiser Friedrich Museum), in which, however, there is no goldfinch. Assuming the source of the composition to be correct, it follows that we have here an Umbrian painter showing enough interest in the goldfinch motif to deliberately add it to his pseudo-Florentine plagiarism. This should serve to remind us that no matter what the local tendency may be in any school, its individual members are not necessarily inexorably bound by it.[9]

Chapter X. The Schools of Milan, Bologna, and Ferrara

1. THE SCHOOL OF MILAN.

THE painters of Milan do not appear to have been greatly interested in the use of the goldfinch motif. This is especially the case if we set to one side as a temporary pseudo-Florentine eclecticism the local obvious Leonardo imitators, who on several occasions did introduce the bird in their works. Thus, as already mentioned, Leonardo's "Madonna Litta" was copied in rather free fashion, once by Bernardino de' Conti and twice by Boltraffio. In these three paintings, which by virtue of their authorship, must be credited to the Milanese school, Leonardo's use of the goldfinch was repeated without change. Similarly, we may dismiss also the obviously Leonardesque paintings already discussed in the account of the three-figured composition of the Madonna and Child with the young St. John. Aside from these, I have identified goldfinches in ten Milanese pictures, three of them versions of the same composition, and all three by Giovanni Boltraffio. Aside from these, one is a panel by Francesco Napoletano (M. G. Brauer collection),[1] which probably also should be dismissed as due to Leonardo's influence. The earliest Milanese work to engage our attention is a triptych by Giovanni da Milano, painted about 1365, and now in the Academy in Florence. The central panel shows a goldfinch held in the Christ Child's left hand. He and His mother are flanked in the lateral panels by Saints Catherine, Dorothy, John the Baptist, and Anthony Abbot. Next in chronologic order is Bartolommeo de' Grassi's "Madonna and Child" painted about 1430. Approximately thirty years later Jacopo Cietario introduced a small bird, apparently a goldfinch, in the Christ Child's hands in a polyptych. Then comes a picture by Ambrogio Bevilacqua of the "Madonna and Child Enthroned with Saints and a Donor," now in the Brera, Milan; then a simpler, two-figured "Madonna and Child" by Bernardino de' Conti, in the Sterbini collection,

Rome, while the last is Bernardino Borgognone's "Madonna and Child with Saints" (Moroni collection, Bergamo).

While this disposes of the few instances I have found of goldfinches in Milanese devotional pictures, it may be noted that the artists of Lombardy were not far behind their colleagues in Venice and Verona in their interest in nature and their consequent familiarity with birds generally, and with the goldfinch, among others. In the Civic Library at Bergamo there is a leaf from a scratchbook, by an undetermined Lombard artist, showing studies of a goldfinch, a parrot, and a lammergeier (the huge, bearded vulture of the Alps). I know of no similar sheet by any other Italian other than a Venetian or a Veronese painter. While this sheet is only a relatively casual sketch by some unknown Milanese, and cannot be taken for more than its true importance, it does add to the feeling that although there was a native Lombard interest in drawing from nature, the artists of that province made relatively little use of natural history accessories except when under the influence of Leonardo. Of the few paintings of this school that contain goldfinches, all but one are by artists who worked directly or indirectly under the spell of the great Florentine, the one exception being Bernardino Borgognone. In addition to this, Ambrogio Bevilacqua may be considered a doubtful exception. Consequently we must hold fast to this one picture of Bernardino Borgognone's to show that the goldfinch motif, even if not widely used, was known to the painters of Milan before and aside from the visit of Leonardo. None of the pictures by Ambrogio Borgognone that I have seen have goldfinches in them.

The general absence of the goldfinch motif in the Milanese works that I have seen is more puzzling than it might seem from a reading of the above remarks. Thus, in the work of the first important founding figure of Lombard painting, Vincenzo Foppa, we find other birds introduced in devotional pictures. In his "Adoration of the Magi" (London, National Gallery) there is a swallow perched on a cornice of the classical setting in the upper left part of the composition. Foppa also put a peacock in one of his Madonna pictures, but he never used the goldfinch icon. In other words there was a local tendency, here as elsewhere in Italy, to use bird symbols in devotional paintings but there appears to have been no Milanese predilection for the goldfinch.

2. THE SCHOOL OF BOLOGNA.

This school would hardly be worth mentioning were it not for the fact that its one most famous figure, Francia, was unusually addicted to painting goldfinches in his devotional pictures. I have found no indication of the use of the goldfinch motif in Bologna earlier than the last quarter of the fifteenth century, but have not seen enough early Bolognese paintings (by men such as Andrea and Vitale da Bologna or Simone dei Crocifissi) to be able to make any generalizations of more than passing value. Similarly, what I have seen of the works of the late, baroque Bolognese eclectics, such as the Carracci and Domenichino, are also free of goldfinches, although Guercino did make use of the motif at least once. As may be seen from the list (see Appendix, p. 162), the eleven Bolognese pictures of concern to us are with the exception of Guercino's one work, limited in chronology to one man's life-time.

Francia not only made extensive use of the goldfinch symbol, but also "made" unusually good, naturalistic birds (plates 122-124). Thus, in his monograph on the master, Williamson[2] notes that, ". . . birds, generally goldfinches, are a characteristic of Francia's work, and are always beautifully painted with the utmost loving care." This fact raises a question of attribution in the case of our first picture listed as by him. In it the bird is atrociously drawn and very badly colored; it can hardly be by the same hand that was responsible for so many excellent goldfinches. It is not my purpose to do more than point out the unlikelihood of the present attribution; the painting smacks of Bologna and is probably by some less competent pupil or assistant of Francia. In the whole range of goldfinches in Italian art, I do not know of another more inaccurate than this example; even the rigid, wooden ones of some of the Trecento painters are, in all their stiff lifelessness, preferable to this one. Thus, we may note the most obvious error — the construction of the tail. In this case all the tail feathers do not appear to come from the same base but to be paired offshoots from a long core. It would be entirely comparable if an artist were to paint a hand with only one finger at the tip, then a pair coming off on either side and finally another pair at the wrist. The color is also unnatural, but this may be the result of some bungling restorer.

In all fairness it must be stated that Francia possibly had assistants fill in some of the goldfinches in his paintings as they vary too much for one man's hand. He obviously knew the bird well and could portray it accurately, yet in the "Adoration" in Bologna the two goldfinches each have the yellow patches in their wings enlarged to form broad specula and also have large, pale rump patches, which are not found in the actual bird.

The Guercino example is known to me only from a poor photograph from which the bird is not certainly identifiable. It is a matter of relatively little concern as it is of a vintage that is characterized by the symbolic emptiness of rampant mannerism and eclecticism.

The two paintings by Chiodarolo serve to connect the school of Bologna with that of Ferrara, to which we may now turn.

3. The School of Ferrara.

The school of Ferrara, closely linked to that of Bologna, developed largely under the stylistic tradition of two artists, one the Umbro-Florentine, Piero della Francesca, and the other, the great Paduan, Mantegna, neither of whom were greatly interested in the goldfinch motif. The first important local master, Cosimo Tura, is not too well represented in our list of goldfinch painters (by a single work), but that the bird was not foreign to his iconographic system is indicated by two other paintings from his studio in each of which the symbol is to be found (plate 126). In all, I have found the goldfinch in 16 devotional pictures, by 10 Ferrarese artists. Their distribution in time is from the third quarter of the fifteenth century through the second quarter of the sixteenth. The earliest picture, by Cossa, dates from the third quarter of the fifteenth century; 5 date from the last quarter of that century; 4 from the first quarter of the following one, and finally 6, by Garofalo, from the second quarter. The absence from the subjoined list of such an artist as Lorenzo Costa is possibly due to lack of photographs available to me rather than to the consistent absence of the icon from his *oeuvre*.

On the whole it may be said, on the basis of not too extensive material, that in Ferrara the goldfinch symbol was used fairly generally. In a school in which the difference between the most and the least worthy of its members was not nearly as great as in cities such as Venice or Florence or Siena, this sort of agreement is to be expected. The list (see Appendix, p. 162-163) shows that with the exception, already noted, of Costa, most of the important local masters made some use of the goldfinch symbol.

Some of these Ferrarese pictures present iconographic peculiarities. Thus, in the painting by Dosso Dossi and in the Philadelphia Museum's picture by a member of Cosimo Tura's studio, we find a cat in the lower foreground. While the cat is not particularly connected with the goldfinch in the action of either composition, these two works are the forerunners of others of like content in later baroque painting. In Ercole Grandi's picture the cat is replaced by a monkey. It seems to me that we have here to deal with an attempt to contrast the physical, lustful, bestial part of man's nature, as portrayed by the cat or the monkey,[3] and the spiritual part as represented by the goldfinch. This tendency to emphasize this meaning in the goldfinch symbol seems to be greater, or at least, more naively direct, in the art of Ferrara than in that of any other Italian city.

We may now turn to another bit of peculiar Ferrarese iconography. In a picture, now in Chicago, Garofalo[4] painted the Christ Child holding the goldfinch in His right hand, and offering it two cherries with His left hand (plate 125). Cherries are symbols of heaven, the fruit that was given as a reward for piety, morality and kindred forms of merit. Here the context possibly is meant to imply that the soul (goldfinch) that relies on Christ will taste the pleasures of Heaven. In other words, here as in the works discussed in the preceding paragraph, in the hands of the painters of Ferrara the goldfinch is chiefly used as a symbol of the Soul. Evidence is not forthcoming that it here too was a symbol of Fertility or an anti-disease augur.

In the painting by Cosimo Tura the goldfinch is perched in the foliage in the upper left part of the composition, above the head of the Christ Child, who, far from being interested in it, is asleep!

Chapter XI. The Minor Schools of Italy

1. PISA

THE school of Pisa was early in its origin and short in its duration, and while its painters are of interest to us in the present connection, its real importance is in the development of the sculptor's art, to the early stages of which it contributed so importantly. While none of its painters achieved to the rank or significance of its marble craftsmen such as Niccolo and Giovanni Pisano, yet they turned out numerous works that reveal the emergence of the early Renaissance spirit from the confusion of three none too harmonious traditions — the Classical, the Byzantine, and the Gothic, the latter introduced from France. In their use of the goldfinch motif the painters of Pisa (plates 133, 134), remind one more strongly of their colleagues in Siena than any other group. In spite of the fact that Pisan pictures are relatively poorly known and seldom reproduced, I have found goldfinches in some 11 paintings by 9 artists of this school. Chronologically these works range from the first quarter of the fourteenth to the first quarter of the fifteenth century. The earliest is a "Madonna and Child" by a Pisan follower of the great Sienese, Duccio, now in S. Francesco, Pisa; the next is a "Madonna and Child and Angels" by Turino Vanni the second (Paris, Louvre) (plate 133). In this work the Child holds both a goldfinch and a scroll in His left hand. On the scroll we may decipher the words, "ratione enunt[i]a[ta] guberno" — "I rule by the pronouncement of reason." The text, of course, refers to Christ, not to the bird, while the bird as a symbol of the Soul, and of the Resurrection, also is an attribute of Christ. The fact that the two quite disconnected symbolic elements should be placed together in the Child's hand reveals an earnest simplicity and forthrightness not to be found in more sophisticated pictures. Another work by the same artist (Pisa, S. Martino, Cappella del Sacramento), is unique in our series of goldfinch-bearing paintings in that it is the central medallion of a large crucifix. This medallion represents the Madonna and Child.

In the third quarter of the fourteenth century were produced three of our examples. Giovanni di Niccolo (Pisa, Museo Civico) painted a goldfinch in the Christ Child's right hand in a "Madonna and Child" composition (plate 134), forming the central panel of a polyptych; in a "Madonna and Child with Angels" by Francesco Neri da Volterra (Modena, Pinacoteca Estense) a rather stiff goldfinch is perched on Mary's right wrist, its bill near the Child's right hand; while in a simple two-figured "Madonna and Child" picture attributed to the Master of San Torpé (Pisa, San Francesco) a heavy-billed goldfinch is held stiffly in the Child's left hand. From the last quarter of the fourteenth century we have four pertinent pictures. One, by Nanni di Jacopo (ex Sterbini collection, Rome) of the "Madonna and Child and Angels" shows a stiffly erect goldfinch standing on the Child's left hand. A string is tied to its left leg and runs loosely to the Child's right hand, showing a rather early use of the "pet bird on a string" motif in connection with the goldfinch symbol. Two of the other pertinent pictures,[1] are one also by Nanni di Jacopo and one by a Pisan follower of Taddeo de Bartolo, dated 1399. A few years earlier (ca. 1390) Jacopo di Michele Gera used the motif in a "Madonna and Child with Saints" (Pisa, Gallery). The last of our Pisan examples, a polyptych by Giovanni da Pisa, dated 1423 shows the Child holding a stiff, poorly drawn goldfinch in His left hand.

2. LUCCA

The school of Lucca, fairly parallel in its development to that of Pisa, provides us with at least two examples of the goldfinch symbol (plate 127-128). One of these, a "Madonna and Child," signed and dated by Deodato Orlandi in 1308, is important in that while it is not the earliest incidence of the goldfinch motif, it is the earliest one that is definitely dated. This picture, now in the R. M. Hurd collection, New York, reveals Sienese influence, as does so much of Deodato's work, but it is not clear if the goldfinch motif as such necessarily came to Lucca from Siena, as the symbol appeared in both towns more or less simultaneously, Another similar work by the same artist (Lucca, Museo Civico) shows the Child holding a goldfinch in His left hand. This picture bears no date.

3. PADUA

I have found no goldfinches in those works of the early Paduans I have been able to study (Guariento and Giusto di Menabuoi), and, as a matter of fact, but two from the later, academically classicized "school" of Squarcione. His greatest pupil and the only truly great artist of the city, Andrea Mantegna, never made use of the motif,[2] but one of his lesser schoolmates, Giorgio Schiavone, did so at least three times. In a "Madonna and Child" in the Pinacoteca Regia, Turin, the Child holds the goldfinch in the hand of His outstretched right arm, the bird facing away from Him. This action is doubly unusual; the bird is commonly held closely by the Child, not at arm's length, and is also usually looking toward Him, or, at least not directly away from Him.[3] It is obvious that this is no translated "charradrius" as in that case the bird would have to look at the Child or else signify His death. In another work by the same artist[4] there is no such puzzling action, but the bird is held fairly close to the Child's body, while in a third picture (Venice, Museo Civico) we have a relationship of bird and Child as in the second one.

4. VERONA

Eight devotional paintings by artists of this school have been found to contain goldfinches. They date from the last quarter of the fourteenth to the first quarter of the sixteenth centuries. The early Veronese masters, such as Altichiero and Avanzo worked in fresco and painted no pieces of a devotional nature. However, in a work of an unknown Trecento master of this school (S. Anastasia, Verona) and in one by the chief figure of the transition from the Trecento to the Quattrocento Veronese style, Stefano da Verona (da Zevio), we find the symbol already present. In his

"Madonna and Child with Angels" (Rome, Galleria Colonna) a rather diminutive goldfinch is perched on Mary's right shoulder, a remarkably free and untraditional placing of the bird for a fairly early and relatively provincial work, but one in keeping with the artist's known tendency to give to his figures liveliness and naturalistic expression. One cannot but recall Taddeo di Bartolo's picture (Washington, National Gallery of Art) done a little earlier in Siena, in which the bird is also perched on the Child's shoulder. In a painting attributed to the school of Stefano "Madonna and Child with Two Saints" (Verona, Museo Civico) the Child holds a goldfinch, all but hidden, in His left hand, only the head of the bird showing, while in another, simpler "Madonna and Child" also ascribed to the school of Stefano (Vienna, Lanckoronski collection) the bird is perched on Mary's left wrist.

Pisanello introduced two goldfinches in his "Madonna della Quaglia" (Verona, Museo Civico), (plate 130). The Virgin and Child are seated on the ground. At their feet is a partridge at which they are looking, while in the foliage on either side is a goldfinch. The one on the Virgin's right is in profile looking away from her; the one on her left has its back to the spectator, its wings spread and its feet impossibly placed on either side. Pisanello was interested in drawing naturalistic animals and was obviously led by this tendency into portraying the bird in this unfortunate pose. One cannot avoid the feeling that the artist was not interested in, if indeed he was even aware of, the symbolism inherent in the goldfinch; to him it seems to have been a pretty bird with which to brighten an otherwise dull spot in a picture. In all his paintings we find a lavish use of naturalistic forms in the same spirit that we find in tapestries. The goldfinches in the "Madonna della Quaglia" are, strangely enough, not nearly so well drawn as in some of the artist's sketches. The distorted one on the Madonna's left also anticipates the medallist in its painter; it is a pose more suited to low relief than to paint.

Francesco dai Libri put a goldfinch in the upper right background of at least one of his "Madonna and Child" compositions (Baltimore, Walters Art Gallery), (plate 129).

The remaining Veronese works pertinent to our theme are Benaglio's "Madonna and Child with Angels" in the Museo Civico, Verona; and Francesco Morone's "Madonna and Child" in the Kaiser Friedrich Museum, Berlin. In the latter picture the Child holds the goldfinch in His left hand; the drawing or placing of the bird shows none of the peculiarities of either Stefano da Verona or Pisanello.

5. VICENZA

The one outstanding master of Vicenza, Bartolommeo Montagna, used the goldfinch motif in a "Madonna and Child" picture, now in the National Gallery, London. This picture, according to Berenson, is the earliest extant work of the master. Howe[5] notes, ". . . the helpless and uncomfortable position of the bird is well studied; it squeaks with open beak and tries to find a hold for its feet." This is partly something "read into" the pose of the bird, but it well reflects the degree of liveliness the artist has achieved in his representation of the goldfinch. A structural peculiarity that may be noted is the large size of the maxilla (the upper part of the bill) as compared with the mandible (the lower part). This is an error that is by no means restricted to Montagna; we find it in such an unrelated painter as the Sienese, Lippo Memmi as well.

Bartolommeo's son, Benedetto Montagna, used the goldfinch in at least two devotional pictures — a "Madonna and Child with Sts. Peter, Paul, Francis, Anthony of Padua, and an Angel," now in the Brera, Milan, and a "Madonna and Child with Sts. Jerome and Francis," now in the Museo Civico, Vicenza.

6. MODENA

One of the leading painters of this city, Barnaba da Modena, made use of the goldfinch icon at least once. In a "Madonna and Child" (Berlin, Kaiser Friedrich Museum) the Child holds in His right hand a string which is attached to a small bird, probably intended to be a goldfinch, that is flying a hand's length away. This picture, dating from the third quarter of the fourteenth century is interesting in the present connection in that it shows, in the flying pose of the bird, a departure, or perhaps more properly, a desire on the part of the artist to depart, from the local Byzantine manner to which Barnaba otherwise remained so loyal. I have found no instance of the use of the symbol (in the few works seen) by Tomasso da Modena. As already mentioned in our discussion of Bohemian painting, the icon was already present there before Tomasso's visit to that country.

7. CREMONA

Although Cremona hardly deserves to be called a distinct art center, it may be mentioned here because of two early sixteenth century paintings by Boccaccio Boccaccino in which the goldfinch symbol appears. Considering the slight artistic inventiveness of their painter the diversity of his treatment of the bird in these two works is of interest. Both paintings are of the simple two-figured "Madonna and Child" type; in one (formerly in the Crespi collection, Milan) the Child holds the bird in His right hand; in the other (New York, Metropolitan Museum) the goldfinch is perched on Mary's right hand and the Child reaches with His right hand to stroke it (plate 131).

8. NAPLES

Although the Neapolitan school owes much of its early activity to non-Neapolitans who were brought there to the rather exotic court; Giotto from Florence, Cavallini from Rome, Simone Martini from Siena, etc., its native members, such as Roberto Oderisio, seem to have followed these exemplars into fresco rather than easel painting, and so more or less away from the opportunity of making pictures of topics in which the goldfinch might readily have been included. In fact, I have found but two Neapolitan paintings with the bird symbol. One of them, dating from approximately 1440 (ex Stoop Coray collection, Erlenbach; illustrated by van Marle, vol. 15, p. 357) is said to be "Neapolitan with Hispano-Flemish Influence." In it the Christ Child holds a goldfinch in His right hand. The bird is not so definitely identifiable in the other painting, a "Madonna and Child" attributed to Andrea da Salerno (Augsburg, Gemäldegalerie, No. 295) which dates from the first quarter of the sixteenth century. The bird, in spite of its lack of diagnostic specific characters (at least in the black and white reproduction seen) is quite well drawn in a convincing life-like pose.

9. SICILY

I have found only three examples of Sicilian painting in which the goldfinch occurs. One is a "Madonna and Child Enthroned" by Antonio da Saliba (plate 135), a follower of Antonello da Messina (Cathedral, Syracuse). The goldfinch is perched in right profile on Mary's right hand and is looking at the Child, Who is attentively watching it. The picture is said to be an early work of the artist and to date from the last quarter of the fifteenth century.

The other two are from the second and third decades of the sixteenth century. One, the "Madonna di Monserrato" by Antonello Palermitano, now in the Gancia Monastery at Palermo shows some Lombard influences in its general style (according to van Marle, vol. 15, p. 438) and shows the Madonna and Child with Saints Catherine and Agatha and two donors. The other, the "Madonna of Loreto," a joint work by Alessandro da Padova and Giovanni Maria da Treviso, now in the Bellomo Museum, Syracuse, is unique in one respect among all the devotional pictures in which I have found the goldfinch. The Madonna and Child are on the roof of a church which is supported by angels at the three visible corners of the edifice.[6]

Another Sicilian picture, while not containing a goldfinch, is of interest here. This, a "Madonna and Child" by Pietro de Saliba (also known as Pietro da Messina[7]) shows the Child holding a small, pure white bird in His left hand. This recalls the medieval charadrius which was later supplanted by the goldfinch, and also recalls the gradual transmutation of the goldfinch into the white dove in later Russian icon painting. Pietro apparently worked in Venice for some years, where he came under the influence of Antonello da Messina and of Giovanni Bellini. Whether this picture was painted in Sicily or in Venice I do not know.

The one really great Sicilian master, Antonello da Messina, appears to have made no use of the goldfinch icon; his sojourn in Venice cannot therefore be looked upon as the occasion of its introduction into Sicilian painting.

10. PIEDMONT

The Piedmontese painters are an unimportant group artistically, and have been correspondingly poorly illustrated in literature. In spite of the paucity of material thereby made available to me, I have found the gold-finch motif in two pictures by artists of this school. Inasmuch as these two are nearly a century and a half apart, it follows that there probably were other instances of its use in the interval. The earlier of the two is a fresco, done in 1359 on the west exterior of the Church of Giovanni dei Campi near Piobese Torinesi, by Giovanni de Camuseto; its chief interest is that it is one of the rare instances in which a goldfinch was included in a fresco. The other work, a polyptych by Giovanni Conavesio da Pinerolo (Turin, Pinacoteca Regia) is said to date from 1491.

11. LIGURIA

Closely allied to the painters of the Piedmont in style and in unimport-ance are those of Liguria. Here there was, if anything, a little more of Sienese and Modenese influence — a pair of conservative tendencies that might well account for the lack of progress in Liguria. Early in the fifteenth century, a local master, Niccolo da Voltri, painted at least three devo-tional pictures containing the goldfinch symbol. The simplest of these, is a two-figured "Madonna and Child" now in the church of Sta. Maria delle Vigne, at Genoa; the Child holds the goldfinch in His left hand, while in His right He holds a scroll reading "ego sum alpha et omega." Another, "Madonna and Child with Two Angels" (Finale Pia, Parish Church) shows the goldfinch perched sideways on the Christ Child's left index finger. Finally, we have a "Madonna and Child and Angels," now in the museum at Savona, in which the Child is holding a very poorly constructed goldfinch in His right hand.

12. MARCHE

The Marches, another of the artistically backward parts of Italy, produced at least two painters who made use of the goldfinch motif. Folchetto da Sanginesio painted an "Adoration of the Shepherds" (Philadelphia, Fine Arts Museum, Johnson Collection) around 1485, in which we find not one, but three goldfinches, flying around the shed in front of which the Child is lying surrounded by adoring figures, (plate 136). The panel is literally full of birds — beside the three goldfinches and one quite unidentifiable bird, there are in this little picture a swallow, an owl, a guinea fowl, a mallard duck, an egret, and a hawk. The three goldfinches, in as many widely different positions, reveal a surprisingly good command of bird form and action, even though there is a stiffness and an almost diagrammatic pattern in them. Stylistically, these three goldfinches are different from those of any other painter in that the whitish area on the back of the neck, between the dark occipital marking and the darkish back, is crossed by many fine longitudinal dark lines. This may have been an attempt by the artist to give a looseness, a soft feathery texture to this area, and is indeed, quite pleasing and successful. At least two other works by the same master contain goldfinches. One, a "Madonna and Child with Saints," painted in 1492 (San Ginesio, Town Hall) is apparently an anti-plague picture in that it contains the two chief patron saints of victims of the disease — Sebastian, and Roch. The other, painted in 1498, also in the Town Hall of San Ginesio, shows the Virgin and Child attended by Saints Francis and Liberatus. In both works the Child holds a goldfinch in His right hand. In spite of his limitations, which were great, Folchetto rewards the searcher for goldfinches very handsomely and thus receives a grateful salute denied him by the standards of art criticism.

The other Marchigian painter of interest to us is Giacomo da Recanati. In his "Madonna and Child and Angels" in the cathedral at Recanati we find a goldfinch perched on the Child's left hand. The picture was painted around 1460. In the parish church at Albacina there is a triptych in Giovanni's manner in which the Infant Jesus holds a little bird, apparently intended to be a goldfinch.[8]

It may be mentioned that the picture listed in our discussion of the

Florentine school as by the "Biadaiolo Illuminator" (Robert Lehman collection, New York; the attribution being that of Offner) has been published by its present owner as by an "Unknown Master of the Marches, ca. 1300." If this attribution be accepted (the present author has no personal opinion and merely follows Offner as being the latest expert to publish on it) it puts the first appearance of the goldfinch motif in Marchigian art back nearly two centuries before Folchetto. The picture is obviously fraught with difficulties as van Marle considered it an early Trecento Riminese work done under the influence of Pietro Cavallini!

13. ROME

It may seem surprising at first that Rome, the greatest city in all Italy, should be classed as only a relatively minor art producing center, but the fact is that if we were to take away from the Eternal City all the Florentine, Umbrian, Venetian, and other extraneous artists and their works, the residue would be far from impressive. Because she had the power and the wealth to call painters from other cities, Rome never developed an important school of her own until after the glorious sun of the Renaissance had set in the colorful blaze of the Baroque. In the thirteenth century, it is true, Rome had a few mosaicists of note and one eminent fresco painter, Pietro Cavallini; during the Renaissance period as such she could boast of nothing greater than Antoniazzo in the way of a native artist. During all this period, while numerous goldfinches were painted at Rome, Roman hands seem to have taken little part in their production. I have found but three devotional paintings by native artists in which the goldfinch symbol occurs; two by Antoniazzo Romano (plate 138) (New York, Percy S. Straus collection; *ex* Paris, Spiridon collection; and Valencia, Museo Provincial de Pintures) and a post-Renaissance picture, a late sixteenth century work by Federigo Baroccio. This picture, in the National Gallery, London, is elsewhere referred to because of its unusual use of the bird. The Christ Child is holding it up away from an eager cat in a playful manner that has been questionably interpreted in literature as if to tease both the goldfinch and the cat.

14. Parma.

Two works by one painter of this school, Filippo Mazzola, have been found to contain a goldfinch — a "Madonna and Child with two Saints" now in the National Gallery, London (plate 137), and a "Madonna and Child Enthroned with Baptist and Bartholomew," now in the Museo Civico Ala-Ponzone, Cremona. The painter was influenced greatly by the Venetians and may have gotten this motif from them as the great figures of the local school — Correggio and Parmigianino, apparently never made use of it. As a matter of fact Berenson[9] assigns Mazzola to the Venetian school outright, which may be where he belongs except for the accident of geography.

15. Sardinia.

A late fifteenth century "Madonna and Child with Angels" in the Parish church at Castelsardo, by an unknown Sardinian artist, shows a goldfinch held in the Child's left hand, its wing somewhat arched.[10]

16. Viterbo.

In the museum at Viterbo is a detached fresco of a "Madonna and Child with a Donor" attributed to Francesco da Antonio da Viterbo. The town of Viterbo can hardly be called the seat of a distinct "school," but where else is one to consider Francesco di Antonio? The picture is worth mentioning in the present connection because the goldfinch is flying from the Child towards the kneeling donor, to whom the Child's hands are also pointing; a fairly suggestive case of the goldfinch as a transformed charadrius.

Chapter XII. Iconographic and Stylistic Details
of the Goldfinch

So far we have been concerned with the goldfinch symbol and the use made of it by artists of different schools, countries, and centuries. With this survey behind us, we may now re-examine our material and see if it yields any data or even hints concerning the style and the approach of its various painters, not a few of whom are still none too clearly envisioned as distinct artistic personalities. Any clues we may gather from a new approach are therefore worth recording and fitting into our previous conceptions. Unfortunately one very important consideration — color, must be left out of our discussion almost entirely, as this study is based largely on black and white photographs. This leaves us position or pose, construction, and compositional placement, on which to base any stylistic studies.

The great variety of positions in which the bird is placed suggests that more than one group of factors early played a part in the development of its use in devotional art. It seems that there were two main determining causes for this diversity. One was the wealth of symbolic meanings concentrated in the goldfinch. Inasmuch as any one, or any possible combination of any two or more, of its many mystical significances might have been chosen for emphasis either by the artist or by his patron, it follows that the position, the action, and the degree of prominence given to the bird in the resulting pictures could well have been affected accordingly. The other factor, which complicates the problem iconographically while adding to its interest aesthetically, was the fact that as artists became increasingly free from formalized tradition, they naturally frequently applied this freedom first to such details as the goldfinch rather than to the more important images of the sacred personages themselves. At a time when it would have been blasphemous (and dangerous) to take liberties with the accepted traditional mode of representation of the Virgin and the Child artists could only express their growing mastery over the problems involved in the representation of movement, of liveliness, of naturalism, in the pictorialization of such minor elements as the accessories, among which the goldfinch, being animate, was one of the most favorable for this purpose.

The situation is therefore a dual one; the little bird unwittingly was both an embodiment of religious symbolism and at the same time a mirror of early progress in representational art. In interpreting any given picture we must keep this duality in mind, and it is therefore important to discuss it in some detail. Paintings of the full High Renaissance and later, are relatively simpler than their predecessors in this regard, as with the great strides in draftsmanship, in the subtle use of color, in the rendering of the solidity of forms, in creating the illusions of ordinary and atmospheric perspective, there was also a falling off of mystical feeling and even of understanding of purely religious concepts and emotions. No one would care to claim Andrea del Sarto, for example, as the equal of Fra Angelico in the presentation and expression of pure, serene, other-worldly, religious sentiment. With this falling off of regard for the strictly spiritual values underlying devotional art there came a tendency for artists to utilize time-honored symbols at least as much as pictorial elements in a painting as to present them for their original symbolic content. Symbols lingered long after their meanings were forgotten. However, in works produced in the thirteenth, fourteenth, and fifteenth centuries in Italy, we may feel fairly certain that in the majority of cases, the meanings were known to the artists and to their patrons and advisors. When we come to such later painters as Tiepolo, we find suggestive evidence of the relative symbolic emptiness of the objects retained from a time when the objects themselves were merely the vehicles for the expression of their inner mystical content. Thus, according to Mrs. Jameson[1] ". . . in the hands of ignorant secular artists of later times those symbols . . . became mere playthings; and when they had become familiar, and required by custom, and the old sacred associations utterly forgotten, we find them most profanely applied and misused. To give one example, the bird was originally placed in the hand of Christ as the emblem of the soul, or of the spiritual as opposed to the earthly nature; in a picture by Baroccio, He holds it up before a cat, to be frightened and tormented." Doubtful as this interpretation seems, Baroccio may possibly have intended some premonition of soul-trying experiences before acceptance by Christ,[2] but no such doubt clouds the evidence in the case of Tiepolo. In the latter's "Madonna and Child with a Goldfinch" in the Kress Collection in the National Gallery of Art, Washington (plate 110), we find the artist has carefully painted the remiges (the flight feathers of the wings) clipped to prevent flight. This is actually the way in which the captive birds used as animate playthings were commonly treated (as uncaged, captive birds are to this day), but to deliberately represent the winged symbol of the Soul in a condition whereby it was deprived of its chief attribute reveals how little the goldfinch meant to Tiepolo aside from its interest as a prettily colored decorative bit in a picture. It also reveals a peculiar intentness on his part to give an illustration dictated by a standard of intellectual verisimilitude rather than by optical vision, as at the distance the artist (or the spectator) is from the bird the cut ends of the feathers would not be especially noticeable.

Just as we find, in some late, Baroque works the symbols outliving their special significances, so also, at the other end of the story, we find a definite lag in the application to these objects of the technical advances made in art. If we accept as the starting point of modern art the time of Duccio in Siena and of Cimabue and Giotto in Florence, it is informing to compare, for example, the birds in the earliest devotional paintings of their schools in which birds appear (the first quarter of the fourteenth century) with the birds in such non-devotional, but even earlier works, as the illuminations in the twelfth century Sicilian manuscript on falconry, "De Arte Venandi Cum Avibus" of the Emperor Frederick II of Hohenstauffen. It is readily apparent that the artists of the earlier, secular work showed far more accurate and direct observation of nature than did the painters of the religious panels. It is doubtful if the latter painters were less capable of observation; they merely followed tradition in making symbols in bird form rather than in trying to draw birds as naturalistically as possible. It took some time before even such minor elements as the birds in religious art were considered by the artists as available for purely artistic purposes, as material on which to test and expend their growing technical skill.

When, later, a certain pose of the goldfinch was found to satisfy both the need for symbolic expression and for artistic purpose it tended to be repeated over and over. The result now, as we look back on these pictures, is apt to be rather monotonous because of their repetitious multiplicity, but their very numbers attest to the dual satisfaction they probably gave originally. A specific example may help to clarify this matter.

One of the favorite themes reflected in the Child holding the goldfinch is the apocryphal story to the effect that the Christ Child, playing with other children, brought to life the clay birds they gave to Him. Here was a sufficient reason for placing the bird, regardless of its symbolic meaning, in the Child's hand. In order to give a pictorial presentation of the idea of the bird's coming to life the artists had to give some semblance of action to the otherwise inert object. Taddeo Gaddi (plates 44 and 47) designed the icon of the goldfinch held more or less upside down (a non-living bird would be apt to droop) but raising its head towards the hand that holds it, its beak almost, or actually, touching and appearing to be pecking at, the fingers. Here was an opportunity for the artist to display his powers of draftsmanship in a "difficult," dynamic, foreshortened pose, just as later artists indulged in similar attempts with the Child's figure, resulting in the so-called "Bambino-Vispo" icon. That this figure seemed to please Taddeo and his patrons is reflected in the fact that he introduced it wtih very minor variations in at least five different paintings.[3] It was no accident, but a deliberate, well thought out solution of a dual problem the artist had to face. In spite of the fact that it gives a realistic touch to the bird, the pecking action may seem a little strange at first, probably because pecking is associated in our minds with inflicting pain or at least offering resistance. However, among the earliest of Christian decorations, such as those in the oldest catacomb paintings, is one of a vessel from which is growing a mass of grape leaves and vines, on which are small birds pecking at the vines.[4] The vine is on old symbol of the Church, of which the wine is the life-giving dogma. The wine is, furthermore (as in the sacrament), the blood of Christ. In other words, in the old catacomb paintings the birds pecking at the vines represent souls partaking of the Eucharist.[5] What Gaddi seems to have done is to have gone back to the original meaning of the wine as representing the blood of Christ, and to have drawn his goldfinches in attitudes where they not only appear to be resurrected souls but also to be trying to nourish themselves directly on the source of the vital fluid of dogma. So rich a symbolic icon, coupled with the opportunity for purely artistic treatment offered by an animated, decorative object, could in itself have been a minor triumph of the first generation of Florentine painters following Giotto. The fact that Gaddi failed to make the most of it from the purely artistic side does detract somewhat from the scope of this triumph, but I cannot help but feel that his partial failure reflects not too unfavorably upon him. Overwhelmed as he and his generation of painters must have been by the towering genius of Giotto, his work was naturally so greatly influenced by that of his famous master that we are apt to dismiss it as a minor effort even compared with his great teacher's lesser productions, and to see in him nothing but a follower of an important leader. While this judgment is partly correct, Taddeo must be credited with an iconographic usage which reveals that in him the creative spirit lived on in the presence of a mighty influence that must have all but annihilated original effort in lesser men, and that if any judgment is to be based on this one bit of evidence it is that in Gaddi the creative artistic mind was, if anything, greater than the artistic techniques at his command. This becomes increasingly clear if we compare him with another outstanding pupil of Giotto, Bernardo Daddi, who, if anything, is Taddeo's superior in technique and delicacy. It so happens that Giotto never made use of the goldfinch icon, while of all Florentine painters none used it more frequently than did Taddeo Gaddi and Bernardo Daddi. In other words, here was a detail in which these two painters could not rely on anything their great teacher had previously done; they had to strike out for themselves. In none of the many paintings by Daddi known to me in which the goldfinch occurs[6] do we find anything comparable to Gaddi's richly concentrated icon. In Daddi's pictures (plates 41, 42, 43, 52, 55, 56) the goldfinch is either held in a rather matter of fact upright pose in the Child's hand (11 of the 19 panels), is flying towards the Child (Who holds it at length on a string), or is perched on the Virgin's hand facing toward the Child. The lack of any outstanding originality in Daddi's treatment of the bird may be partly due to the fact that he was so greatly influenced by French sculpture, in which he found ample precedent for his relatively stereotyped representation of the goldfinch.

Another of the first generation of "Giotteschi" who utilized the goldfinch motif extensively, and who also reveals, by contrast, the superiority of Taddeo Gaddi, is Jacopo del Casentino. In two panels (one in the

Royal Gallery, Brussels, and one in the Church of San Stefano at Pozzo-latico, near Florence) he introduced the bird held in the Christ Child's left hand. In the Brussels picture the bird is represented with partly raised wings, head turned towards the hand and with open bill — a fair representation of animation. In the other, the Child holds in His right hand a string which runs to the leg of the bird held in His left hand. It is held by the left wing and is turning to peck at the thumb of the hand that holds it. At least five paintings of the Madonna and Child by assistants in Jacopo's *bottega* have been found that contain goldfinches. Inasmuch as these may be taken together with the two by Jacopo himself to give an idea of the master's use of the icon they may be briefly mentioned here. In all of these panels the bird is very stiff, with no attempt to render convincing movement. The painting of the goldfinches in these five pictures is very inferior to that in the two by the master himself, but the fact that they were allowed to leave his shop indicates that the bird was not considered of any great moment. The often repeated dictum that Jacopo del Casentino was influenced by Bernardo Daddi but developed a style similar to that of Taddeo Gaddi is borne out by the fairly animated manner in which the detail of the goldfinch is employed in his own works, but is not reflected in those of his assistants. Either the closeness of these "assistants"[7] to the master has been over-estimated, or the detail was one which they were permitted to do in a perfunctory manner.

The open-mouthed attitude, suggestive of, or actually representing, pecking of the fingers by the goldfinch, was not peculiar to Florentine art. Thus, among the Sienese masters, we find it in the works of Barna ("Madonna Nursing the Christ Child"; Mrs. R. M. Hurd Collection, New York), (plate 75); Francesco di Segna di Bonaventura ("Madonna and Child," Pinacoteca, Siena), and the Master of the Pratt Madonna ("Madonna and Child"; *ex* D. F. Platt collection, Englewood, New Jersey), (plate 87). In the last named, the action seems particularly forced; the Child has to put His finger against the bird's open bill to establish the contact the artist desired. This is also true of a picture by the Florentine, Giovanni dal Ponte.

A "pecking" goldfinch in a fourteenth century Catalonian picture may be a reflection of Florentine precept through Starnina's influence.

It may be noted in passing that this open-billed, ostensibly pecking attitude may also have a dual significance. Aside from the interpretation given above, it may possibly also be looked upon as a continuation, even though a transformed one, of the medieval charadrius "sucking the peccant humors" from the mortal body of the Child. We may recall that in his description of the charadrius in a sculpture at Alne, Collins[8] describes it as identifiable for what it is meant to be by its label, although looking more like a raven about to peck out the eyes of the victim.

This particular attitude, of the "pecking" goldfinch, is, however, but one version of the commonest placement of the motif, to the general aspects of which we may now turn.

THE GOLDFINCH HELD IN THE HAND

By far the most frequent pose given the goldfinch, is that of being held in the Christ Child's hand in a semi-upright position, usually facing towards Him. The bird is held in the left hand in a considerably greater number of pictures than in the right hand but this seems to be due to the fact that the Child is more often seated on the Virgin's left knee or arm than on her right, so that His left hand is usually the one towards the frontal plane of the picture. The variations on this pose of the bird are minor but endless; the wings may be closed against the body, they may be partly arched or fully raised; the bird may be in simple profile or in any degree of rotation from that to full face; its bill may be open or closed; it may be held by the body with its feet dangling free; it may even be held by a wing alone. In most cases it is held in one hand, but in a good number of paintings it is grasped with both hands. In some pictures it is almost completely hidden by the enclosing fingers; in others it is held by the lower part of the body and the base of the tail leaving the bulk of the anterior part of the body exposed to view.

It is difficult to say with provable certainty that the symbolic significance of the icon is most strongly felt or rendered in those pictures in which the bird is clasped most tightly or held most closely to the Child's body, but, in a general way this seems to be true. At least, in its Trecento and Quattrocento usage, when not only was symbolism generally held more constantly in mind than later, but also when external conditioning factors, such as epidemics of plague, were more frequent and more severe, the goldfinch symbol was depicted with less variance from this intimate position than in succeeding generations and centuries.

Also, it is true that relatively fewer divergences from this close juxtaposition of the bird and the Christ Child are to be found in the art of schools more mystically inclined such as that of Siena, than in relatively mundane schools like that of Venice.

In a number of paintings the goldfinch is depicted as held by, or perching on, Mary's hand, or arm. Thus, it is perched on her right index finger in works by a follower of Bernardo Daddi, by Paolo Veneziano, and by Lorenzo di Niccolo; on her left index finger in a painting by Piero di Cosimo; on or in her right hand in works by Jacopo Bellini and Antonio de Saliba; in her left hand in a picture by Piero di Cosimo;[9] and perched on her left arm in paintings by Giambono, and by Carpaccio in Italy, and by a member of the school of Pacher in Germany.

In one instance[10] the bird is being handed to the Christ Child by St. Joseph; in another, likewise iconographically unique, picture, by a follower of Bernardo Daddi, the goldfinch is perched on the right index finger of St. Peter who extends this hand to the Child, while in a painting by Neri di Bicci (plate 64) and in another by Alvaro de Perez de Evora, and also in one by the St. Nicholas Master, an angel holds the bird towards the Infant Jesus (plate 16).

In a very small number of paintings the bird is represented as drooping or dead, a pose understandable only if we assume the artist to have had the Pseudo-Matthew legend in mind and to have chosen to depict the bird before it was brought to life by the Christ Child. At best it was a rather unsuccessful and disappointing choice, and its relative scarcity in art suggests that it did not appeal to many artists or their patrons. The Venetian, Donato Bragadin, so represented the bird in his triptych, now in the Metropolitan Museum (plate 91). Possibly the goldfinch in the "Madonna and Child" by the Master of the Bambino Vispo, in the Perriolet collection, Paris, and the "Madonna and Child with Saints" attributed to Lorenzo di Niccolo Gerini (S. Lorenzo, Collina) (plate 38) are to be looked upon as other cases, but it is also possible that the wretchedly rendered bird in each case is intended to be pecking at the hand that holds it. In Bragadin's picture the Child is obviously telling His Mother about the inert bird as though to call attention to the miracle about to be performed. Another pertinent example is Banchi's "Madonna and Child" in the National Gallery of Art, Washington (plate 54). The Christ Child holds a drooping, seemingly inert barn swallow (symbol of the Resurrection) in His hand.

What may be intended to represent the end, instead of the beginning, of the episode in the "Pseudo-Matthew Legend" is the "Madonna and Child" by the Master of the Castello Nativity (New York, Mrs. C. R. Holmes). In this picture the goldfinch, held in the Christ Child's hand, looks up at His other hand, raised in benediction, as though it had been thereby brought to life.

THE GOLDFINCH ON A STRING

The fact that the goldfinches, and other birds, commonly kept as household pets, especially as animated playthings for the children, were usually tethered by a long thread-like string is reflected in a large number of devotional paintings in which the goldfinch is used symbolically. In these pictures we have what amounts to a direct "taking over" from contemporary domestic reality, a true genre touch; a capital illustration of the Trecento and Quattrocento tendency to give a child's attributes to the representation of the Christ Child. The extent to which this tendency was carried is a reflection of the depth of the reaction to the old Byzantine influence which had prevailed for so long in Italy, in accordance with which the Christ Child was depicted as a small adult.

The important point for our present study is the fact that those artists who depicted the tether seem to have had somewhat more of a genre approach than a purely symbolic usage in mind when they painted goldfinches, than did those others (far more numerous) who did not attempt to connect the icon with such needless and trifling reality. It is significant that I have not found any evidence of a string attached to the bird's leg in any mature work by a really major artistic personality. It was, as might be expected, the lesser men who catered in this regard to an unsubtle clientèle. Thus, among Florentines, I have found only the following painters guilty of this tendency — a follower of Orcagna, Jacopo del Casentino, Gozzoli, and Leonardo da Pistoia. It is possible that a tether, no longer definitely visible may have existed formerly in one of Daddi's works as well. Of Sienese masters, Ambrogio Lorenzetti, the so-called "Ugolino Lorenzetti," and Andrea Vanni are the only artists I have found to have depicted this genre motif; other painters so involved as the Pisan, Nanni di Jacopo, the Roman, Antoniazzo Romano, the Venetians, Basaiti, Bastiani, Carlo Crivelli, and Antonio da Solario; the Modenese, Barnaba da Modena; and two Ferrarese, Ercole Grandi and a member of Cosimo Tura's studio. A tethered goldfinch also occurs in a very early Raphael (Solly Madonna) and in a work of unknown authorship, said to be attributed to Lucas Cranach, in imitation of Raphael(!) (Squindo Sale, 1903), but which is reminiscent of neither artist.

In some Russian devotional paintings, such as the "Konevskaia" icon (plate 32), the bird is held by a string; similarly a tethered goldfinch occurs in an old Panagiarion, both described by Kondakov, who continues as follows.

"Purely Russian icons of this theme show a white goldfinch or some sort of white bird instead of a finch, and there follows the interpretation that it is a white dove, and a halo around it marks it as the Holy Ghost in the form of a dove; . . . It is a case of a small fraud, but a pious one and an explanation made to suit it; yet there is something strange in the emblem of the Holy Ghost being led upon a string even by the hands of the God-man." [11]

Not only does the presence of the tether suggest limited understanding of the symbolism involved on the part of the painters who included it, but, on the other hand, its consistent absence in the works of artists ordinarily not credited with too much awareness of symbolism generally, must be counted as evidence in their favor in this regard. Thus, when we find as frequent a depicter of goldfinches as Francia never to have put a string on his birds we cannot help but conclude that to him the motif was far more than an attribute of childhood taken from contemporary life and given to the Christ Child. Likewise Taddeo Gaddi was above using so obviously secular a touch in his devotional pictures.

Aside from the Russian usage, which was derived from Italian sources, I have found the "goldfinch-on-a-string" motif only in Italian pictures and in one Spanish painting (Zurbaran), although the genre reality on which it was based was equally true of northern Europe. In Italian art its earliest appearance seems to have been in the second quarter of the fourteenth century; its latest, the first quarter of the sixteenth.

The goldfinch was the bird most commonly kept in captivity, and, aside from one exception, is the only one that I found in devotional art represented with a tether. The next most frequently included bird symbol, the barn swallow, the most direct avian symbol of "Resurrection" is seldom shown tied by its leg.[12] Aside from the fact that such a theme as it represents would be greatly impeded by a tether, it should be noted that swallows, being aerial feeders, and wholly insectivorous birds, and therefore difficult to provide food for, were never kept as domestic pets. As a matter of fact even zoological parks, with all their equipment, find swallows practically impossible to "keep" to this day.

THE GOLDFINCH UNATTACHED

It did not take long for painters to become aware of the possible sameness of the resulting pictures as they made successive versions of the Madonna and Child theme, and they sought to vary their works in all possible details. Their success is noticeable today in the fact that it is possible for a visitor to a great gallery to look at numbers of such panels without being bored by them. This success involved, among other items, the treatment of the goldfinch. One of the easiest ways to insure new interest in this element in the picture, because of different positions and compositional placements, was to take the bird out of the Child's hand and let it appear in the picture in almost any part of the composition. Thus, we find the goldfinch perching on the Infant's shoulder in pictures by such unrelated artists as the Umbrian, Boccati (plate 115), and the Sienese, Taddeo di Bartolo (plate 77); on His knee in a picture by Gozzoli (plate 60); on Mary's shoulder in a work by Stefano da Verona (Zevio) or perched on a curtain rod behind the throne on which the Madonna and Child are seated, in a painting by Vittorio Crivelli (plate 98). The goldfinch is depicted as standing untethered on a parapet in front of the Holy personages, towards the bottom of the picture in works by the Italians, Giovanni Bellini, Carpaccio, Graffione, Francesco Napoletano, and an unknown follower of Perugino, and by the Fleming, Ysenbrandt; it is shown standing on or near the ground or hovering over it in paintings by Albertinelli and Fra Bartolommeo (jointly) (plate 70, 70a), Bonifazio, Fungai, Ghirlandajo, Giovanni di Francesco, Piero della Francesca (plate 119, 119a), Philippus Veronensis, Sassetta (plate 90), Sellaio and Taddeo di Bartolo. The bird is placed in foliage, such as the vines on a trellis in a number of paintings of the "Madonna in a Rose Garden" type, chiefly by Germanic painters such as Hans Burgkmair (plate 29), Hans Baldung Grien (plate 28), Schongauer (plate 27), and an unknown Upper Rhenish master (plate 3); in trees by Crivelli, Francia, Pisanello (plate 130), and Simone Martini (plate 74). It was painted perched on, or flying, about the roof of the shed in front of which the Holy Family is depicted, in works by Daret (plate 22), Herlin, a follower of Filippo Lippi, Folchetto da Sanginesio (plate 136), Wolgemut, and Vecellio.

On the whole it seems true that the nearer to the sacred personages the bird was placed, either compositionally or by the action of the picture, the more intense was its symbolic significance intended to be. At the other end of the scale are those pictures where the bird seems to be put in chiefly as a decorative bit to brighten a piece of the background.

THE GOLDFINCH AND THE SCROLL

In a relatively small number of paintings, the goldfinch is placed near or directly in contact with a small scroll or piece of paper on which a variety of legends is inscribed. The fact that there is no basic similarity in the wordings on these scrolls indicates that it is not the message that is compositionally or symbolically related to the bird, but the scroll itself. As pointed out elsewhere in this work, the goldfinch is, to some extent, a substitute object for the little scroll or scroll box usually held by the Christ Child in early pictures done under Byzantine influence. Not a few of the earliest goldfinches are decidedly cylindrical in shape, as though the artists still had the scroll case form in mind.

We may recall that in an early Pisan picture by Turino Vanni the second (plate 133), the inscription on the scroll reads "ratione enunt[i]a[ta] guberno," *i.e.,* "I rule by the pronouncement of reason," a phrase that refers not to the bird but to Christ, in Whose hands both the scroll and the bird are held. In Zaganelli's "Virgin Adoring the Child" (in the Metropolitan Museum of Art) the goldfinch actually holds a scroll in its bill (plate 132). The legend on the scroll, however, bears merely the artist's signature! Lippo Memmi's "Madonna and Child" (Servite Church, Siena) shows the Child holding a goldfinch in His left hand, a scroll in His right. The inscription here is a direct quotation from the words of Christ "EGO SUM VIA VERITA[S]" (I am the true way); Niccolo da Voltri's "Madonna and Child" in Genoa (Sta. Maria delle Vigne) shows a goldfinch in the Babe's left hand, while in His right He holds a scroll reading "Ego Sum Alpha et Omega"; while in Domenico Ghirlandajo's "Adoration of the Magi" there is no visible legend on the paper (there may once have been, however?). In still another instance, Philippus Veronensis's picture of St. Jerome, the scroll again presents nothing more significant than the artist's signature. It is, of course, quite possible that the juxtaposition of the bird and paper is without particular significance, but it is more likely that some connection did exist in the mind of the painter or the patron in each case. The only connection that I can suggest is the fact that the Italian words for goldfinch, the bird with a "message" — *cardellino*, and for scroll (a message) — *cartellino*, are so very similar that they probably appealed to the pun-loving, anagramatically inclined Renaissance mentality and may have been placed together for this reason. Italian art is certainly not wanting in instances of this kind.

Possibly related to the bird-and-scroll motif is the placing of the goldfinch close to an open book as we find in the lower foreground in Fungai's "Madonna and Child, with the young St. John and Angels." In this connection it may also be recalled that in Raphael's "Madonna of the Goldfinch" (plate 117), the goldfinch has temporarily taken the attention of the group away from the book which the Virgin had been reading. This is, however, apparently not intended as a conflict or competition between the goldfinch and the book (apparently Holy Writ) but as a naturalistic bit of genre serving as a vehicle for the introduction of one of the bird's many symbolic meanings — in this case, Fertility.

The Symbolic Goldfinch

As has already been pointed out, painters not infrequently used multiple symbols to strengthen and to clarify, as well as to supplement, each other. Thus, in its role as a disease augur the goldfinch was sometimes placed in the hands of a Christ Child Who is wearing a red coral amulet about His neck. Examples are the triptych in Washington by Nuzi and the Master of the Fabriano Altarpiece (plate 112); and other paintings by "School of Giotto," "School of Niccolo di Pietro Gerini," Filippo Mazzola, Giovanni di Niccolo da Pisa, Bartolommeo de' Grassi, Giacomo da Recanati, and Ceccolo di Giovanni.

Another instance involving, however, a different symbolic meaning, is a "Madonna and Child" by Benozzo Gozzoli (plate 60), now in the Fogg Museum, Cambridge. The goldfinch is on the Child's right knee, looking at a pomegranate held in His left hand. The pomegranate was a symbol of Fertility and Immortality.[13] According to the authors of the definitive catalogue of the Fogg Museum, the, ". . . bird was painted over the mantle of the Madonna, as the mantle shows through the more or less transparent colors of the bird." This suggests that it was an afterthought, and quite possibly the motif was inserted to strengthen and elucidate the one already present, the pomegranate. The goldfinch and the pomegranate occur together also in paintings by Albertinelli and Fra Bartolommeo (plate 70), Andrea Vanni, and Cosimo Rosselli (plate 62). The goldfinch and the apple (symbols, respectively, of Resurrection and of Death) are contrastingly held in His two hands by the Christ Child in a picture by van Orley.

Other fruits symbolically used in conjunction with the goldfinch are the cherry (Garofalo), the plum (Fungai), and the gourd (Crivelli). The cherry is the fruit of heaven; the gourd the antidote for the apple of death. The plum's significance is unknown to me.

Flowers of various sorts, some, to me at least, quite unidentifiable, are used as companion symbols to the goldfinch in paintings by Alvaro de Pirez de Evora, Bernardino di Mariotto and Sano di Pietro, while flowers are a conspicuous part of the background in the "Madonna in a Rose Garden" compositions so favored by the Germanic painters, and in a modified way by Pier Francesco Fiorentino and his double, Pseudo Pier Francesco Fiorentino. In a painting by Jacopo Bellini the Christ Child is offering the goldfinch some leaves (?) (which may prove, on examination of the painting or of a better reproduction than the one I have seen, to be flowers). The goldfinch is associated with the thistle in a picture by Piero della Francesca[14] (plate 119).

Other birds are frequently introduced with the goldfinch in devotional paintings. In the pictures of the "Madonna in a Garden" type (plate 27), there are usually a variety of small birds — siskins, robins, tits, magpies, swallows, etc. Likewise in Adorations, either of the Magi or the Shepherds, numerous birds are often introduced — egrets, hawks, ducks, owls, pheasants, guinea hens, quail, etc. The only other birds that I have found to replace the goldfinch in the Christ Child's hand are the barn swallow (Resurrection), the titmouse (Fertility), the siskin and the greenfinch (apparently fairly extensive in their symbolism along the same lines as the goldfinch), a small (unidentifiable) parrot, a white dove, and an oriole (IKTEROS) and a small white bird both of which I assume to have been intended as variants of a "charadrius" (see p. 18-21).

Cats figure in conjunction with the goldfinch in pictures by Dosso Dossi, Baroccio, and (plate 126) a member of Cosimo Tura's school;[15] a monkey in a work by Ercole Grandi. While I have found no compositional connection between the goldfinch and the lamb, I have found the two together in a few pictures.

Inanimate symbols of particular Saints are rarely connected with the goldfinch, but I have found at least two such cases. In Bonifazio's "Coronation of St. Catherine of Alexandria," the goldfinch is standing on the piece of the wheel of Catherine's martyrdom, while a joint work by Albertinelli and Fra Bartolommeo (plate 70), the goldfinch is placed with the reed cross and the cup of the Baptist. In Bonifazio's picture the connection is established through the goldfinch's symbolizing Sacrifice; in the Florentine tondo through its meaning of Baptism.

THE SIZE OF THE GOLDFINCH

While it is true that the significance of a given symbol bears no relation to the size of its representation, but is something apart from the dimensions of its outward container, it does seem that in some instances its importance in the mind of the painter or of the patron is reflected in the prominence given it, and this prominence is increased or decreased pictorially by the actual size of the icon. Consequently we may briefly review the facts bearing on the size variations of the goldfinches in devotional art. The size, as here understood, is, of course, not the actual size (a bird in a picture on a small scale would be reduced as are the other figures) but its size in relation to the human figures in the same painting. It is not possible to say to what extent mere largeness was intended to give emphasis to the symbol and to what extent it may have been partly or largely unintentional, as it is only in a relatively few cases that we have a sufficient number of pictures by the same hand to indicate whether the artist was really aware of the actual dimensions of the bird. As already pointed out in our discussion of the use of the goldfinch in Germanic painting, in one fourteenth century Bohemian panel (in the Rudolphinum Gallery, Prague) (plate 25), the bird is unusually large, being considerably longer than the Child's head, and yet in all its details of construction and of plumage pattern is obviously based on such close observation of the actual bird that it seems more reasonable to interpret the result as intentional than otherwise. If intentional, emphasis is the only probable explanation. Certainly purely pictorial considerations such as composition, design, etc., would have been served equally well by a goldfinch a third less in bulk. Emphasis must then be emphasis on meaning, not on physical attributes.

On the other hand, in the work of a very prolific producer of goldfinches, such as Bernardo Daddi, the size of the bird varies enough to suggest that either the artist had assistants to paint in such minor elements in his pictures or else that he was very indifferent to accuracy in its portrayal. The latter seems quite likely as the small birds in contemporary French Madonna and Child statuettes by which he obviously was influenced to a considerable extent, vary greatly in size, but this by no means rules out the possibility, even the probability, of the former suggestion also being operative. It so happens that the range of size variation of the goldfinch in Daddi's art may be seen in the group of his paintings in the National Gallery of Art, Washington. In one panel (No. 511) (plate 52) the bird is fairly accurate in its dimensions, while in another (No. 519) (plate 55), it is unusually small, actually the smallest goldfinch I have found in any painter's work. The second picture is on a much smaller scale than the first one, which suggests that possibly when it came to reducing all the figures, the relative size of the bird was lost sight of. Furthermore, in the smaller picture the bird is flying, not held in the hand. It appears, not only from these cases, but from a great many others that the encircling fingers of the hand in which the bird was usually held seemed to serve the artist as the "object of known size" in relation to which he determined the size the bird was to be. When the bird was no longer in close juxtaposition this determining scale was lost or at least was less effective.

Aside from the unknown Bohemian master already discussed, the following Italian painters tended to make their goldfinches large and massive — Bernardino Borgognone, Gian Francesco Maineri, Francesco Napoletano, Gualtieri di Giovanni, Cosimo Rosselli, Folchetto da Sanginesio, and Cenni di Francesco. Thus, in Borgognone's picture the goldfinch on the ground at the bottom of the painting is as large as the two quail placed near to it; in Napoletano's painting the bird tends to overflow the capacity of the Child's two hands to hold it. Similarly a number of decidedly small goldfinches occur in works by several painters. Aside from the picture by Daddi (or, as Offner suggests, by a follower of his), I have found less than properly sized goldfinches by the following artists — Maestro Gregorio, the Master of the Cappella Medici Polyptych, Ercole Grandi, Stefano da Verona, and a member of the school of Andrea Verrocchio.

VARIATIONS IN THE PROPORTIONS OF THE GOLDFINCH

On the whole it seems that most of its painters made an effort to construct the goldfinch fairly accurately, but as might be expected, different artists made errors in almost every part of the bird. Thus the tail is relatively too long in works by Daddi, the Biadaiolo Illuminator, the Master of the Dominican Effigies, Rossello di Jacopo Franchi, Nuzi, the Master of the Fabriano Altarpiece, Zaganelli, Boccaccino, Bonifazio, and Carpaccio; the tail is unduly forked in pictures by the Master of the Bambino Vispo, Pesellino, and by an unknown member of Giotto's school; the wings are too long for the body in panels by Bartolo di Fredi, Andrea Vanni, Nuzi, and the Master of the Fabriano Altarpiece. Not only are the wings too long but their outer primaries are too long in relation to the more proximal ones, causing the wings to be too pointed, in all of these. The head of the bird is too small for the body in pictures by Sano di Pietro, Lorenzo di Niccolo, Bartolommeo de Tomasso da Foligno, and Garofalo; while the bill is exaggerated by Barna and Lippo Memmi among Sienese masters and by Juan de Juanes among Spanish painters. The two Sienese likewise made the maxilla (upper part of the bill) extend beyond the tip of the mandible (lower part of the bill) in their goldfinches. Of all parts of the bird, the feet seem to have given the most trouble to the painters, possibly because in so many pictures the bird is not standing on its feet but is held by the body with its toes either dangling loosely or partly hidden by the tail, positions in which the artist had difficulty in imagining the placement of the toes.

Enough has been said to indicate that the construction of the goldfinch as a whole, and of its component parts individually, should prove a fruitful field for students of style, even though the usefulness of the results would be applicable only to pictures containing this motif.

While it is probable that the goldfinches drawn by any one artist tend to be more uniform than do the human faces or figures by the same hand, because the artist was less interested in the birds and made them in a more routine fashion, they do occasionally exhibit considerable diversity. The factor that complicates the use of the goldfinch for the student of style is the fact that the bird was a relatively minor accessory figure, and, as such, was sometimes rendered with complete indifference as to its appearance. While this very indifference was a stabilizing factor tending towards sameness in the results, occasionally it permitted, if it did not lead to, variations of considerable degree. Thus, the two paintings by Sano di Pietro illustrated on plates 83 and 84 show two birds, both intended to be goldfinches, yet one has a short, stubby bill and the other a long, aciculate one; one has the cephalic markings indicated while the other lacks them entirely. It may be that Sano had assistants to do these minor bits, but it still remains that he was willing to let these works pass out from his studio as by him. Such lack of interest was obviously quite improbable, if not impossible, in connection with the rendition of the human form. On the whole, however, it seems that most artists, after learning how to draw a goldfinch, merely repeated their own version of it in successive pictures, altering merely its pose and position.

Add to this the variations in the coloring of the bird, and we have a great many variables among which to find the "combinations" that may give a clue to the authorship of an anonymous goldfinch set before us. Color is the one element I have not been able to study as most of my material has consisted of black and white photographs. However, among those paintings of which the original were seen, some color aberrations stand out. The whole sides of the head, the "face" of the bird is red in pictures by Benvenuto di Giovanni, Lorenzo Veneziano, and Girolamo di Benvenuto, whereas in most other artists' works, and in the real bird, the cheeks are largely white. In a painting from the workshop of Pesellino the spots on the tail are reddish instead of white; the whole coloration of the bird is pale and "washed out" in some pictures by Sano di Pietro and Pseudo Pier Francesco Fiorentino; the entire bird is dark and greenish olive with some reddish on the face, in works by Andrea di Bartolo, Benvenuto di Giovanni, Basaiti, and a work attributed to Francia but possibly not actually by his hand. In a picture by Bernardino di Mariotto the pale area on the wings is dull pink instead of yellow. It is not my purpose in this work to go into stylistic matters; this cannot be done without study of many more originals than have been available to me; for the student of style these few brief remarks may serve as an initiating stimulus.

Chapter XIII. Michelangelo's Exceptional Treatment of the Goldfinch

THROUGHOUT the whole span of its use in devotional art the goldfinch is either regarded with varying degrees of eagerness and pleasure by the Christ Child or at least forms an acceptable, and accepted, item in the picture. Only once do we find it an untoward element, a cause of negative response from any of the principal actors in the composition. This one remarkable exception, the marble tondo relief of the "Madonna and Child with the Young St. John" (plates 139, 139a), made by Michelangelo for Taddeo Taddei (now in Burlington House, London),[1] deserves fuller discussion than it was possible to give it earlier in his study. In spite of the fact that its authenticity has never been doubted and that therefore it has been mentioned, and even briefly described, by the innumerable authors who have written accounts of the master's life and works, until very recently[2] no one seems to have noticed that it, and it alone, completely reverses the treatment of the goldfinch motif found in the works of all the other artists of Europe. We expect it of Michelangelo to be original and "different," but always with a valid reason and with sound, intuitive and sympathetic understanding guiding his hand. Few, if any, practitioners of art have been profounder students of the Bible and of related theological literature than was the great Florentine. No artist had more stimulating sources of contact with the humanities, with the treasures of classical literature and philosophy than did he who passed an important part of his impressionable youth in the daily company of such men as Poliziano, Pulci, Ficino, and Pico della Mirandola. If any artist was prepared by tradition, by learning, and by both intellectual and emotional inclination, to make the most of a polyvalent symbol such as the goldfinch it was Buonarroti.

We may, therefore, approach his one rendition of the theme involving the bird[3] with more than ordinary interest. Knowing the quality of our artist's mind, we may expect a combining, if not, indeed, a conflicting of meanings crowded together in his use of the icon. Inasmuch as the interpretation I have to suggest is based on what I am able to read in his work, and not on any statements either by the sculptor or his contemporaries or predecessors that might throw some light on his intentions, it may be well to fortify ourselves with a few of the more important reflections and remarks made by previous writers.

The most elaborate attempt to explain this tondo, without, apparently realizing its uniqueness, was made by Justi.[4] He notes that the little St. John, as if prophetic of his life in the wilderness, is a bird-catcher, but that the bird, a stock fixture of old, primitive "church" Madonnas, serves to emphasize the contrast of their hieratic calm with this modern, nervously agitated conception; the infant Precursor startles the Christ Child with the fluttering bird so suddenly placed close to Him in semi-opened hand, so that He makes a great leap back to His Mother. She also seems to regard this play as not entirely proper; she pushes back the little Baptist with an almost involuntary, gentle motion of Her hand. The drawing of the Child toward the Mother, ordinarily expressed through the loving glance and through movement, is here translated into actuality; the Child forsakes play and playmates.

"In this tondo every current of churchly meaning has vanished. Here the humanizing of the divine is made serious, even in play. This group could be assimilated into the society painting of the eighteenth century without one's noticing its high origin. Mary is merely the happy, earthly mother, resting on the sod in a refreshing respite from her orthodox role of divine ministration to the Child. In the Pietá the whole lucid countenance was entirely free; it gave the face its character of spiritual heavenliness. Here, the turban-like headgear, concealing the tresses, reminds one of a zingarella, a gypsy. Instead of the forehead band with its cherub head[5] we see only an unfinished, sketchily suggested roll together with a little pearl string.[6] The . . . London Madonna . . . represents the highest point which he (Michelangelo) reached in the direction of grace. He soars in the ether of the ideal, far removed from definite time or place, so that one hardly recognizes him again. But that he has become free from himself, or, better stated, from the conception of himself which the bulk of his work has forced upon mankind, is due to the fact that here he intended, or believed he had to make, nothing great and lofty. The slightly esteemed relief-form, the genre-like motif, the fact that the work was destined to become a house ornament of a private citizen, a bourgeois — all this Michelangelo considered play, a bagatelle. On the contrary, it is when, in the ardor of competition, he believed he had to produce something extraordinary, and thereto plagued himself with an unwonted technique, that he floundered in rebellious artistic affectation."

According to Mackowsky[7] the important element in the composition is that the Christ Child, in His leap back to His Mother, steps back over Her outstretched leg. "With this motif of the great "stepping back" (*i. e.*, transformation) Michelangelo has made something entirely original. In accordance with his nature, even here, where he wants to be gentle and sensitive, he touches on the heroic. . . ."[8]

In his recent monograph, de Tolnay[9] notes that the ". . . motif of the goldfinch is known to fourteenth century art in Florence . . . here the bird is held as a sort of attribute by Jesus. In Michelangelo the idea is changed. The fear of Jesus before the bird seems to anticipate the fear of his later destiny. The resigned figure of the Virgin seems to look beyond all this little drama to the passion of Christ. . . ." In another passage (p. 104) he writes, "the goldfinch motif may be traced to Florentine Madonnas as early as the Trecento. In these works the Christ Child holds the bird in his hand, but it is still. It was Michelangelo's idea to dramatize this scene by making the goldfinch beat its wings."

With these considerations held in mental reserve we may now proceed to study the tondo and see for ourselves what it may suggest.[10]

But, first, in order to understand more fully the significance of this work it is necessary to consider it, not only by and for itself, but also in connection with two other circular "Holy Family" compositions of the master, especially since all were made in the same period, ca. 1504-1506, and since all were made as house ornaments for private citizens. In other words, all represent the same stage of Michelangelo's art, and all were brought about under similar external conditions. These two other works are the marble relief of the "Madonna and Child and St. John," sometimes known as the "Pitti Madonna" (plate 141), in the Bargello, Florence, and the painting known as the "Doni Holy Family," now in the Uffizi Gallery in the same city. The dimensions of the painting and of the London tondo are alike; the marble in Florence is considerably smaller. The work we have been considering is the only one in which the bird motif appears; it is also the most appealing and satisfying, and is certainly the most successful solution of the compositional problems presented by a circular shape. The "Doni Holy Family" (plate 140), is one of the most sculpturally conceived paintings in the world. As Goldscheider says, "... it is composed in accordance with the rules of relief-carving just as much as the two sculptural works themselves." It is, however, not at all adapted to the round shape it occupies; no concessions in its composition have been made to the demands of the circle. The Bargello relief might also have been carved just as well on a square or oblong without altering it in any way. It is only the Taddei tondo that is eminently a circular composition. Inasmuch as we have no other evidence as to the relative chronology of these three works,[12] it seems to me that we can ill afford to ignore the far greater success of the London marble in its solution of this purely technical problem. This would make it the latest of the three, and it might be inferred that, in a sense, it is the outgrowth of the trials made in the other two.

The marble tondo of the Bargello is the simplest of the three. The Child has tired and has interrupted His Mother in Her reading by resting His right arm across the open book in a quiet, thoughtful pose. The little St. John, whose head appears from behind the Madonna's right shoulder, is compositionally rather unfortunate; he looks "stuck in" rather than inherent in the group. He seems to be standing behind a wall, and, in this regard, as well as in facial expression, he is a reversed image of the St. John in the "Doni Holy Family." In other words, in the Bargello marble and the Uffizi painting the little Baptist is separated both psychologically and physically from the Virgin and the Infant Jesus. In both, the Infant Precursor contributes little to the action or the meaning of the composition. His presence is probably due to the popularity he held in Florence, of which city he was the patron saint, which, in turn, made him a very frequent figure in devotional pieces. In the Bargello marble the Virgin has, as in the London version, a prophetic mien; She seems to be still thinking about what She has been reading. The Christ Child is likewise immersed in thought, a faint smile forming on His lips. The little Baptist seems too timid to intrude upon the contemplative mood of the Holy Personages.

We have here a direct and simple presentation of the basic devotional icon, the Christ Child, Hope and Saviour of the world, and His Mother, the sibylline font of care and nurture that guards and nourishes the Spirit in the body of mankind.[13]

In the "Doni Holy Family" we have the figure of Joseph together with Mary and Jesus. The Holy Family is placed in a grassy plot in front of a low wall, immediately behind which, to the extreme right is the little St. John gazing at the Christ Child, while in the further background are grouped five nude figures. The background of this picture has often been cited by critics as evidence of Michelangelo's preoccupation with the nude, even at the expense of significance; of the influence on him of Signorelli and his powerful use of the nude human figure. The interpretation of this work here followed is that of de Tolnay who anticipated my own similar one, independently arrived at. Inasmuch as the "Doni Holy Family" is a partial expression of what transpired in the mind of the creator of the Taddei tondo, its exposition is of interest to our main problem. In short, what we find in the "Doni Holy Family" is this. The Holy Family is seated in a fertile world of grass and flowers separated by a wall from the bleak, stark, desolate pagan world, which in turn is inhabited by largely nude figures, as opposed to draped ones. The little Precursor, coming as he did before Christ, is placed on the pagan side of the wall, but he sees the Divinity and is rapt in attentive contemplation. He is furthermore differentiated from the background figures by being draped. When we consider that in making this picture Michelangelo condescended, for the only time in his life, to paint such minor bits of verdure as grasses and flowerets, his inclusion of numbers of them, delicately fashioned, in the foreground cannot be without meaning. It seems definitely done to heighten the contrast of the verdant monotheistic world and the barren stretches of the pagan background from which it emerged. Within this monotheistic world in the foreground there transpires the triumph of the Church over the Synagogue, as symbolized by the Christ Child being placed above Mary and Joseph, the figures of the preceding generation that tended Him.

Now, to return to the London tondo (plates 139, 139a). The little St. John has scaled the wall, so to speak, and is brought into close contact with the Virgin and the Infant Jesus. Now that he has "arrived," what does he do but frighten the Christ Child with his offer of a violently excited, fluttering bird!

The unique feature of this treatment of the goldfinch theme is the retreat of the Christ Child from it. On the basis of a realistic interpretation of the composition, this is, in turn, due to the fact that the bird, instead of being docile, gentle, or, at least fairly calm, is violently fluttering, nervously agitated, quite capable of frightening the Child to Whom it is suddenly brought so near. In other words, our first question becomes, not "Why does the Child retreat?" but "Why is the goldfinch represented in so unusual a fashion?" The answer, as in all of Michelangelo's works, is to be found simultaneously, and intentionally, in the double realm of realism and of mystic symbolism. The purely realistic, physical aspect of the action portrayed would lead us to expect a newly captured bird to be attempting to escape; hence the vigorous fluttering. From the standpoint of symbolic meaning, the goldfinch as a symbol of the Soul would be yearning towards Divinity, away from St. John towards Christ; as a symbol of Baptism it would be anxious to go from the Baptist to the One to be baptized. Therefore, from both the realistic and the symbolic aspects, the goldfinch would be in an excited, nervous state, if it were intended to be an embodiment of what it symbolizes and not merely a hollow label to guide the spectator into the proper line of thought. In the hands of a profound genius like Michelangelo even a symbol became expressive of what it stood for. The figure arts were to him (and in his hands became) capable of complete expression, or they did not apply to a given theme. All through his *oeuvre* we find this shedding of time-honored "labels." Save for one youthful work (in which his hand was not free as he was bound to make a companion piece for an earlier figure[14]) his angels have no wings; nowhere do we find his Holy Personages or Saints identified with nimbi. So too, the goldfinch either had to express the thoughts it carried or be left out. When we first realize this, when we first learn to feel the symbolism with the zeal and the energy with which our artist did, how tame and stilted all the other goldfinches suddenly become, how like mere labels as contrasted with the real symbol itself.

However, there is one very serious difficulty to be "explained away" before we can accept this interpretation. If the bird represents the Soul yearning towards Divinity, why does the Divinity retreat from it? If the bird is a symbol of Baptism (and through that, of Redemption) why does the One to be baptized flee from it? Are we to believe that these things are unacceptable to the Christ Child? Surely they never were so considered before (or since). In order to answer this question it is necessary to digress for a moment and consider the external factors attendant upon the creation of our tondo.

During the last four years of Savonarola's life and for more than a decade after his execution, Florence passed through a terrible period, usually referred to in the histories as the "Interregnum" (1494-1511). Young[15] describes it in these words: "So far, therefore, as Florence is concerned, the record of this period consists of little else than internal discord and misgovernment. Unceasing turmoils between rival factors . . . an administration utterly corrupt . . . anarchy, injustice and misery at home, are the prevailing features of this period . . ." (p. 250). Following the death of the eloquent friar of San Marco, the conditions in Florence were described by a contemporary writer, Cambi (quoted by Young, p. 262) to the effect that, ". . . citizens who sought redress in the law courts were frequently stabbed in the street the next night, judges pronounced iniquitous sentences, and there was no reverence for holy things or fear of shame." It is well known that Michelangelo was profoundly stirred by the gloomy prophecies and dire forebodings that were thundered from the pulpit of the Duomo by the fervent Savonarola. The celerity with which these prophesied disasters seemed to transpire must have appeared not without significance to our artist. Added to this, the house of Medici, to whom he was so greatly indebted personally, and which had been the main controlling force in the previous orderly conduct of Florentine affairs, was not only no longer in power but was actually in exile. In spite of the many favors he had received from the Medici, Michelangelo opposed their rule as inimical to the liberties of his fellow Florentines. In other words, returning to his beloved Florence, Buonarroti found conditions there desperate almost beyond hope, and the one tried, strong, stabilizing force not only gone but not wanted back. To a devout, impressionable soul such as his, prepared as he was by the dismal prophecies of Savonarola, it must have seemed that the woes that had befallen the Florentines were signs of Divine displeasure.[16] While we cannot even begin to prove that these feelings and thoughts were transmitted directly by the great sculptor to any particular part of any of his works, it seems reasonable to assume that they were part of the mental background in which were formulated the designs that eventually were transferred to carved marble or to painted panel. Is it not plausible to assume (since no proof is possible) that something of this conviction that his fellow townsfolk were largely doomed to damnation as a result of their sinful disregard of proper values may be reflected in the tondo made for Taddeo Taddei? The little patron Saint of the city of Florence, offers the symbol of its soul to the Christ Child who not only wants none of it but retreats from it. The agitation of the bird may reflect the despairing urgency of the need for Divinity, and, in fact, may even be increased by the lack of the hoped-for response, but the Infant Divinity is not willing to accept it, at least not yet. Mary, the "Maria Mediatrix" does not prevent the little St. John from coming forward with the bird; She merely gently restrains him, as if to delay or to postpone him, as though the time was not yet right for a successful termination of his action. Time is needed, time for penance, for at least attempting to right the wrongs done, before acceptance by Christ can be expected.

It may be argued that this interpretation is too severe, that the artist would not have permitted external factors to enter so largely into the spirit of his work. To this I can only say that Michelangelo was still a young man, not yet thirty, when he carved this tondo, and that he had not yet achieved that degree of detachment that served him so well in his later works, where the reflection of external conditions is softened and generalized to the point where the connection, although still present, is much less obvious.[17]

An independent, but parallel instance of artistic reaction to the chaotic condition of Florentine affairs is reflected in the work of Botticelli. As has been pointed out by Venturi[18] the inscription along the top of Botticelli's "Nativity," painted two years after Savonarola's death, informs us that the artist interpreted the execution of the friar as the moment of the unloosing of the demon according to the Apocalypse. ". . . In the Nativity the spirit of piety, of compassion for the fate of mankind, dominates the picture. The Angels still dance . . . but their gracefulness has acquired a melancholy element. The adoration of the new-born Child is no longer a motive for joy; the sense of human guilt weighs too heavily on the shoulders of the adorers, who are bent beneath their grief.

"In the 'Crucifixion' in the Fogg Museum, the mystical anguish of the

Magdalen, who throws herself in despair at the foot of the Cross, is one of the highest achievements of art. In the background is Florence, and it may be that the angel is an allegorical representation of the punishment of the city for the burning of Savonarola. . . ."

To return to the tondo under discussion, we may note that from the standpoint of realism, Mary might attempt to delay the frightening bird from nearing the Child, as she is doing here. Symbolically, she would not attempt to prevent either the soul from attaining to Christ or the baptism from being consummated (by the symbol passing from the baptizer to the baptized). But the action is not merely this; it is still more complex. The bird is also a symbol of the Crucifixion; a theme from which the Child might well retreat. This would form part of the reason for His frightened leap back to the safety of His Mother, but it would not in any way explain the activation of the bird. Connected with this element in the symbolic meanings involved in the composition is the fact that the Madonna has a far-away, dreamy look. Obviously She is a sibylline, prophetic Madonna, and insofar as the bird represents Crucifixion, She may well be looking beyond to the Passion. Far from agreeing with Justi that She suggests a gypsy type, it seems to me that we have here, of all of Michelangelo's numerous figures combining incompatible qualities of divinity and humanity, one of the most tender, one of the most easily accepted emotionally, in spite of the fact that She is to a large extent a sibylline and not a purely maternal figure.

What is it that makes this particular Madonna so acceptable? She has sweetness and purity but so does the Pietá, so does the Madonna at Bruges, or the one of the "Pitti" tondo in Florence. It certainly is not her rapt, far-off prophetic qualities or we should feel equally touched by the early "Madonna of the Stairs"; She lacks the heroic qualities we admire in the Madonna of the Medician chapel in Florence or the exuberant strength of the "Doni" Madonna. The thing that makes her so appealing is the fact that she is the motherly refuge for the frightened Child, an expression of a haven and a solace for which we all harbor, consciously or otherwise, a nostalgic memory.

As if to emphasize the conflicting play of emotions involved in the situation depicted, the artist has caused the Christ Child to look back at the bird as He runs away from it. This action enormously enhances the dramatic effect of the composition[19] and serves to connect the figures involved with still greater force than would otherwise have been the case.

Lest it be thought that the interpretation here suggested is simplified by omitting all reference to such symbolic meanings so often associated with the goldfinch, as the fertility and the disease augury concepts, it may be pointed out that throughout his entire *oeuvre*, Michelangelo always chose to emphasize the higher, the more purely spiritual, elements at the expense of the more earthly meanings. The goldfinch's significance as a disease augur and as a symbol of Fertility, if present in this work, owe their inclusion not to anything directly expressed in it, but to the fact that the bird icon was so widely and intimately connected with these ideas as to bring them in by inference and assumption. The fact that the bird is so very much alive before passing into the Christ Child's hands eliminates any reference to the Pseudo-Matthew legend with its resultant Resurrection symbolism. Michelangelo took the currently popular goldfinch and reduced it back to the basic idea of the small bird symbol.

Justi is probably quite correct when he says that the great sculptor considered this tondo, made expressly as a house ornament for a private citizen, as of less importance than a work done for a sacred or public edifice, but Justi forgets that a great artist does even small things in a great way. We may recall Michelangelo's own reputed statement, apocryphal though it may be, that, ". . . trifles make perfection, but perfection is no trifle." In his striving for perfection in the union of form and meaning, Michelangelo has succeeded in his rendition of the goldfinch as he did in so many more important figures. By disregarding the representation of the outer physical reality of the bird the master serves to emphasize the presentation of its inner significance. Instead of being an exception, his Taddei tondo becomes the climax and the epitome of the goldfinch as a symbolic figure in devotional art.

Appendix
List of Paintings Containing the Goldfinch Symbol

To RELIEVE the main body of the text, and for convenience in ascertaining just what paintings have been found containing the goldfinch symbol, all the pertinent works are here listed, arranged by schools in the order in which these schools have been discussed in this work. As pointed out in the preface, this list could easily be extended, probably doubled, if one cared merely to amass more cases. It is doubtful, however, if additional examples would add anything to the scope of the symbolism, or to the historical and geographical range of the usage, of the goldfinch motif.

In cases where the present location of a picture is unknown, I have given a reference to a published reproduction of it. There are a very few cases where this has not been possible; pictures that I learned of solely by mention in literature as containing a goldfinch and as being in a "private collection." The most extensive sources of reproductions in literature are the following. For Italian works, van Marle's "Development of the Italian Schools of Painting," Offner's "Critical and Historical Corpus of Florentine Painting," and Adolfo Venturi's "Storia dell'arte italiana"; for Spanish paintings, Post's "History of Spanish Painting"; for Flemish works, Friedländer's "Die altniederländische Malerei"; for early Germanic pictures, Stange's "Deutsche Malerei der Gotik"; while for such individual artists as are covered by its volumes, the "Klassiker der Kunst" series is very useful.

List of Paintings

SPANISH

BASSA, FERRER
    1. Madonna and Child and Angels   Pedralbes, Chapel of San Miguel

CATALONIAN, FOURTEENTH CENTURY
    1. Triptych   Baltimore, Walters Art Gallery

CATALONIAN, FIFTEENTH CENTURY
    1. Child Jesus Learning to Walk   Barcelona, Chapter Room of Cathedral

FIGUERA, JUAN
    1. Madonna and Child with
       St. Peter Martyr and St. Mark   New York, Mr. Piero Tozzo

GIL MASTER
    1. Madonna and Child and Angels   Madrid, Apolinar Sanchey collection

JACOMART AND REXACH, WORKSHOP OF
    1. Triptych   Frankfurt am Main, Stædel Art Institute

JUAN DE JUANES
    1. Madonna and Child and Saints   Philadelphia, Fine Arts Museum
                                                 (Johnson collection)

MAJORCA, SCHOOL OF
    1. Madonna and Child and Angels   Madrid, Raimundo Ruiz collection

MASTER OF ALBATARRECH (?)
    1. Madonna and Child and Angels   Chicago, Art Institute

MURILLO, BARTOLOME ESTEBAN
    1. Holy Family with a Bird   Madrid, Prado

OSONA, RODRIGO DE, THE YOUNGER (?)
    1. Madonna and Child   Valencia, Private collection
                                                   (Post, vol. 6, pt. 1, p. 235)

REXACH, JUAN
    1. Part of Retable from Cubélls   Barcelona, Museum of Catalan Art
    2. Madonna and Child and Angels   Abal, Parish Church

List of Paintings

SEVILLE, FOURTEENTH CENTURY
1. "Virgen de la Antigua" — Seville, Cathedral
2. "Virgen de Rocamador" — Seville, San Lorenzo
3. "Virgen del Coral" — Seville, San Ildefonso

ST. NICHOLAS MASTER (OR PUPIL)
1. Triptych — Whitebridge, near London, Lord Lee

VERDERA, NICHOLAS (?)
1. Madonna and Child and Angels — Vich, Museum

ZURBARAN, FRANCISCO DE
1. Madonna and Child and Young St. John — San Diego, Fine Arts Museum

FLEMISH

ANONYMOUS, 16TH CENTURY
(under influence of Dürer)
1. Madonna and Child and St. Elizabeth — Paris, Stephen Bourgeois (in 1910)

HUGO VAN DER GOES
1. Madonna and Child — Brussels, Royal Gallery

JORDAENS, JACOB
1. Holy Family with Saints Zacharias, Elisabeth and Young St. John the Baptist — Westphalia, private collection*

MASTER OF THE MANSI MAGDALEN †
1. Madonna and Child and St. Anne — Paris, Art Market (Friedländer, vol. 7, p. 132, no. 97)

2. Madonna and Child and Joseph — New York, Art Market (Friedländer, vol. 7, p. 132, no. 97)

SITHIUM, MIGUEL
1. Madonna and Child — Berlin, Kaiser Friedrich Museum

VAN ORLEY, BARENT
1. Madonna and Child — London, *ex* A. Wertheimer collection

* *Illustrated in Münster Landesmuseum . . . Meisterwerke holländischer und flämischer Malerei aus westfälischem Privatbesitz, 1939, no. 29, pl. 12.*
† *The birds in these two paintings are not wholly certainly identified, but appear, in not too good reproduction, to be goldfinches.*

[*139*]

List of Paintings

YSENBRANDT, ADRIAAN
1. Madonna and Child and Two Angels   New York, F. Kleinberger, 1927

FRENCH

AMIENS, SCHOOL OF
1. Madonna and Child   Chicago, Art Institute

ANONYMOUS, CA. 1515
1. Madonna and Child with Two Angels
   and St. Margaret and Louis XII of France   Weld Blundell Collection

DARET, JACQUES
1. Nativity   Lugano, Thyssen Collection

ENGLISH

UNKNOWN, LATE 13TH CENTURY ILLUMINATOR
1. Madonna and Child
   (in Psalter of Robert de Lisle)   London, British Museum

DUTCH

GEERTGEN VAN HAARLEM
1. Adoration of the Kings   Amsterdam, Rijksmuseum

GERMANIC

BALDUNG GRIEN, HANS
1. Rest on the Flight Into Egypt   Nürnberg, Germanisches Museum

BOHEMIAN, UNKNOWN
1. Madonna and Child   London, Buckingham Palace
2. Madonna and Child   Prague, Strahowkloster
3. Madonna and Child   Prague, Rudolphinum Gallery
4. Madonna and Child   Brussels, Capuchin Church

BURGKMAIR, HANS
1. Madonna and Child   Nürnberg, Germanisches Museum

List of Paintings

HERLIN, FRIEDRICH
   1. Nativity
                               Nördlingen, Städtisches Museum

HOLBEIN, HANS, THE ELDER
   1. Madonna and Child with Angels
                               Nürnberg, Germanisches Museum

PACHER, FOLLOWER OF
   1. Madonna and Child
                               Nürnberg, Germanisches Museum

SCHEL, SEBASTIAN
   1. Triptych
                               Chicago, Art Institute

SCHONGAUER, MICHAEL
   1. Madonna and Child in Rose Garden
                               Colmar, St. Martin's Church

UPPER RHENISH SCHOOL
   1. Madonna and Child
      among the Strawberries
                               Solothurn, Städtisches Museum

WOLGEMUT, MICHAEL
   1. Nativity
                               Zwickau, Marienkirche
   2. Madonna and Child and St. Anne
              Nürnberg, Germanisches Museum

FLORENTINE

ALBERTINELLI, MARIOTTO, AND FRA BARTOLOMMEO
                               Washington,
   1. Madonna and Child with Saints and Angels
      National Gallery of Art

ALUNNO DI BENOZZO
   1. Madonna and Child, Saints Jerome, Clare,
      young Baptist, and Cherubim
                               Perugia, Gallery

AMBROGIO DI BALDESE
   1. Madonna and Child
                                 Los Angeles, Dr. Ernest L. Tross
   2. Madonna and Child and Saints
                 Boston, Museum of Fine Arts

AMBROGIO DI BALDESE, PSEUDO
   1. Madonna and Child Enthroned
                 Poggibonsi, S. Pietro a Cedde
   2. Madonna and Child
                 London, Kerr Lawson collection
   3. Madonna and Child
             The Hague, Verburgt collection
   4. Madonna and Child
              Florence, Uffizi (magazine)

List of Paintings

ANGELICO, FRA, FOLLOWER OF

    1. Madonna and Child and Angels   Frankfurt, Ad. Schaeffer collection

ANTONIO VENEZIANO

    1. Madonna and Child   Boston, Museum of Fine Arts

BALDOVINETTI, SCHOOL OF

    1. Holy Family with Young St. John   Richmond, Lee of Fareham collection

BIADAIOLO ILLUMINATOR

    1. Madonna and Child with Two Saints   New York, Robert Lehman collection

BONAIUTI, ANDREA

    1. Madonna and Child and Saints   Whereabouts unknown
    (illustrated in Dedalo, vol. 12, 1932, p. 515)

BONSI, GIOVANNI

    1. Polyptych   Vatican, Pinacoteca

BOTTICELLI, SCHOOL OF

    1. Madonna and Child   New York, Metropolitan Museum

BUGIARDINI, GIULIANO

    1. Madonna and Child with Infant St. John   Rome, Borghese Gallery

CENNI DI FRANCESCO

    1. Madonna and Child   Washington, National Gallery of Art

CIMABUE, SCHOOL OF

    1. Diptych   Rome, Sterbini collection

DADDI, BERNARDO

    1. Madonna and Child   Florence, Berenson collection
    2. Triptych   Altenburg, Lindenau Kunstmuseum
    3. Polyptych   Florence, Uffizi
    4. Madonna, Child, with Eight Angels   Florence, Or San Michele
    5. Madonna and Child   Boston, Gardner Museum
    6. Madonna and Child [1]   New York, Durlacher collection
    7. Madonna and Child and Donor   Washington, National Gallery of Art, no. 511
    8. Madonna, Child, Saints and Angels   Washington, National Gallery of Art, no. 519

9. Madonna and Child [1]   New York, Duveen collection
10. Madonna and Child   Vatican, Picture Gallery

DADDI, BERNARDO, SCHOOL OF
1. Madonna and Child with Six Angels   Florence (environs),
                                                    S. Martino alla Palma
2. Madonna and Child Saints, and Angels   Budapest, Museum of Fine Arts
3. Madonna and Child   Florence, A. Corsi collection
4. Madonna, Child, with Eight Angels   Chianciano, Palazzo Municipale
5. Madonna and Child   Parma, Pinacoteca
6. Madonna and Child   Parma, Congregazione di San Filippo Neri
7. Madonna and Child   Princeton, New Jersey, University Museum
8. Madonna and Child with Saints   New York, Mrs. Edith Beers
9. Madonna and Child   Cambridge, Fogg Museum
10. Madonna and Child Enthroned with Saints   Petrignano (near Perugia)
                                                    St. Pietro

DADDI, BERNARDO, CLOSE FOLLOWER OF
1. Madonna and Child with Six Angels   Lecore (near Florence), S. Pietro
2. Madonna and Child   Munich Art Market. (Illustrated by Offner,
                                   Crit. Corpus., sec. 3, vol. 4, p. 118, pl. xlvi.)
3. Madonna and Child   Naples, Museo Nazionale
4. Madonna and Child   Florence, Accademia, No. 3466
5. Madonna and Child with Saints Augustine,
   John the Baptist and the Archangel Michael   Nantes,
                                              Musée Municipal des Beaux-Arts
6. Madonna and Child with Saints. John, Peter,
   Paul, and Lawrence, and Twenty-five Angels   Paris, Louvre

DADDI, BERNARDO, REMOTE FOLLOWER OF
1. Madonna and Child   Whereabouts unknown (illustrated in Offner,
                                   Hist. Corpus, sec. 3, vol. 4, p. 164, pl. lxi.)

GADDI, AGNOLO   Washington,
1. Madonna and Child with Saints and Angels   National Gallery of Art
2. Madonna and Child with Eight Angels Borgo San Lorenzo (near Florence),
                                                    S. Lorenzo

GADDI, AGNOLO, SCHOOL OF
1. Madonna and Child with Saints, Angels,
   and a Nun as Donoress   Parma, Pinacoteca
2. Madonna and Child and Angels   Whereabouts unknown
                           (illustrated in Dedalo, November 1931, p. 1311)

[*143*]

List of Paintings

GADDI, TADDEO
1. Madonna and Child with Saints and Angels   Siena, Pinacoteca
2. Madonna and Child with Saints and Angels   Florence, Uffizi
3. Polyptych   Florence, S. Felicità
4. Madonna and Child   Florence (environs) S. Lorenzo alle Rose
5. Madonna and Child   Munich, private collection (illustrated in Sirén, Burlington Mag., vol. 48, 1926, p. 184, fig. A)
6. Madonna and Child   Florence, Horne Foundation
7. Madonna and Child   Florence, Accademia
8. Madonna and Child   Castiglione Fiorentino, Pinacoteca
9. Madonna and Child Enthroned with Saints   Florence (environs), San Martino a Mensola

GADDI, TADDEO, SCHOOL OF,
1. Madonna and Child   Bernay (Rouen), Museum

GERINI, NICCOLO DI PIETRO
1. Madonna and Child with Angels   Paris, Louvre
2. Madonna and Child (triptych)   Florence (environs), Vincigliata, S. Lorenzo

GERINI, NICCOLO DI PIETRO, SCHOOL OF
1. Madonna and Child with Six Angels   Brunswick, Landesmuseum
2. Polyptych   Florence, Santa Croce
3. Madonna and Child with Two Angels   Florence (environs), La Quiete
4. Madonna and Child with Two Saints   Vatican, Pinacoteca
5. Madonna and Child with Saints and Angels   Altenburg, Lindenau Museum
6. Madonna and Child   Rifredi, S. Stefano in Pane

GHIRLANDAJO, DOMENICO
1. Adoration of Magi   Florence, Uffizi

GIOTTO, SCHOOL OF
1. Madonna and Child   Palermo, Chiaramonte Bordonaro collection

GIOVANNI DI BARTOLOMMEO CRISTIANI
1. Madonna and Child with Angels   Moscow, Museum of Fine Arts

GIOVANNI DI FRANCESCO
1. St. Francis and Elderly Baptist   Chartreuse

List of Paintings

GIOVANNI DAL PONTE
1. Madonna and Child with Saints and Angels   Whereabouts unknown
(illustrated in Berenson, Dedalo, vol. 12, 1932, p. 178)

GIOVANNI DEL BIONDO
1. Madonna and Child, Baptist
and Catherine of Alexandria   Vatican, Pinacoteca
2. Madonna and Child   (Berlin?), Victor Frisch collection
3. Madonna and Child   Florence, Sacristy of Sta. Felicita

GIOVANNI DEL BIONDO, SHOP OF
1. Madonna and Child with Saints John
and Anthony and Donors   Romena (Casentino), Pieve di S. Pietro

GOZZOLI, BENOZZO
1. Madonna and Child Enthroned among
Saints Peter, Dominic, John,
Jerome, Francis, and Angels   London, National Gallery
2. Madonna and Child with Cherubim   Detroit, Edsel B. Ford collection
3. Madonna and Child   Cambridge (Mass.), Fogg Museum

JACOPO DEL CASENTINO
1. Madonna and Child   Brussels, Royal Gallery
2. Madonna and Child   Pozzolatico, near Florence, S. Stefano

JACOPO DEL CASENTINO, SHOP OF
1. Madonna and Child   Florence, Charles Loeser collection
2. Madonna and Child   Florence, Luigi Bellini collection
3. Madonna and Child   Geneva, Villa Ariana.
4. Madonna and Child   Rome, formerly Paolo Paolini collection
5. Madonna and Child with Saints   Amsterdam, Otto Lanz collection

JACOPO DI CIONE
1. Madonna and Child with Saints   Washington, National Gallery of Art

LEONARDO DA PISTOJA
1. Madonna and Child   Berlin, Kaiser Friedrich Museum

LEONARDO DA VINCI
1. "Madonna Litta"   Leningrad, Hermitage

List of Paintings

LIPPI, FILIPPINO, FOLLOWER OF

  1. Madonna adoring Child   (Illustrated in Scharf, Filippino Lippi, fig. 202)

  2. Madonna adoring Child   (Illustrated in Scharf, Filippino Lippi, fig. 203)

  3. Madonna and Child and Young St. John   Florence, Ferroni Museum

LIPPI, FILIPPO (ATTRIBUTED TO)

  1. Madonna and Child   New York, S. H. Kress collection

LIPPI, FILIPPO, FOLLOWER OF

  1. Nativity   Paris, Louvre

  2. Madonna and Child, Catherine and Angels   New Haven, Yale University Museum

LORENZO DI NICCOLO GERINI

  1. Triptych   New Haven, Yale University Museum of Fine Arts

  2. Madonna and Child with Saints and Angels Altenburg, Lindenau Museum

  3. Madonna and Child with Angels   Paris, Louvre

  4. Madonna and Child   Copenhagen, Kunstmuseet

  5. Madonna and Child with Saints Nicholas, Lawrence, Julian, and Michael   Collina, S. Lorenzo

LORENZO MONACO

  1. Madonna and Child Enthroned   Amsterdam, Lanz collection

  2. Madonna and Child with Saints John and Nicholas   Siena, Accademia

  3. Madonna and Child with Six Saints   Florence, Uffizi (magazine)

  4. Madonna and Child with Two Saints   Turin, Museo Civico

  5. Madonna and Child with Saints   Whereabouts unknown
    (illustrated in Berenson, Dedalo, vol. 12, 1932, p. 28)

MARIOTTO DI NARDO

  1. Madonna and Child and Saints   Florence, Accademia

MASACCIO(?)[2]

  1. Madonna and Child with Saints Michael and John the Baptist   Montemarciano, Oratory

MASO DI BANCO

  1. Polyptych   Florence, S. Spirito

MASO DI BANCO, MILIEU OF

  1. Madonna and Child (detached fresco)   Formerly Florence (illustrated in
    Hendecourt collection, Sale Catalogue, London, Sotheby, May 8-10, 1929, p. 14, no. 106.

List of Paintings

MASO DI BANCO, CLOSE TO
1. Polyptych   Philadelphia, Art Museum, Johnson collection

MASTER OF THE BAMBINO VISPO
1. Madonna and Child   Paris, Perriolet collection
2. Madonna and Child with Saints and Angels   Whereabouts unknown
(illustrated in Berenson, Dedalo, vol. 12, 1932, p. 183)
3. Madonna and Child   Philadelphia, Art Museum, Johnson collection
4. Madonna and Child with Twelve Angels   Dornoch (Scotland), Viscount Rothermere
5. Triptych   Rome, Palazzo Doria

MASTER OF THE CAPPELLA MEDICI POLYPTYCH
1. Madonna and Child, with Peter,
Paul, and Two Bishop Saints   Formerly Paris, M. Bacri collection

MASTER OF THE CASTELLO NATIVITY
1. Madonna and Child   Göttingen, Gallery
2. Madonna and Child in a Niche   Paris, Louvre
3. Madonna and Child   New York, Mrs. C. R. Holmes

MASTER OF ST. CECILIA
1. Triptych   Whereabouts unknown (Frick Art Ref. Libr. 101-9c)

MASTER OF ST. CECILIA, REMOTE FOLLOWER OF
1. Madonna and Child and Two Angels   Florence, Charles Loeser collection

MASTER OF THE DOMINICAN EFFIGIES
1. Polyptych   London, Lord Lee of Fareham

MASTER OF THE HORNE TRIPTYCH, FOLLOWER OF
1. Madonna and Child and St. Francis   Whereabouts unknown (illustrated in
Offner, Crit. Corpus, etc., sec. 3, vol. 1, p. 82, pl. 25)

MASTER OF THE MAGDALENE (MAESTRO DELLA MADDALENA)
1. Madonna and Child, Two Angels and Two Saints   Florence, Acton collection

MASTER OF SAN MARTINO
1. Madonna and Child with Saints and Angels
New York, New York Historical Society [3]

List of Paintings

MASTER OF SAN MINIATO

1. Madonna and Child   Amsterdam, Rijksmuseum
2. Madonna and Child and Two Angels   Whereabouts unknown
(illustrated in Berenson, Dedalo, vol. 12, 1932, p. 825)
3. Madonna and Child   Formerly Paris, Spiridon collection
4. Madonna and Child   Le Mans, Musée Municipal
5. Madonna and Child   Agram, Strossmayer Gallery
6. Madonna and Child with Two Angels   Formerly London, Dowdeswell collection[4]

MASTER OF SAN MINIATO, SHOP OF *

1. Nativity   Boston, Museum of Fine Arts

NARDO DI CIONE

1. Madonna and Child with Angels   New York, N. Y. Historical Society

NERI DI BICCI

1. Madonna and Child and Angels   New York, Lilienfeld Galleries 1942

NICCOLO DI PIERO, SCHOOL OF

1. Triptych   Whereabouts unknown (illustrated in Berenson, Dedalo, vol. 12, 1932, p. 9)

ORCAGNA, ANDREA, SCHOOL OF

1. Madonna and Child with Saints Zenobius, Reparata, Baptist, and Evangelist   New York, N. Y. Historical Society
2. Standing Madonna and Child   Florence, S. S. Apostoli
3. Madonna and Child with Donor**   New York, Robert Lehman collection
4. Mystic Marriage of St. Catherine   Paris, Louvre
5. Madonna and Child with Saints and Angels   Siena, Saracini collection
6. Madonna and Child with Saints and Angels   Florence, Panciatichi collection
7. Madonna and Child with Peter and Andrew   Ceriena, S. Andrea
8. Madonna and Child   New York, Maitland Griggs collection
9. Madonna and Child   Florence, Piccoli collection
10. Madonna and Child with Angels   Florence, Stibbert Museum
11. Madonna and Child with Saints and Angels   Florence, Stibbert Museum
12. Polyptych   Florence, Accademia
13. Madonna and Child and Angels   New York, Kleinberger Galleries, 1917 [5]
14. Triptych   New York, New York Historical Society [6]

* *Now attributed by the Boston Museum merely to "Tuscan School."*
** *Also attributed to Spinello Aretino.*

List of Paintings

ORCAGNESQUE, REMOTE
    1. Madonna and Child[7]   Haarlem, Musée van Stolck

PESELLINO, FRANCESCO
    1. Madonna and Child, Infant St. John, and Angels   New York,
                                            Mrs. Harold I. Pratt
    2. Madonna and Child with Saints and Angels   Corshan Court, Methuen
                    collection, (illustrated in Dedalo, vol. 12, 1932, p. 666)
    3. Madonna and Child   Berlin, Bracht collection
    4. Madonna and Child   Esztergom, Kereszteny Museum

PESELLINO, WORKSHOP OF
    1. Madonna and Child
    2. Madonna and Child   Baltimore, Walters Gallery
    3. Madonna and Child   Baltimore, Walters Gallery
    4. Madonna and Child   Both illustrated in Mackowsky, Burlington Magazine,
                    vol. 57, 1930, facing p. 218, figs. A. and B.)

PIER FRANCESCO FIORENTINO
    1. Madonna and Child with Two Angels   New York, Metropolitan Museum
    2. Madonna and Child and St. John   Cambridge (Mass.), Fogg Museum
    3. Madonna and Child
       with Two Saints and Donor   San Gimignano, Palazzo Comunale
    4. Madonna and Child in Landscape   Whereabouts unknown (illustrated in
                    Dedalo, Sept., 1932, vol. 12, p. 688)

PSEUDO PIER FRANCESCO FIORENTINO
    1. Madonna and Child   Washington, National Gallery of Art
    2. Madonna and Child with Saints
       and Angels   Whereabouts unknown (illustrated in Berenson,
                    Dedalo, vol. 12, 1932, p. 687)
    3. Madonna in Landscape   Whereabouts unknown (illustrated in Berenson,
                    Dedalo, vol. 12, 1932, p. 688)

    4. Madonna and Child
       (version of No. 2)   New York, formerly Otto H. Kahn
    5. Madonna and Child   Boston, Gardner Museum
    6. Madonna and Child   Brussels, Adolph Stoclet collection
    7. Madonna and Child   Formerly E. Aymard collection (illustrated in Aymard
                Collection Sale, Galerie Georges Petit, Dec. 1-4, 1913)

List of Paintings

PIERO DI COSIMO

1. Madonna and Child and Infant St. John   Amsterdam, Rijksmuseum
2. Madonna of the Goldfinch   Acquavella collection (illustrated in Loan Exhibition of International Art, Los Angeles Art Assoc., 1937)
3. Madonna and Child   N. Riabouchinsky collection (Sale, Plaza Hotel, April 26, 1916, no. 21.)
4. Madonna and Child and Infant St. John   Whereabouts unknown; negative in possession of Percy Rainford, New York

PIERO DI LORENZO

1. Nativity   Paris, Louvre
2. Madonna and Child, Saints, and Adoring Monk   Dijon, Museum

ROSSELLI, COSIMO

1. Madonna and Child   Philadelphia, Art Museum, Johnson collection

ROSSELLO DI JACOPO FRANCHI

1. Madonna and Child   Ortimino, Chiesa Vito (illustrated in Rivista d'Arte, vol. 15, 1933, p. 79, fig. 3)
2. Madonna and Child   Florence, Accademia
3. Madonna and Child with Bird   Rome, Miss Vedder
4. Triptych   Siena, Pinacoteca

SELLAIO, JACOPO DI

1. Madonna adoring Child   Baltimore, Walters Gallery
2. Youthful St. John the Baptist   Washington, National Gallery of Art

SPINELLI, PARRI

1. Madonna of Mercy with Saints Lorentino and Pergentino   Arezzo, Pinacoteca

SPINELLO ARETINO

1. Triptych   Florence, Accademia
2. Madonna and Child   Copenhagen, Kunstmuseet
3. Monte Oliveto Altarpiece   Cambridge (Mass.), Fogg Museum
4. Madonna and Child Enthroned   Città di Castello, Pinacoteca

SPINELLO ARETINO, SCHOOL OF

1. Triptych   Vatican, Pinacoteca (magazine)

"TOMASSO" (CLOSE TO LORENZO DI CREDI)

1. Madonna and Child with Infant Baptist and Angel   Angers, Musée Napoléon III

List of Paintings

"Tuscan School" *
1. Madonna and Child   Baltimore, Walters Gallery

SIENESE

Andrea di Bartolo
1. Madonna and Child with Four Evangelists,
   Angels, and the Annunciation   Baltimore, Walters Gallery
2. Madonna and Child   Englewood, New Jersey, Dan Fellows Platt Estate
3. Madonna and Child   Montefollonico, S. Sigismondo
4. Polyptych: Madonna and Child with Louis, Paul,
   Peter, Francis; and Two Evangelists above   Tuscania (Viterbo), Duomo

Barna
1. Madonna Nursing Child   New York, Mrs. R. M. Hurd

Bartolo di Fredi
1. Triptych; Madonna and Saints   Perugia, Pinacoteca Vanucci
2. Madonna and Child   Montalcino, Museo Diocesano
3. Madonna and Child   Florence, Corsi collection
4. Madonna and Child   Castiglione d'Orcia, Sta. Maria Maddalena

Beccafumi
1. Madonna and Child with Michael   Rome, Sili collection

Benvenuto di Giovanni
1. Madonna and Child, Four Saints,
   and Angels   Cambridge (Mass.), Fogg Museum
2. Madonna and Child and Female Saints   Baltimore, Walters Gallery
3. Madonna and Child, Saints and Angels   Sinalunga, S. Lucia
4. Madonna and Child with Two Angels   Formerly Paris, Dollfuss collection.
   (illustrated in Berenson, Internat. Studio, March 1931, p. 37, fig. 2)
5. Madonna and Child   Viterbo, Duomo, Sala Capitolare
6. Madonna and Child   Minneapolis, J. R. Van Derlip collection
7. Madonna and Child, Saints and Angels   Formerly New York,
   Maitland F. Griggs collection
8. Madonna and Child with Saints John
   and Andrew   Torrita (Val di Chiana), S. Flora

* Formerly ascribed to "school of Verrocchio."

List of Paintings

COZZARELLI, GUIDOCCIO
    1. Madonna and Child and Two Angels   Milan, Cagnola collection

COZZARELLI, SCHOOL OF
    1. Madonna and Child and Two Angels   Siena, Accademia

DUCCIO, FOLLOWER OF
    1. Madonna and Child   Paris, private collection (illustrated in Perkins, Diana, vol. 8, 1933, p. 115, pl. 1-2)
    2. Madonna and Child   Detroit, Institute of Art

FRANCESCO DI SEGNA DI BONAVENTURA
    (or SEGNA DI BONAVENTURA)
    1. Madonna and Child   Siena, Pinacoteca

FRANCESCO DI VANNUCCIO
    1. Madonna and Child[8]   Siena, San Domenico

FUNGAI, BERNARDINO
    1. Holy Family   London, National Gallery
    2. Madonna and Child, Infant St. John, and Two Angels   Whereabouts unknown (illustrated in Berenson, Internat. Studio, April 1931, p. 21, fig. 17)
    3. Madonna and Child   Ferdinand Howald collection
    4. Holy Family with St. Francis (version of No. 1)   Chambéry, Musée
    5. Madonna and Child   New York, Mrs. Morton H. Meinhard
    6. Madonna and Child   Siena, Accademia
    7. Madonna and Child (version of No. 5)   Whereabouts unknown (illustrated in Dedalo, April 1931, p. 761
    8. Madonna and Child with Two Angels   Whereabouts unknown (illustrated in Catalogue of Sale, Galleria Ciardiello, Florence Feb. 14-18, 1938, p. 12)
    9. Madonna and Child, Jerome and Angel   Siena, Pinacoteca

GIROLAMO DI BENVENUTO
    1. Madonna and Child with George and Bernardino   New York, Robert Lehman collection
    2. Madonna and Child with Peter and Paul   New York, Mrs. H. M. Hurd
    3. Madonna and Child with Four Saints   Cambridge (Mass.), Fogg Museum

List of Paintings

MATTEO DI GIOVANNI
1. Madonna and Child   New York, Wildenstein and Co.

MATTEO DI GIOVANNI, STUDIO OF
1. Madonna and Child with Two Angels   Whereabouts unknown
(illustrated in Berenson, Internat. Studio, Feb. 1931, p. 29, fig. 14)

MEMMI, LIPPO
1. Madonna and Child   Siena, Servite Church
2. Madonna and Child   New York, Percy S. Straus collection

NEROCCIO DEI LANDI
1. Madonna and Child   Siena, Pinacoteca
2. Madonna and Child and Two Saints   Philadelphia, Fine Art Museum
(Johnson coll.)
3. Madonna and Child with Saints Bernard
and Catherine   Siena, Pinacoteca

NICCOLO DI BUONACCORSO
1. Madonna and Child, Baptist, Augustine,
and Angels   Boston, Museum Fine Arts

PANZANO MASTER
1. Madonna and Child   Whereabouts unknown (illustrated in Berenson,
Internat. Studio, 1931, p. 32, fig. 13)

SANO DI PIETRO
1. Madonna and Child with Saints and Angels   Washington,
National Gallery of Art
2. Madonna and Child   New York, Robert Lehman collection
3. Madonna and Child with Angels   New York, Kleinberger Galleries, 1917
4. Madonna and Child with Two Angels   New York, Blumenthal collection
5. Madonna and Child with Four Saints,
and Four Angels   Siena, Accademia
Saints Jerome and Bernardino
6. Madonna and Child with Saints Jerome
and Bernardino   Siena (environs), Osservanza (third altar right)
7. Triptych; Madonna and Child with
Saint James and Evangelist   Brooklyn, N. Y., Museum
8. Madonna and Child with
Two Saints and Angels   Cleveland, Mrs. Ralph King

[*154*]

List of Paintings

SASSETTA, STEFANO DI GIOVANNI
1. Fragment of Adoration (Journey of Kings) New York,
Metropolitan Museum, Maitland F. Griggs collection

SEGNA DI BUONAVENTURA; FOLLOWER OF
1. Madonna and Child Florence, Private collection

SIMONE MARTINI
1. Triptych; Beato Agostino Novello
and His Legend Siena, Sacristy of San Agostino

STRATONICE MASTER
1. Madonna and Child, St. Anne, and Two Angels London, Lord Lee

TADDEO DI BARTOLO
1. Madonna and Child with Musician Angels Perugia, Provincial Gallery
2. Madonna and Child Washington, National Gallery of Art
3. Madonna and Child with Angels Cambridge (Mass.), Fogg Museum
4. Madonna and Child with Cherubim Volterra, Seminario Vescovile
5. Polyptych; Madonna and Child,
Six Saints, Annunciation, etc. San Gimignano, Pinacoteca
6. Madonna and Child Le Puy, Musée Crozatier
7. Triptych; Madonna and Child with
Angels and Cherubim between
Andrew and Baptist Siena, Compagnia di S. Caterina della Notte
8. Nativity with Adorers Siena, Servite Church

TADDEO DI BARTOLO, SCHOOL OF
1. Madonna and Child New York, Blumenthal collection

UGOLINO LORENZETTI
1. Madonna and Child Cologne, Museum Wallraf Richartz
2. Madonna and Child New York, Robert Lehman collection

VANNI, ANDREA
1. Madonna and Child (in ancona) Siena, S. Stefano
2. Madonna and Child Cambridge, Fitzwilliam Museum
3. Madonna and Child Siena, S. Spirito

[155]

List of Paintings

VENETIAN

BASAITI, MARCO
 1. Madonna and Child   Washington, National Gallery of Art

BASTIANI, LAZARRO
 1. Annunciation   Klosterneuburg, Austria
 2. Annunciation   Venice, Museo Civico
 3. Madonna and Child   Venice, Doge's Palace
 4. Madonna and Child   London, National Gallery

BELLINI, GIOVANNI
 1. Madonna and Child   New York, P. S. Straus collection
 2. Madonna and Child   Venice, Cà d'Oro
 3. Madonna and Child Enthroned with
  St. Christopher, St. John the
  Baptist, and Doge Mocenigo   London, National Gallery

BELLINI, JACOPO
 1. Madonna and Child   Lovere, Galleria Tadini

BONIFAZIO VERONESE
 1. Crowning of St. Catherine of Alexandria   Washington,
                     National Gallery of Art

BRAGADIN, DONATO
 1. Triptych   New York, Metropolitan Museum

CARPACCIO, BENEDETTO
 1. Madonna and Child and Saints   Carlsruhe, Gallery

CARPACCIO, VITTORE
 1. Meditation on the Passion   New York, Metropolitan Museum
 2. St. Ursula taking Farewell of Her Parents   Venice, Layard colection
 3. Annunciation   Venice, Cà d'Oro

[*156*]

List of Paintings

CIMA DA CONEGLIANO*
1. Madonna and Child   Berlin, Kaiser Friedrich Museum
2. Madonna and Child   London, Sir M. Shaw Stuart
3. Madonna and Child   New York Art Market, *ex* Brady collection

CRIVELLI, CARLO
1. Madonna and Child   Philadelphia, Fine Arts Museum
2. Madonna, Child and Saints   Vatican, Pinacoteca
3. Madonna and Child   Ancona, Museo Nazionale della Marche
4. Madonna and Child   Verona, Museo Civico
5. Madonna and Child   New York, Bache collection
6. Beato Ferretti   formerly London, Benson collection

CRIVELLI, VITTORIO
1. Madonna and Child   Philadelphia, Art Museum
2. Madonna, Child, and Saints   Vatican, Pinacoteca
3. Madonna, Child, and Two Angels   formerly London, Benson collection

DUIA, PIETRO
1. Madonna, Child, Saints Francis
and Peter and Adorers   Venice, Correr Museum

GIAMBONO, MICHELE
1. Madonna and Child   Private collection (illustrated in van Marle, vol. 7, p. 377)
2. Madonna and Child   Rome, Palazzo Venezia
3. Madonna and Child   Venice, Museo Civico

GIROLAMO DA SANTA CROCE
1. Madonna and Child with Saints   Baltimore, Walters Gallery
Peter, Anthony of Egypt, and
Nicholas of Myra   New York, Ehrich Galleries

JACOPO DE' BARBARI
1. Madonna and Child, Anthony Abbot, and Baptist   Paris, Louvre

---

* The so-called "Madonna of the Goldfinch" by Cima, in the National Gallery, London, contains a linnet, not a goldfinch.

List of Paintings

LORENZO VENEZIANO
1. Madonna and Child with Two Donors   New York, Mrs. A. E. Goodhart
2. Madonna and Child   Washington, National Gallery of Art
3. Polyptych   Venice, Cà d'Oro

MANSUETI, GIOVANNI
1. Madonna and Child, St. Jerome
   and the Baptist   Oldenburg, The Augusteum

MOCETTO, GIROLAMO
1. Madonna, Child, Stephen, and Catherine   Verona, Sta. Maria in Organo

RONDINELLI, NICCOLO
1. Madonna and Child   Rome, Doria Palace

SEBASTIANO DEL PIOMBO
1. Madonna and Child   Philadelphia, Fine Arts Museum

SOLARIO, ANTONIO
1. Madonna and Child and Infant St. John   London, National Gallery
2. Holy Family, Infant St. John, and Magdalena   Baltimore, Walters Gallery
3. Holy Family with Angels and Donor   Duke of St. Albans Collection
4. Madonna and Child Enthroned with Saints   Fermo, Carmine Church
5. Madonna and Child, Joseph,
   and young Baptist   Paris, *ex* Spiridon collection

SPAGNUOLI, PAOLO (?)
1. Madonna del Soccorso   Imola, Chiesa di Valverde

TIEPOLO, GIOVANNI BATTISTA
1. Madonna of the Goldfinch[9]   Washington, National Gallery of Art

VERONESE, PAOLO
1. Madonna and Child and Adorer   Munich, Alte Pinakothek

VIVARINI, ALVISE
1. Madonna and Child and Musician Angels   Venice, Redentore Church

VIVARINI, ANTONIO
1. Madonna and Child   Città di Castello, Pinacoteca Comunale

List of Paintings

UMBRIAN

BARTOLOMMEO DI TOMASSO DA FOLIGNO
1. Madonna and Child with Baptist,
Beato Pietro Crisci, Angels, and
Donor (Rinaldo Corrado Trinci)　　　Foligno, S. Salvatore

BERNARDINO DI MARIOTTO
1. Madonna, Child, and Saints　　　Perugia, Galleria Comunale
2. Madonna and Child　　　Baltimore, Walters Gallery

BOCCATI, GIOVANNI
1. Madonna dell' Ochestra　　　Perugia, Galleria Comunale

CAPORALI, BARTOLOMMEO
1. Madonna and Child, Four Angels and
Saints Bernardino and Francis　　　Agram, Strossmayer Gallery

CECCOLO DI GIOVANNI (?)
1. Madonna and Child and Saints　　　Assisi, San Francesco

FIORENZO DI LORENZO
1. Madonna and Child　　　Vienna, Von Auspitz collection
2. Madonna, Child, Francis, and Bernardino　Berlin, Kaiser Friedrich Museum
3. Madonna and Child　　　Paris, Jacquemart André Museum

GHISSI, FRANCESCUCCIO
1. Madonna, Child, and St. Catherine　　　Vatican, Pinacoteca

MASTER OF THE FABRIANO ALTARPIECE
1. Madonna and Child Enthroned
(part of a triptych)　　　Washington, National Gallery of Art

MATTEO DA GUALDO
1. Madonna and Child with Saints John,
Jerome, and Catherine　　　Whereabouts unknown;
(illustrated by Reinach, Repertoire, vol. 1, p. 293)

List of Paintings

NELLI, OTTAVIANO
1. Madonna and Child with Three Saints   Assisi, S. Francesco, Lower Church
2. Madonna and Child with Two Angels   Rome, Pio Fabbri collection

NUZI, ALEGRETTO
1. Madonna and Child   Fabriano, Duomo
2. Madonna and Child (in diptych)   Berlin, Kaiser Friedrich Museum
3. Marriage of St. Catherine   Formerly Berlin Art Market; (illustrated in
   Berenson, Studies in Medieval Painting, fig. 63)
4. Madonna and Child   Philadelphia, Fine Arts Museum, Johnson collection
5. Madonna and Child (*ex* polyptych)   Annesley-Gore collection

NUZI, ALEGRETTO, SCHOOL OF
1. Madonna and Child with Two Saints   Vatican, Pinacoteca

NUZI, ALEGRETTO, ECLECTIC FOLLOWER OF
1. Mystical Marriage of St. Catherine   Offida, Sta. Maria della Grazia

PERUGINO, FOLLOWER OF
1. Madonna and Child with Infant St. John   Cantiano, at Cagli, Collegiata

PIERMATTEO D' AMELIA
1. Madonna and Child   Amelia, Palazzo Comunale

PIERO DELLA FRANCESCA
1. Nativity   London, National Gallery

PIERO DELLA FRANCESCA, FOLLOWER OF
1. Madonna and Child with Angels   Whereabouts unknown; photo in Frick
   Art Reference Library

PINTURICCHIO
1. Holy Family with Infant St. John   Cambridge, (Mass.), Fogg Museum

RAPHAEL
1. The Solly Madonna   Berlin, Kaiser Friedrich Museum
2. Madonna of the Goldfinch   Florence, Uffizi Gallery

List of Paintings

RAPHAEL, FOLLOWER OF

    1. Madonna and Child with Saints John,
       Anne and Joseph   Whereabouts unknown;
                    (illustrated in Reinach, Repertoire, vol. 4, 311 Bercioux Sale, 1905)
    2. Rest on Flight into Egypt   Vienna, Kunsthistorisches Museum

MILANESE

BARTOLOMMEO DE GROSSI

    1. Madonna and Child   Whereabouts unknown (illustrated in van Marle,
                                                     vol. 7, p. 208)

BERNARDINO DE' CONTI

    1. Madonna and Child   Rome, Sterbini collection
    2. Version of Leonardo's "Madonna Litta"   Milan, Poldi-Pezzoli collection

BEVILACQUA, AMBROGIO

    1. Madonna and Child Enthroned with Saints and a Donor   Milan, Brera

BOLTRAFFIO, GIOVANNI ANTONIO

    1. Madonna and Child   Milan, Poldi-Pezzoli collection
    2. Madonna and Child   Formerly Milan, Crespi collection
    3. Madonna and Child   Formerly Philadelphia, Widener collection
    4. Version of Leonardo's "Madonna Litta"   Milan, Museo Civico
    5. Version of Leonardo's "Madonna Litta"   Unknown private collection

BORGOGNONE, BERNARDINO

    1. Madonna and Child with Saints   Bergamo, Moroni collection

CIETARIO, JACOPO

    1. Polyptych   (Illustrated in van Marle vol. 7, p. 180)

GIOVANNI DA MILANO

    1. Triptych   Florence, Accademia

NAPOLETANO, FRANCESCO

    1. Madonna and Child   M. G. Brauer collection

BOLOGNESE

ANTONIO DA CREVALCORE
1. Holy Family with Infant St. John   Formerly Paris, Spiridon collection

CHIODAROLO, G. M.
1. Madonna and Child with St. Joseph   Rome, Doria Gallery
2. Madonna and Child   Venice, Cà d'Oro

FRANCIA, FRANCESCO
1. Madonna and Child   Washington, National Gallery of Art
2. Madonna and Child with Angels   Munich, Alte Pinakothek
3. Adoration of the Child   Bologna, Royal Gallery
4. Madonna of the Rose Garden   Munich, Alte Pinakothek
5. Madonna and Child with Saints Francis
   and Girolamo   New York, Blumenthal Collection
6. Madonna and Child   Wallington, Sir Charles Trevelyan
7. Madonna and Child   Boston, Fenway Court, Gardner Museum

FRANCIA, SCHOOL OF
1. Madonna and Child with Saints   Verona, Museo Civico
2. Madonna and Child   Dresden, Gallery
3. Madonna and Child,
   Magdalene, and Jerome   Formerly New York, C. W. Hamilton collection

GUERCINO
1. Madonna and Child with Angels   (Bird not certainly identifiable)
        Florence, Pitti Palace

FERRARESE

COSSA, FRANCESCO DEL
1. Madonna and Child (part of altarpiece)   Bologna, Gallery

DOSSI, DOSSO
1. Holy Family with Donor   Philadelphia, Fine Arts Museum,
        Johnson collection

[*162*]

List of Paintings

GAROFALO
1. Madonna and Child   Rome, Borghese Gallery
2. Madonna and Child with
   Catherine and Dominic   London, National Gallery
3. Madonna and Child   Chicago, Art Institute, Ryerson collection
4. Holy Family with Infant Baptist   London, National Gallery
5. Madonna and Child   Venice, Cà d'Oro
6. Madonna of the Rose   Whereabouts unknown (illustrated in Rey Collection
   Sale, Galerie Georges Petit, May 8, 1900)

GRANDI, ERCOLE
1. Madonna and Child Enthroned with
   Saints Dominic and Catherine   Venice, Palazzo Layard

MAINERI, GIAN FRANCESCO
1. Madonna and Child   Turin, Accademia Albertina

MAZZOLINO, LUDOVICO
1. Madonna and Child with
   Magdalene and Anthony Abbot   Berlin, Kaiser Friedrich Museum

ROBERTI, ERCOLE
1. Madonna and Child Enthroned with Saints   Milan, Brera

TURA, COSIMO
1. Madonna and Child   Venice, Accademia

TURA, COSIMO, STUDIO OF
1. Madonna and Child   Philadelphia, Fine Arts Museum, Johnson collection
2. Madonna and Child   Venice, Accademia

ZAGANELLI, BERNARDINO
1. Madonna Adoring Child,
   with Two Musician Angels   New York, Metropolitan Museum,
   Blumenthal collection

PISAN

FRANCESCO NERI DA VOLTERRA
1. Madonna and Child and Angels   Modena, Pinacoteca Estense

List of Paintings

GIOVANNI DI NICCOLO
1. Polyptych   Pisa, Museo Civico

GIOVANNI DA PISA
1. Polyptych   (Illustrated in Berenson, *Internat. Studio*, November 1930, p. 32, fig 13)

JACOPO DI MICHELE GERA
1. Madonna and Child and Saints   Pisa, Museo Civico

MASTER OF SAN TORPÉ
1. Madonna and Child   Pisa, San Francesco

NANNI DI JACOPO
1. Madonna and Child and Angels   *ex* Rome, Sterbini collection
2. Madonna and Child   (Illustrated in Berenson, *Internat. Studio*, November 1930, p. 30, fig. 12.)

PISAN FOLLOWER OF DUCCIO
1. Madonna and Child   Pisa, San Francesco

PISAN FOLLOWER OF TADDEO DI BARTOLO
1. Madonna and Child   (Illustrated in Berenson, *Internat. Studio*, November 1930, p. 28, fig. 2.)

VANNI, TURINO, THE SECOND
1. Madonna and Child with Angels   Paris, Louvre
2. Madonna and Child (central medallion of a large Crucifix)   Pisa, San Martino, Cappella del Sacramento

LUCCHESE

ORLANDI, DEODATO
1. Madonna and Child   New York, Mrs. R. M. Hurd colection
2. Madonna and Child   Lucca, Museo Civico

List of Paintings

PADUAN

Schiavone, Giorgio
    1. Madonna and Child   Turin, Pinacoteca Regia
    2. Madonna and Child   Whereabouts unknown (illustrated in Reinach
                                         "Repertoire" vol. 5, p. 297)
    3. Madonna and Child   Venice, Museo Civico

VERONESE

Benaglio, Francesco
    1. Madonna and Child and Angels   Verona, Museo Civico

Libri, Francesco dai
    1. Madonna and Child   Baltimore, Walters Art Gallery

Morone, Francesco
    1. Madonna and Child   Berlin, Kaiser Friedrich Museum

Pisanello, Antonio
    1. "Madonna della Quaglia"   Verona, Museo Civico

Stefano da Verona
    1. Madonna and Child with Angels   Rome, Galleria Colonna

Stefano da Verona, school of
    1. Madonna and Child with Two Saints   Verona, Museo Civico
    2. Madonna and Child   Vienna, Lanckoronski collection

Unknown Trecento Veronese Master
    1. Madonna and Child   Verona, S. Anastasia
                          (illustrated by van Marle, vol. 4, p. 195)

List of Paintings

VICENTIAN

MONTAGNA, BARTOLOMMEO
    1. Madonna and Child   London, National Gallery

MONTAGNA, BENEDETTO
    1. Madonna and Child with
    Saints Peter, Paul, Francis, Anthony of
    Padua, and an Angel   Milan, Brera
    2. Madonna and Child with
    Saints Jerome and Francis   Vicenza, Museo Civico

MODENESE

BARNABA DA MODENA
    1. Madonna and Child   Berlin, Kaiser Friedrich Museum

CREMONESE

BOCCACCIO BOCCACCINO
    1. Madonna and Child   ex Milan, Crespi collection
    2. Madonna and Child   New York, Metropolitan Museum

NEAPOLITAN

ANDREA DA SALERNO
    1. Madonna and Child   Augsburg, Gemäldegalerie

"NEAPOLITAN WITH HISPANO — FLEMISH INFLUENCE"
    1. Madonna and Child   ex Erlenbach, Stoop Coray collection
                                    (illustrated by van Marle, vol. 15, p. 357)

List of Paintings

SICILIAN

ALESSANDRO DA PADOVA AND GIOVANNI MARIA DA TREVISO
1. "Madonna of Loreto" Siracusa, Bellomo Museum

ANTONELLO PALERMITANO
1. "Madonna di Monserrato" Palermo, Gancia Monastery

ANTONIO DE SALIBA
1. Madonna and Child Enthroned Siracusa, Cathedral

PIEDMONTESE

GIOVANNI DA CAMUSETO
1. Fresco, central part of which
is a Madonna and Child near Piobesi Torinesi, Church of Giovanni dei Campi

GIOVANNI CONAVESIO DA PINEROLO
1. Polyptych Turin, Pinacoteca Regia

LIGURIAN

NICCOLO DA VOLTRI
1. Madonna and Child Genoa, Sta. Maria delle Vigne
2. Madonna and Child with Two Angels Finale Pia, Parish Church
3. Madonna and Child and Angels Savona, Museo

MARCHIGIAN

FOLCHETTO DA SANGINESIO
1. Adoration of the Shepherds Philadelphia, Fine Arts Museum,
 Johnson collection
2. Madonna and Child with Saints San Ginesio, Town Hall
3. Madonna and Child with Francis and Liberatus San Ginesio, Town Hall

GIACOMO DA RECANATI
1. Madonna and Child and Angels Recanati, Cathedral

List of Paintings

ROMAN

ANTONIAZZO ROMANO
1. Madonna and Child New York, P. S. Straus collection
2. Madonna and Child Valencia, Museo Provincial de Pinturas

BAROCCIO, FEDERIGO
1. Madonna and Child London, National Gallery

PARMESE

MAZZOLA, FILIPPO
1. Madonna and Child with Two Saints London, National Gallery
2. Madonna and Child Enthroned
with Baptist and Bartholomew Cremona, Museo Civico

SARDINIAN

UNKNOWN SARDINIAN MASTER
1. Madonna and Child with Angels Castelsardo, Parish Church

VITERBIAN

FRANCESCO DI ANTONIO DA VITERBO (ATTRIBUTED TO)
1. Madonna and Child with Kneeling Donor Viterbo, Museo Civico

PORTUGUESE
(under Italian Influence)

ALVARO DE PIREZ DE EVORA
1. Madonna and Child with Angels Pisa, Santa Croce a Fossabanda

[*168*]

Notes to the Text of the Preceding Chapters

CHAPTER I. INTRODUCTION

1. A. McComb, in his book on Agnolo Bronzino, 1928, p. 17, actually calls the bird a bullfinch, but in this he is mistaken. It is definitely identifiable as a goldfinch; in fact, it is an unusually well rendered one.

2. H. M. R. Martin: La Miniature Française du XIIIe au XVe Siècle, 1923, p. 83.

3. From the purely ornithological point of view it may be well to state that the goldfinch is known to be a common, familiar bird throughout Europe from Scandinavia to the Mediterranean, and from the British Isles to Asiatic Russia. There are no data indicating or even suggesting that its present numerical status or geographical distribution has undergone any marked changes within historic times.

4. M. Vloberg: La Vierge et l'Enfant dans l'Art Français, vol. 2, 1937, p. 9-10.

5. See, in this connection, the discussion of Carpaccio's "Meditation on the Passion," pp. 83-84.

6. It may be mentioned that a goldfinch, along with numerous other birds, occurs in a fifteenth century Italian tapestry of the Annunciation, now in the Martin A. Ryerson collection, Art Institute of Chicago.

7. The interest in natural history that developed early in northern Italy is revealed in Pisanello's marvelous animal drawings and aquarelles, to say nothing of his exquisite little painting of "The Vision of St. Hubert," in the National Gallery, London, and in the sketches and other drawings of Jacopo and Gentile Bellini, and in the sketchbook of Giovannino de' Grassi in the Civic Library at Bergamo.

8. This number is arrived at after eliminating multiple attributions by different authors. The bulk of the artists involved being Italians, the attributions of Berenson (Italian Paintings of the Renaissance, 1932) have been followed as the basis to which have been added additional works published by others, or in which corrections have been made on safe ground by others, chief of whom are Offner, A. and L. Venturi, van Marle, and Sirén. Dr. Offner gave me the benefit of his valued advice on numbers of the attributions, but the responsibility for any errors in the final form in which they appear in this book is entirely the author's.

Notes

CHAPTER II. THE SYMBOLISM OF THE GOLDFINCH

1. Early sources for this legend have been found by W. N. Howe (Animal Life in Italian Painting, 1912, p. 51) in the Evangelium Infantiae Arabicum, chapter xxxvi, (in Tischendorff's edition, published at Leipzig in 1876), and by Huysmans (La Cathédrale, ed. 5, 1898, p. 396) in the writings of Enfance and Thomas l'Israélite.

2. Robert Eder (Mittheilungen des Ornithologischen Vereins in Wien, vol. 15, 1891, p. 139) writes it as "Muttergottesvogel" (Mother of God's bird) and as "Marienvogel" (Mary's bird).

3. Possibly pertinent in that it further serves to connect the goldfinch and the swallow is the fact there was an old belief in a "swallow-goldfinch," the offspring of a swallow father and a goldfinch mother. (See Jacob Theodor Klein, Historia Avium, 1750, p. 97).

4. An inconclusive, and tangential, bit of evidence, however, is the fact that the goldfinch was considered a long-lived bird, especially so for its size. Thus, the sixteenth century scientific writer, Girolamo Cardano, specifically comments on the wonder that so small a bird as the goldfinch should have a life span of a dozen years or more. However, if this thought was in the minds of any of the artists or their patrons at the time, it has escaped being so recorded, and at this late date it cannot be reintroduced with any degree of assurance. If anything, it might more readily have been a plea for longevity rather than a symbol of immortality.

5. Skinner, C. M.: Myths and Legends of Flowers, Trees, Fruits, and Plants 1925 (5th impression), p. 16.

   Inasmuch as the actual identity of the bird involved in this and related legends varies in literature, and inasmuch as the robin, the crossbill, and the goldfinch appear to be, to some extent, substitute identifications, we may briefly note parts of the legend even though I have not found them to be definitely associated with the goldfinch. Thus, as Seymour (William Wood Seymour: The Cross. In Tradition, History, and Art, 1898, p. 100-101) has pointed out, there was an old legend of the robin, which reached as far from the center of old European tradition as Sweden, and which was thence utilized in one of his poems by the American, Whittier. The legend related that the robin brings daily a drop of water to cool the tongues of those parched with thirst in Hell, and that its red breast is the result of the scorching fires that the bird braves in its act of mercy.

   The crossbill was said, in another legend, to have tried to minister to Christ on the Cross, after all others had left Him, and to have worked at the nails trying to extract them. This was put in verse by Longfellow, after a poem by Julius Mosen, as follows:

   > "Stained with blood and never tiring
   > With its beak it doth not cease
   > From the Cross 't would free the Saviour;
   > Its Creator's Son release.

Notes

"And the Saviour speaks in mildness;
    'Blest be thou of all the good!
Bear this token of this moment,
    Marks of blood and holy rood.'"

6. Josef Strzygowski: Der Bilderkreis des Griechische Physiologus. 1899, pp. 68, 84.

7. See pp. 126 ff for a full discussion of this work and its symbolism.

8. O. Keller: Die antike Tierwelt, vol. 2, 1913, p. 179.

9. Walther Arndt: Die Vögel in der Heilkunde der alten Kulturvölker. Journal für Ornithologie, vol. 73, 1925, pp. 57-58.

10. Konrad Gesner: Vogelbuch, 1581.

11. I have been able to locate but little information on this name. It is probably a latinization of the Greek Euphron, an Athenian poet of the fourth century B. C., who wrote many comedies, only some fragments of which have come down to us. These were published by August Meineke under the title "Fragmenta comicorum graecorum," and were translated into Latin in Didot's ambitious library series of Greek and Latin authors. This Euphron is not to be confused with the sixth century B. C. Greek potter and vase painter of the same name.

12. Ulysses Aldrovandus: Ornithologiæ, vol. 3, 1640, book 20, chapter 76, pp. 536-537.

13. Robert Eder: Mystisch-allegorische Vogelgeschichte und deren Ursprung. Mittheilungen des Ornithologischen Vereins in Wien, vol. 14, 1890, pp. 141-143.

14. Friedrich Lauchert: Geschichte des Physiologus. 1889.

15. Gonzalo de Berceo: El Sacrificio de la Misa; lines 49 ff.

16. Friedrich Heinrich von der Hagen: Minnesinger. Deutsche Liederdichter des zwölften, dreizehnten, und vierzehnten Jahrhunderts. Leipzig, 1838, 5 vols.

17. Reproduced in "The Animal Kingdom, Illustrated Catalogue of an Exhibition of Manuscript Illuminations, Book Illustrations, Drawings, Cylinder Seals, and Bindings." Pierpont Morgan Library, New York, 1941, p. 15.

18. Arthur H. Collins: Symbolism of Animals and Birds Represented in English Church Architecture. 1913, p. 114-115.

19. The exact words of Honorius are as follows: "Est avis albicolor, quæ caradrius vocatur,

per quam æger, utrum evadere possit, probatur. Adducta enim ad ægrum, si mori-
turus erit, faciem ab eo avertit; si vero victurus, visum in eum fortiter dirigit et infigit;
hianti ore ægritudinem ab eo bibit, in altum contra radium solis volat, infirmitas hausta
de eo exudat, æger sospitate exultat. Caradrius albus est Christus de Virgine natus.
Hic ad ægrum adducitur dum a Patre ad infirmum genus humanum mittitur; qui
faciem suam a Judeis avertit eosque in morte reliquit, ad nos autem vultum convertens
a morte revocavit."

20. See W. R. Valentiner: Tino da Camaino; a Sienese Sculptor of the Fourteenth Century. 1935, pl. 56c and 58; text on p. 119.

21. Samuel Bochart: Hierozoicon. 1663.

22. It may be noted, however, that, according to Twining (Symbols and Emblems of
Early and Mediæval Christian Art) the eagle and the dove were both symbols of
the same thing — the Holy Spirit, the eagle being so used chiefly in connection with
characters from the Old Testament. That the dove and the goldfinch are to some
extent substitute identifications, we know also. This opens the door to the possibility
of a common meaning (even if but rarely used) for the goldfinch and the eagle.

23. Oluf Gerhard Tychsen: Physiologus Syrus, seu Historia Animalium xxxii in S. S.
memoratorium, Syriace ... edidit, vertit, et illustravit O. G. Tychsen. 1795, pp. xi, 175.

24. Oskar von Hovorka: Geist der Medicin, Analytische Studien über die Grundideen
der Vormedizin, Urmedizin, Volksmedizin, Zaubermedizin, Berufsmedizin. 1915, p.
136-137. The quotation is based on a statement taken from Jacob Grimm's three
volume compilation of "Deutsche Mythologie," published in 1878.

25. D'Arcy W. Thompson: A Glossary of Greek Birds; 1895, p. 186. The suggestion
here given that the charadrius legend may be only a slightly distorted version of
eastern tales of the stork appears to be based chiefly on the learned author's reaction
to the similarity in the names *chasad* (said by him to be the Hebrew word for
stork) and *charad*, the beginning of the word charadrius, rather than on any strictly
evidential grounds. It is of more than passing interest to find a modern scholar reflecting in his judgment a similar type of evaluation of puns and parallelisms of word
formation that were so widely adhered to centuries ago. Perhaps it is an indication
of his sympathetic insight into medieval mentality.

26. Francesco degli Stabili (1257-1327), known as Cecco d'Ascoli, was an encyclopedist
and poet. He studied mathematics and astrology, and was professor of mathematics
in 1322 at the University of Bologna. He entered the service of Pope John xxii at
Avignon. He was burned at the stake in Florence in 1327, after being condemned
by the Inquisition as a relapsed heretic for having violated the terms of a previous
lighter sentence upon him at Bologna in 1324. The event is mentioned by later medieval writers, while numerous manuscripts contain what purport to be summaries of the

sentence on Cecco by the Inquisition or accounts of his life and death. These various sources of information are open to suspicion as of late date (XVII-XVIII Century) and do not agree as to the nature of Cecco's heresy. (See Cambridge Mediæval History, vol. 8, pp. 677-679).

27. MSS Liber acerbae ætatis or Vita Acerba by Cecco d'Ascoli, end of the XIVth Century, ornamented with illuminations, in the Medicean Library of Florence, plut. xi, cod. 52, in 80 article "de natura calandrini (cardellino – chardonneret)." I am indebted to Mrs. Nathalie Scheffer of the Dumbarton Oaks Research Library for this information. I have not seen a reproduction of the original manuscript myself. In John Pierpont Rice's "Critical Edition of the Bestiary and Lapidary from Cecco d'Ascoli's Acerba," 1908, no mention is made of cardellino, but only of calandrinus. His edition is based on the fourteenth century manuscripts in the Florentine library.

28. The legend is not given as something new in the "Acerba." Cecco was merely including it, not inventing it, so it must have been known in Italy for some time prior to 1322.

29. For a discussion of the painting by the "Maestro della Maddalena" see E. Sandberg-Vavalá's book, L'Iconografia della Madonna col Bambino nella pittura Italiana del Dugento; 1934, p. 49.

30. There were some twenty editions, the last being dated 1546. The Venetian printing of 1510 is looked upon as the "best," but on what criteria this judgment is based I do not know.

31. Dr. W. W. Francis, Librarian of the Osler Library at McGill University, Montreal, writes me that this 1516 edition is an exact reprint of the same publisher's 1510 edition, with which he once compared it. Nevertheless, if the early manuscript in the Florentine library does connect the goldfinch with this legend it demonstrates that that identification was already definitely current even though possibly not wholly acceptable to the more scholarly editors of the printed versions of Cecco's manuscript.

32. In his book, "The Literary Works of Leonardo da Vinci," 1883, vol. 2, p. 315, Jean Paul Richter actually translates this part as referring to the goldfinch and not the lark. However, as Girolamo Calvi has shown in his illuminating study "Il Manoscritto H di Leonardo da Vinci. Il 'Fiore di Virtù' e 'L'Acerba' di Cecco d'Ascoli" (Archivio Storico Lombardo, anno. xxv, fasc. xix, ser. 3, vol. 10, 1898, pp. 73-116) Richter erroneously transcribed "Calandrino" as "Cardellino," thereby unwittingly committing as an error that which was apparently consciously done by the pun-loving, anagrammatically minded folk of Trecento and Quattrocento Italy.

33. Nevertheless Leonardo enlarges upon the legend in a moralizing fashion as follows: "Like unto this is the love of virtue. It never looks at any vile or base thing, but rather clings always to pure and virtuous things and takes up its abode in a noble heart, as the birds do in green woods on flowery branches. And this love shows itself

more in adversity than in prosperity; as light does, which shines most where the place is darkest."

34. Konrad von Megenberg was born in 1309 and died in 1378. His book, "Das Buch der Natur" was not printed until a century after his death (in 1478 at Augsburg), but its contents were not altered by its fifteenth century editors as far as we know.

35. I am informed by Professor Richard Offner that this picture has recently been cleaned and that the bird "came off" at least in part, indicating that it was not an integral part of the original painting, but a subsequent, though still very early, addition. This does not affect its interest in the present study, but it probably pushes it at least into the fourteenth century chronologically.

36. Among the few instances of the dove's appearance in paintings of the Madonna and Child that I have come across are the following: a painting by Piero di Cosimo, in the Louvre, Paris, in which the Child reaches for a white dove; a picture of the Madonna and Child with St. Catherine and Michael Spavanti by Paolo Veronese (S. Sebastian, Venice) in which St. Catherine offers the Christ Child a white dove; and lastly two paintings of "The Holy Family with a Dove." One, by Rubens (W. H. Moore collection, New York), a late baroque work, suggests that the artist, in spite of his admittedly extensive knowledge of symbolism, chose to disregard its usual significance when he introduced the white dove in his picture. In this canvas the Christ Child, standing on His mother's lap, holds a white dove over and in back of His head, away from the young St. John who is attempting to climb up on the Madonna's lap to reach it, his arms outstretched to grab it. The usual action is reversed, the little St. John, instead of offering a bird to Christ, is trying to take it away from Him. The rather rough way in which the poor bird is handled also suggests how little of a symbol it was to the artist. The young Baptist is the center of interest in the picture; the Madonna, Christ Child, St. Anne, and Joseph are looking intently at him in his efforts to reach the bird. The other picture, still later, is by the Frenchman, Fragonard, and is similarly far from the mark symbolically (reproduced in Vloberg, see bibliography).

This work of Rubens possibly derives indirectly from Tintoretto, who, in his relatively few paintings of the Nativity, introduced ordinary barnyard pigeons as naturalistic, "atmospheric" accessories. In Tintoretto's pictures these birds have no symbolic value; they are merely part of the artist's conception of the setting. In Russian icon paintings, however, as first pointed out by Kondakov, the use of the white dove in Madonna and Child paintings was derived through misunderstanding from the goldfinch in earlier Italian art.

37. Nikodim Pavlovich Kondakov: Ikonografia B. M. Sviazi grecheskoi i russkoi ikonopisi s italianskoi ranniago Vozrozhgeniia SPB, 1910, p. 30. The passage referred to was kindly translated for me by Mrs. Nathalie Scheffer of the Dumbarton Oaks Research Library.

38. The only ancient therapeutic legend involving the goldfinch that I have come across is a statement in Kyranides, of the fourth century, A. D., to the effect that the flesh of the goldfinch is used in relieving colic.

39. Angelo de Gubernatis: Zoological Mythology, 1872, 2 vols.

40. Ludwig Hopf: Thierorakel und Orakelthiere in Alter und Neuer Zeit; 1888.

41. The French Gothic was one of the formative influences behind early Pisan and Sienese art. Not only were itinerant artists responsible for the spread of the Gothic style, but at a very early date pieces of medieval French sculpture were imported into Italy.

42. See, for example, H. M. R. Martin's book, La Miniature Française du XIIIe au XVe Siècle, 1923.

43. Skinner, Charles M.: Myths and Legends of Flowers, Trees, Fruits, and Plants. 5th impression. 1925, pp. 275-278.
    Also Bächtold-Stäubli, Hans: Handwörterbuch des deutschen Aberglaubens, vol. 2, p. 302. In this account we find that the "cabbage thistle" (Kohldistel) acts as a drug against the "terror" and other demoniac diseases of children.
    In a Bohemian plague medication tract of the seventeenth century (H. Schöppler, Ein Prager Pestarzneibuch aus dem Jahre 1679. *Janus*, vol. 14, 1909, p. 731) there is listed among the ingredients in the formula for ' Aqua bezoartica Pestilentialis" Cardui benedicti, the Holy Thistle.

44. Springer, Anton: Über den Phyiologus des Leonardo da Vinci. *Berichte über die Verhandlungen der Königlich Sächsischen Gesellschaft der Wissenschaften zu Leipzig.* Phil.-Hist. Cl. vol. 36, 1884, p. 244-271.

45. Henry E. Sigerist (Deutsche Medizinische Handschriften aus Schweizer Bibliotheken. *Archiv für Geschichte der Medizin*, vol. 17, 1925, p. 239) mentions an ointment called "Magdalene salve" prepared from the thistle in the late Middle Ages. According to Auber (Histoire et Théorie du Symbolisme Religieux avant et depuis le Christianisme, 1884, vol. 3, p. 182, 567) the thistle was a symbol of Penitence. This is not unconnected with the use of the thistle in a late fifteenth century German print (Augsburg, *ca* 1490) representing "The Way of Salvation." The main feature of this print is a rocky hill on which are growing many large thistles, the difficult hill being an allegory of the troublesome path to perfection. Three banderoles, ". . . billowing around the mountain contain exhortations which state that by overcoming vice and sin and by treading over thorn and thistle, one can arrive at the top of the mountain, to stand at peace with God. . . ." (Elizabeth Mongan and Carl O. Schniewind. The First Century of Print Making 1400-1500. Art Inst. Chicago, 1941, p. 42, 43, No. 31). That this composition was known south of the Alps is shown

by a famous example of the same subject engraved in Italy for the frontispiece of a book called the "Monte Sancto di Dio," printed at Florence in 1477.

46. J. G. Frazer: The Golden Bough, 2d ed., 1900, vol. 3, p. 25.

47. Hans Bächtold-Stäubli (Handwörterbuch des deutschen Aberglauben, vol. 8, p. 482) also states that the goldfinch will absorb tuberculosis if brought into the room of the patient.

48. In their discussion of the charadrius Cahier and Martin (Mélanges d'Archéologie, d'Histoire et de Littérature, 1851, vol. 2, p. 133) write, ". . . Car la jaunisse seule, et c'était bien assez, était la vraie maladie qui avait primitivement pour spécifique la calandre. Plus tard on a fait de ce précieux oiseau un véritable catholicon."

49. Henry Osborn Taylor: The Mediaeval Mind, vol. 2, p. 69; pp. 128-129.

50. William L. Wardle, in Encyclopedia Britannica, ed. 14, vol. 3, 1936, p. 313.

51. St. Roch appears in a "Madonna and Child with Saints" by an obscure Marchigian painter, Folchetto da Sanginesio. This is the only instance in which I have found this saint in a picture in which the Infant Saviour is holding a goldfinch (Town Hall, San Ginesio), but there may well be other cases.

52. For a lengthy and detailed account of the plague symbolism connected with St. Sebastian, the reader may be referred to Mrs. Johnson's "Sacred and Legendary Art," London 1866, vol. 2, pp. 412 ff., a few short quotations from which may be given here: "It is probably from the association of the arrows with his form and story, that St. Sebastian has been regarded from the first ages of Christianity as the protecting saint against plague and pestilence. Arrows have been from all antiquity the emblem of pestilence. Apollo was the deity who inflicted plague, therefore was invoked with prayer and sacrifice against it . . .

"St. Sebastian is everywhere popular, but more particularly in those countries and districts which were most exposed to the plague. . . . In the more ancient pictures his usual pendant is either St. George or St. Nicholas; in the more modern pictures St. Roch; very often the healing saints St. Cosmas and St. Damian. Wherever these are grouped together or round the Virgin and Child, the picture has been dedicated against the plague."

A seventh century mosaic in San Pietro in Vincoli, Rome, is dedicated (in Latin) "To St. Sebastian, Martyr, dispeller of the pestilence. . . ." To this may be added that the figure of the saint, his body pierced with arrows, appears on numerous mediaeval plague sheets.

53. Furthermore it should be noted that no mention is made of the goldfinch in any of the plague tracts of the fourteenth to the sixteenth centuries. Sudhoff (Pestschriften aus den ersten 150 Jahren nach der Epidemie des "Schwartzen Todes" 1348; *Archiv für Geschichte der Medizin*, vols. 13-15, 1922-1924) has collected about 300 such

tracts produced in Italy, Germany, Bohemia, France, etc., and I have gone through them in vain looking for the slightest mention of the bird. It seems that the role of the goldfinch as a plague amulet (and, for that matter, of amulets generally) was not included in these old medical writings, since they deal with medications and not with preventives.

It may also be mentioned that the goldfinch occurs nowhere in the writings of either Dante or Petrarch, although these authors made extensive use of then current legends.

54 The Natural History of Pliny. Translated and edited by John Bostock and H. T. Riley, vol. 2, 1890, pp. 541-542.

55. P. 29, fig. 116 of the edition seen, printed in English at London, by B. Motle, 1709.

56. The fact that in this picture the birds in the nest, both adult and young, are whitish further suggests the identity of the white charadrius with the goldfinch.

57. Borkhausen (Deutsche Fauna, vol. 1, 1797, p. 248), was the first author to do so.

58. I am greatly indebted to Dr. Erwin Panofsky, of the Institute for Advanced Study at Princeton University, for first calling my attention to the possible fertility symbolism of the goldfinch.

59. The goldfinch does occur in one painting attributed to Fra Angelico by some critics, a panel now in Frankfort; but there is no sign of the bird in the many fully authenticated devotional works of this artist.

60. Eugène Müntz: Raphael; 1882, p. 182.

61. This statement is not wholly correct; Müntz may be referring to the early "Solly" Madonna in the Kaiser Friedrich Museum in Berlin; but in this work there is no figure of the young St. John, although the Christ Child is holding a goldfinch.

62. George Richardson: Iconology, or a Collection of Emblematical Figures (based on Ripa), vol. 2, 1779, p. lxxx, fig. 307.

63. According to Richardson, the source of this idea is Horace, Epist., ii, lib. i. "Haec esto mater possessio pulcherrima et potior divitiis si cui sint liberi boni." However, I have not been able to find this statement in Horace.

64. In an engraving of "Abundance" by Robetta (1462-1522), we find a woman with three small children, one of whom holds a small bird in the same fashion as the Christ Child is often depicted.

65. The Natural History of Pliny. Translated and edited by John Bostock and H. T. Riley, vol. 2, 1890, p. 522.

Notes

66. Mrs. Jameson: Sacred and Legendary Art, vol. 1, 1866, pp. 35-36. While not supported by documentary proof or by other direct evidence, the symbolic value of the various colors found in its plumage may possibly have had some effect on the popularity of the goldfinch and its extensive use in art. According to Mrs. Jameson the red color symbolizes fire, divine love, the Holy Spirit; the white stands for innocence, purity, joy, life, and faith; gold or yellow for faith, fruitfulness, and divine goodness; black for pathos, suffering, and mourning.

67. In connection with the fertility symbolism of the goldfinch, it may be pertinent to recall that in everyday usage in the Italian idiom, small birds, frequently the nightingale, are mentioned in the sense of phallic symbols. The phallus is often referred to as "the little bird." This usage is apparently not a modern innovation, but has a considerable antiquity.

68. Possibly one of the earliest records of this habit is given by Konrad Gesner in his "Historia animalium," published in Zurich in 1554. He relates (book II, pp. 235-237) that a goldfinch belonging to Cardinal Franciscus Gonziacus (probably Francesco Gonzaga, 1444-1483) was trained to pull up, with its toes, miniature pails containing its food and water, the pails being attached to a rope.

    Bächtold-Stäubli (Handwörterbuch des deutschen Aberglaubens, vol. 8, 1936-1937 p. 482) quotes Albertus Magnus (De Animalium, 23, 41) to the effect that the goldfinch, when kept in captivity, pulls its water cup to it with its beak and feet.

69. R. Junghaus: Ornithologische Erinnerungen aus Italien. *Ornithologische Monatsschrift d. deutsch. Vereins zum Schutze der Vogelwelt*, vol. 15, 1890, p. 91.

70. Paul Leverkuhn: Die Legende vom Stieglitz. *Ornithologische Monatsschrift d. deutsch. Vereins zum Schutze der Vogelwelt*, vol. 15, 1890, pp. 278-281.

71. M. l'Abbé Charles Auguste Auber: Historie et Théorie du Symbolisme Religieux avant et depuis le Christianisme, vol. 4, 1884, p. 141.

72. Konrad von Megenberg (1309-1378): Das Buch der Natur; Augsburg, 1478.

73. Inasmuch as the text is illuminating as to the mental attitude of the author towards the goldfinch, a short quotation is here appended. "Es ist ein grosses Wunder, dass der Vogel so schön singt, trotzdem er die scharfen Stacheln der Distel frisst. Er ist so ein Sinnbild der guten Prediger auf Erden, die viel erdulden müssen und doch in den Dornen dieser Welt fröhlich Gott dienen. Ach Gott, Du weisst wohl, wo Deine Stieglitze singen, Du kennst auch ihr heimliches Dornenessen wohl; Du selbst hast auf Erden gesungen bis in den bitteren Tod, warum leiden Deine guten Freunde nicht auch auf Erden?"

74. Jacob Theodor Klein: Historia Avium, 1750, p. 97.

Notes

CHAPTER III. THE TYPES OF PICTURES IN WHICH THE SYMBOLIC GOLDFINCH OCCURS

1. Illustrated in Berenson's "Studies in Mediæval Painting," 1930, fig. 63.

2. This list of saints represented in paintings containing the goldfinch symbol is undoubtedly subject to extensive revision. In many pictures included in the present study, and of which I do not have even poor reproductions available at the time of this writing, the titles merely list ". . . and saints" with no further clues as to their identity.

3. The motif of the two Children playing has been taken from this picture and utilized without the Madonna in a number of works, of which we may mention as an example one now in the Museo Nazionale, Naples. In this panel there is a goldfinch flying straight towards the spectator, directly over the heads of the two Children. The attributions in this case are many and various; it has been given to Boltraffio by Salaini, to Joos van Cleve by Friedländer, to Mabuse by Brunelli, and to the safer, but less definite, "follower of Leonardo" by other critics.

4. Bernhard Berenson: Italian Pictures of the Renaissance, 1932, p. 543.

5. Charles de Tolnay: The Youth of Michelangelo, 1943, p. 162.

6. The most ancient representation of this theme is found in the second or third century frescoes in the catacomb of Priscilla; see V. Lasareff, Art Bulletin, vol. 20, 1938, p. 27; and Wilpert, Le pitture delle catacombe, 1903, pls. xxi, xxii. These frescoes have been dated more recently as of the third century by Morey.

7. Millard Meiss: The Madonna of Humility; *Art Bulletin*, vol. 18, 1936, pp. 435-464, esp. p. 460.

8. The attribution to Barna is rejected by Offner, who points out that there is a closely similar composition in the Museo Civico in Padua.

9. M. Salmi: Masaccio, 1934, pl. 1, 2, 7. The attribution of this painting to the master himself has been questioned by Offner, who prefers to call it by a "follower of Masaccio."

10. Some doubt exists as to the correctness of this attribution. The picture has been restored and repainted to such an extent that it is difficult to tell. It has, however, been listed among the master's works by most authors.

11. In S. Reinach's "Répertoire des peintures du moyen âge et de la renaissance," vol. 1, 1905, p. 189.

12. Illustrated in W. Pinder: Die Deutsche Plastik des Vierzehnten Jahrhunderts, 1925, pl. 73.

13. See pp. 28-32 for further discussion of this symbolism.

CHAPTER IV. THE GOLDFINCH IN SPANISH, FRENCH, ENGLISH FLEMISH, DUTCH, GERMANIC, AND RUSSIAN ART

1. It should be kept in mind, however, that the richest single source of illustrative material, Post's great encyclopedic work, is still incomplete, not having reached beyond the sixteenth century in its treatment. Were it complete, we might well have a somewhat greater number of pertinent paintings.

2. A dozen or so Spanish pictures have been found containing swallows and other small birds other than goldfinches.

3. Chandler Rathfon Post: A History of Spanish Painting, vol. 2, 1930, esp. pp. 177 and 182.

4. See Millard Meiss: Italian Style in Catalonia; *Journ. Walters Art Gallery*, vol. 4, 1941, p. 45.

5. Post, *cit. supra* vol. 3, 1930, p. 298.

6. One, attributed to the Palanquinos Master, in the Plandiura collection, Barcelona, and one given to Jaime Cabrera, in the Museum at Vich. Both are illustrated in Post's great work, the former in vol. 4, p. 333, the latter in vol. 2, p. 365.

7. For a fuller account see Georgiana Goddard King; The Virgin of Humility; *Art Bulletin*, vol. 17, 1935, p. 474; also Post, History of Spanish Painting, vol. 2, pp. 388-389, vol. 5, p. 318; and vol. 8, p. 600.

8. Joaquin Perez y Pando: Iconografia Mariana Española, 1930, p. 134, fig. 110, and p. 154, fig. 130.

9. Ramiro de Pinedo: El Simbolismo en la Escultura Medieval Española, 1930, esp. pp. 51-60.

10. In the illuminations in manuscripts the goldfinch occurs chiefly as a part of decorative border patterns, along with other, often fantastic, birds, and flowers, and not as a symbolic icon.

11. Illustrated in M. Vloberg's "La Vierge et l'Enfant dans l'art français," vol. 2, 1937.

12. J. E. Harting: The Ornithology of Shakespeare, 1871.

Notes

13. For a full discussion of this symbolism, see pp. 10 ff.

14. Illustrated and discussed by T. Borenius and E. W. Tristram in their book, "English Medieval Painting," 1927, pl. 42.

15. Jan van Eyck's "Madonna and Child with Saints Donatian and George, and Donor," now in the Town Gallery, Bruges.

16. See Friedländer: Die Altniederländische Malerei, vol. 11, pls. lviii and lxxi.

17. Illustrated in Kleinberger Catalogue, American Art Association. Sale No. 4800, 1932, No. 38.

18. It should be stated that probably a smaller proportion of the total bulk of Germanic painting has been available to me as illustrations in the literature than is the case with French or Flemish art. The relatively greater frequency of the goldfinch in Germanic pictures is therefore possibly even more than here indicated.

19. Lionel Cust (Notes on Pictures in the Royal Collection, 1911, p. 43) calls the bird a bullfinch, but it appears, from his reproduction, to be more likely a goldfinch, although by no means a very passable one.

20. Illustrated, and discussed in A. Stange, Deutsch. Malerei d. Gotik, vol. 1, 1934, Zeit 1250 bis 1350, figs. 187, 188.

21. Described and briefly discussed by Stange, cit supra, vol. 1, 1934, p. 185, fig. 186, and vol. 2, 1936, pp. 66, 71; and also by Oettinger, Zeit. Kunstgeschichte, vol. 6, 1937, p. 397. The specific identification of the little bird is not as definite as I would like in this case, but the reproductions available were dark, small, and rather poor.

22. In the catalogue of the Squindo Sale, 1903, is a picture of the "Madonna and Child with a Goldfinch" attributed to Lucas Cranach in imitation of Raphael! The bird is definitely a goldfinch, but the picture is, to me at least, not at all reminiscent of either Cranach or Raphael. For this reason I mention it in a note rather than in the body of the text. Who may actually have been the artist I cannot guess.

23. Nikodim Pavlovich Kondakov: The Russian Icon. Translated by E. H. Minns, 1937, pp. 80-82.

CHAPTER V. THE GOLDFINCH IN ITALIAN ART. INTRODUCTION

1. Moretto, a leading master of the Brescian school, may have made use of the goldfinch motif. Berenson (Italian Pictures of the Renaissance, 1932, p. 376) lists a "Madonna with a Bird in Hand" as probably by him, now in Venice. I have not seen this painting or even a photograph of it; the bird may turn out to be a goldfinch.

2. It may be that some of the other pictures here treated as easel paintings were originally frescoes and have been since removed from the walls on which they were painted and transferred to panels or canvas.

3. Illustrated in Lisetta Motta Ciaccio; "Gli affreschi di S. M. di Vezzolano e la pittura piemontese del Trecento," L'Arte, vol. 13, 1910, p. 349, fig. 16, p. 351, fig. 17.

CHAPTER VI. THE FLORENTINE SCHOOL

1. This picture is thought by Professor Offner to have originated, not in Florence, but in the vicinity of Venice. I leave it here in the discussion of the Florentine School because it has been so published elsewhere and because, as far as I know, Professor Offner's attribution, and his reasons for it, have not yet appeared. I am indebted to him for raising this doubt. The reader must bear this opinion in mind both when reading this chapter and also the one on the Venetian School (chapter VIII).

2. The date is that given by A. Venturi (L'Arte, vol. 8, 1905, p. 300).

3. It should be remembered that the list of pictures here assembled is by no means exhaustive, and that consequently there may have been some later ones. It is not likely, however, that there were many such, or I would hardly have missed all of them.

   It should also be remembered that the dating of pictures is, in some cases, little more than informed guesswork. The dates I have used have been those given in the literature. As in the case of attributions, I have been careful to judge conflicting datings of identical works by all the evidence available to me of the lives and works of the artists involved. That I have escaped all error is, however, too much to expect.

4. When it is said that an artist did not paint any pictures containing a goldfinch, the evidence is fairly good, as in all such cases I have consulted the entire *œuvre* of the artist as represented in standard monographs of the "Klassiker der Kunst" series and many other volumes, some of which are listed in the bibliography. It is understood, of course, that "never" means "never in the works preserved to us": I obviously cannot say anything about the presence or absence of the bird in lost paintings of which no knowledge has come down to us.

5. Bronzino may have made use of the goldfinch. In his "Holy Family with the Infant Baptist" in the Kunsthistorisches Musuem, Vienna, the Christ Child holds a small bird. I have not seen a reproduction clear enough to enable me to identify the bird, however, and unfortunately, when I was in the Vienna museum years ago, I was not particularly interested in noting goldfinches.

6. Fra Angelico we have already considered and found to be outside the interest in, and use of, the goldfinch symbol; Orcagna has left but little by which to judge him,

but that little contains no sign of a goldfinch certainly his and not his pupils' (who were, however, much given to including it in their works); Uccello was interested far more in the science of perspective than in religious painting, and cared little for symbolic meanings, and his work is therefore understandably free from any attempt to introduce the bird.

7. This work is given by Professor Offner to a "follower of Masaccio." If Professor Offner's decision be accepted, the argument presented in this brief historical survey of Florentine usage of the symbolic goldfinch gains further in strength.

8. One painting, attributed to Filippo, does contain a small bird, probably intended to be a goldfinch. Even if really by him, this work constitutes an exception in his *œuvre*, and hardly invalidates the present discussion.

9. Other Florentine sculptors frequently placed a small bird in the Child's hands or in those of another figure in the act of offering it to Him. Among others may be mentioned Agostino di Duccio, Rossellino, the della Robbias, the "Master of the Marble Madonnas," Raffaello da Montelupo, and Michelangelo.

10. This may possibly be due to a later "cutting down" of the picture.

CHAPTER VII. THE·SIENESE SCHOOL

1. It may be recalled that the goldfinch in the painting by a follower of Duccio, now in the Detroit Art Institute, mentioned above, resembles a swallow in shape and form. One cannot help but recall also the old legend of a "swallow-goldfinch," offspring of a union of these two species. On the other hand, it must be admitted that, as far as I have been able to learn, this legend was chiefly Germanic and not Italian, but the data on it are very scant and inconclusive.

2. A similar placement of the bird occurs in one of Carlo Crivelli's works, discussed in our account of the Venetian school, p. 82.

3. This work has also been attributed to a "follower of Leonardo," which, in truth, applies to Sodoma as well as to many others of his generation.

CHAPTER VIII. THE VENETIAN SCHOOL

1. In discussing a painting by Michele Giambono, in which a goldfinch occurs, E. von Bercken (Die Malerei der Früh- und Hochrenaissance in Oberitalien, 1927, p. 74) considers this element a sign of the influence of Gentile da Fabriano. This, however, seems to be a doubtful conclusion.

2. The reader is reminded of Professor Offner's opinion as to the Venetian origin of the picture done about 1300, mentioned in Chapter VI (p. 65) as an early Florentine work. See note 1, to Chapter VI as well.

3. Picture not seen; description taken from the guidebook of the gallery.

4. According to G. M. Rushforth (Carlo Crivelli, 1900, p. 87) Gabriele Ferretti was the Superior of the Franciscans in the March of Ancona. He died in 1456. Some thirty or more years later, in the pontificate of Innocent VIII (1484-1492) his body body was exhumed and found incorrupt, and was deposited in a sarcophagus in the Church of SS. Francesco and Alto at Ancona.

5. Both of these pictures were kindly brought to my attention by Professor Offner.

6. Illustrated in "Exhibit of Venetian Paintings . . . in aid of Lord Baldwin's Fund for Refugees," Matthiensen Gallery, London, 1939, No. 30.

CHAPTER IX. THE UMBRIAN SCHOOL

1. Early Umbrian paintings are not very extensively reproduced in the literature, and I may therefore have failed to note some examples with the symbolic goldfinch.

2. William N. Howe: Animal Life in Italian Painting, 1912, p. 61.

3. At least, I have never come across this interpretation in other Italian art centers. A Spanish echo is an Aragonese plague banner in the Episcopal Palace at Teruel (illustrated in Post's History of Spanish Painting, vol. 5, p. 314); and I have found the same general idea repeated in at least one Germanic print, done in Alsace about 1500 (Elizabeth Mongan and Carl O. Schniewind, The First Century of Printmaking 1400-1500, 1941, No. 36, illustrated on p. 46).

   Another Germanic work, done about 1430 under north French and Netherlandish influence, now in the abbey church at Heilsbronn, shows the Eternal at the top hurling the arrows of the pestilence. The Madonna stands holding the Infant Jesus, Her wide-spread robe protecting the multitude of adoring suppliants kneeling about her. A goldfinch is flying, apparently on a string held in the Christ Child's left hand. (This work, illustrated in Fritz Burger, Herman Schmitz, and Ignaz Beth "Die Deutsche Malerei vom ausgehenden Mittelalter bis zum Ende der Renaissance," 1913-1922, vol. 2, p. 296, was noted too late for inclusion in our discussion of the goldfinch in Germanic art).

   A Florentine painting showing God as the hurler of the arrows is Benozzo Gozzoli's "St. Sebastian as Interceder and Protector of the Populace of San Gimignano" in the church of St. Augustine in San Gimignano. In this work God, at the top of the picture hurls the arrows. Christ, depicted as a grown man, and Mary are immediately below Him in attitudes suggesting that they are interceding or pitying figures. St. Sebastian stands with his hands as in prayer; surrounding the pedestal on which he stands are a multitude of suppliants. There is no goldfinch in the picture; Sebastian, the patron saint of victims of the plague, and the interceding Christ and Mary need no such assistance from such a symbol. The important point for our present inquiry is that Christ is shown interceding for the people against the dread scourge in this Florentine work. Such an idea was apparently unthought of in contemporary Perugia.

4. George G. Coulton: Five Centuries of Religion, vol. 2, 1923, p. 394.

5. Inasmuch as the difference between the two reactions seemed to involve possible difficulties of theological theory, the matter was submitted to several of the learned faculty of the Catholic University of America, who assured me that there was nothing inherently improbable or even unlikely in such local differences in attitude towards the plague. Thus, Dr. A. K. Ziegler, in a note, in this connection, to my esteemed friend Monsignor John M. Cooper, adds, ". . . is there really anything unusual in finding that both punishment for sin and relief from punishment come from God? The latter comes as a result of sorrow and penance through the intercession of Mary and the Christ Child."

6. A somewhat similar painting, done in Arezzo in the latter half of the fifteenth century, is Domenico Pecori's "Madonna of Mercy" (Arezzo, Gallery). In this work, however, the arrows are being hurled by God Himself. It may be noted that no usage of the goldfinch has been found in the work of any painter of Arezzo. Pecori did include a dark small bird in the Child's hand in a "Madonna and Child" picture shown at the Polish Pavillion at the World's Fair, New York, in 1940 (as part of the exhibition of "Polish Owned Works of Art" and published and illustrated under that title). The bird is so wretchedly drawn as to render it unidentifiable but it appears to have been intended as a swallow.

Another gonfalone by Bonfigli (Corciano, Parish Church) shows the arrows being hurled by God. In still another, by Caporali (Montone, S. Francesco) Christ hurls the darts.

7. See p. 23 for the therapeutic significance of the thistle; see pp. 28, 29 for the fertility symbolism of the goldfinch.

8. It may be noted that a magpie is perched on the roof of the shed. That this bird is also connected with the charadrius legend is evidenced by the fact that Aldrovandus (Ornithologiæ, vol. 1, 1681, p. 855, lines 14-17) in writing of the charadrius, and of one of its most frequent substitute identifications, the galbulus, states, ". . . alii galbulum cum mollicipite, *quæ Pica glandarius* (the magpie) *est;* alii cum charadrio seu hiaticula, quæ prope aquas degit . . . confunderunt" (italics mine).

The magpie was also a symbol of death. It probably is here as a token of the fate of the newborn Saviour.

9. Another case in point is Caporali's "Madonna and Child with Four Angels and Saints Bernardino and Francis," in the Strossmayer Gallery, Agram. We have already noted Caporali as a painter of anti-plague gonfalones, yet here he succumbs to the wide-spread popularity of the symbolic goldfinch.

CHAPTER X. MILAN, BOLOGNA, AND FERRARA

1. There are at least two other pictures by this artist that are said to have a small bird in them. Inasmuch as I have not seen either the originals or reproductions I cannot be certain that the bird in each or either is a goldfinch. The paintings are listed by Berenson (Italian Pictures of the Renaissance, 1932, p. 205) as being, respectively, in the Vom Rath collection, Amsterdam, and the Mrs. R. M. Hurd collection, New York.

2. G. C. Williamson: Francesco Raibolini, called Francia, 1899, p. 59.

3. The monkey was a frequently used symbol of Lasciviousness. The cat was a symbol of Heresy in the Middle Ages.

4. This picture has been attributed, in literature, to the Bolognese painter Chiodarolo as well.

CHAPTER XI. THE MINOR SCHOOLS OF ITALY

1. Illustrated in Berenson: International Studio, November, 1930, p. 30, fig. 12, and p. 28, fig. 2, respectively.

2. In Mantegna's "Madonna della Vittoria" in the Louvre, Paris, there are three birds, not certainly identifiable, but apparently not goldfinches, on the trellis in the background.

3. Illustrated in Laudadeo Testi: Storia della Pittura Veneziana, Parte Prima, La Origine, 1909, p. 440.

4. Whereabouts unknown; illustrated in Reinach's "Répertoire," vol. 5, p. 297.

5. William N. Howe: Animal Life in Italian Painting, 1912, p. 82.

6. Illustrated in van Marle: Development of the Italian Schools of Painting, vol. 15, p. 443.

7. This picture is reproduced in color on the cover of the December, 1923 number of International Studio.

8. Both of these pictures are illustrated in van Marle, vol. 8, p. 278.

9. Bernhard Berenson: Italian Pictures of the Renaissance, 1932, p. 355.

10. Illustrated in van Marle, vol. 15, p. 462.

CHAPTER XII. ICONOGRAPHIC AND STYLISTIC DETAILS OF THE GOLDFINCH

1. Mrs. Jameson: Legends of the Madonna, 4th ed., 1867, pp. 71-72.

2. According to Howey: (The Cat in the Mysteries of Religion and Magic, 1931) "The cat represents the attributes of the predecessors of the Virgin — the plain, ordinary individual that was suddenly transformed." . . . The parable of the Virgin and the cat may also be recognized by the old folk-tale of Cinderella, which, in some of its variants, is entitled "The Hearth Cat." It may also be recalled that at the time when the Infant Jesus lay in His bed of straw, a cat was nursing its kittens beneath the manger. Mrs. Jameson's interpretation is therefore open to serious doubt. Baroccio's painting recalls the one by Murillo in which the Christ Child holds the bird away from the reach of a little woolly dog. The cat was also a symbol of Heresy in the Middle Ages.

3. "Madonna and Child Enthroned with Saints and Angels," Siena, Gallery; "Madonna and Child with Saints and Angels," Florence, Uffizi; "Madonna and Child," near Florence, San Lorenzo alle Rose; "Madonna and Child," Florence, Horne Foundation; "Madonna and Child," Florence, Accademia.
   In another painting of the Madonna and Child, in a private collection in Munich (illustrated by Sirén, Burlington Magazine, vol. 48, 1926, p. 184) the position is reversed but the action is the same. The bird is held upright but is bending its head down as if to peck the hand that holds it.

4. Wilhelm Neuss: Die Kunst der Alten Christen, 1926, p. 106.

5. Frederick Roth Webber: (Church Symbolism. An Explanation of the more important Symbols of the Old and New Testaments, the Primitive, the Mediæval, and the Modern Church, 1927, p. 239) states that the vine represents Christ and also the Church, and that the birds pictured among its branches represent human souls. Hastings (Encyclopedia of Religion and Ethics, vol. 12, 1928, p. 134) considers the vine as the earthly pledge of the heavenly feast — the Eucharist, and the dove sipping water from a vessel as the soul refreshing itself with the water of life.

6. And also in an equally large number of works by Daddi's pupils and followers, as listed on p. 143.

7. Their status as assistants is largely inferred from their paintings rather than from any direct evidence of their having been employed in Jacopo's *bottega*.

8. Arthur H. Collins: Symbolism of Animals and Birds represented in English Church Architecture, 1913, pp. 114-115.

9. A white bird, discussed on p. 19, as a possible charadrius is so placed in a Florentine panel done *ca* 1300.

10. School of Cimabue (Sterbini collection; Rome).

11. Nikodim Pavlovich Kondakov: The Russian Icon. Translated by E. H. Minn, 1927, pp. 80-82.

12. The only paintings in which I have noticed a tethered swallow are a "Madonna and Child" by Antoniazzo Romano, in the Museo Nazionale, Naples; one by an unknown Sardinian painter, in the Parish Church, Tuili; and one by Bartolommeo Caporali, in the Museo Nazionale, Naples.

13. It also came to have a special meaning, signifying the unity of the Church with its multitude of members (seeds).

14. Before leaving the matter of flowers, it may be noted that in his "Madonna of the Siskin" Dürer painted the young St. John offering some lilies of the valley to the Christ Child, who is holding the siskin. Flowers in devotional paintings usually refer to the Canticles "I am the Rose of Sharon and the Lily of the Valley."

15. See note No. 2, this chapter, for a discussion of the symbolic meaning of the cat.

CHAPTER XIII. MICHELANGELO'S EXCEPTIONAL TREATMENT OF THE GOLDFINCH

1. A later, slight echo of this work is the painting by the Spaniard Zurbaran, already discussed in an earlier chapter (p. 41). The young Baptist comes forward eagerly with a goldfinch; the Infant Jesus, somewhat startled, partly turns back to His mother, who is dreamily contemplating the action. The bird, however, is depicted in a quiet attitude.

2. Charles de Tolnay (The Youth of Michelangelo, 1943, pp. 104ff and 162ff) is the only author who has done so, and even he does not stress its uniqueness. His book was not available to me until after I had already completed my interpretation.

Notes

3. As previously stated, I agree with Tolnay in calling the bird a goldfinch although, being fashioned in uncolored stone and left in a very unfinished stage, it cannot be absolutely identified as such. The identification is an inferential, not an evidential one.

4. Carl Justi: Michelangelo; Neue Beiträge zur Erklärung seiner Werke, 1909, pp. 186-187.

5. As in the earlier tondo, now in the Bargello, Florence.

6. This "pearl string" is surely nothing but an effect produced by Michelangelo's manner of undercutting, as found also in the faun of the Bacchus, as was there pointed out by Valentiner (Art Quarterly, vol. 1, 1938, p. 37), and not a pearl string at all.

7. Hans Mackowsky: Michelangelo, 1925, p. 52.

8. It may be noted that, according to Panofsky (Studies in Iconology, 1939, p. 172, footnote) Michelangelo derived this figure of the Child running over His mother's outstretched leg, and looking backward over His shoulder at the same time, from a "Medea" relief on an old Roman sarcophagus. Be this as it may, the meaning inherent in Michelangelo's figure appears not to be involved in this possible compositional source.

9. Charles de Tolnay: The Youth of Michelangelo, 1943, p. 162.

10. Greatly to my regret, I have been unable to see a copy of Wölfflin's "Die Jugendwerke Michelangelos," in which the tondo is said to be discussed. (As the present book was going through the press, a copy finally came to hand. The discussion in it of this tondo adds nothing new.)

11. Ludwig Goldscheider: The Paintings of Michelangelo, 1939, p. 16.

12. The "Doni Holy Family" is supposed to have been commissioned by Angelo Doni on the occasion of his marriage to Maddalena Strozzi, about 1503-1504, but is also supposed not to have been completed until a couple of years later.

13. Students of Michelangelo may also note that this work is a descendant of the earlier "Madonna of the Stairs" where the Madonna is also sitting on a block and where the little figures in the background are likewise apart from the main personages psychologically.

14. The kneeling angel holding a candlestick, in San Domenico, Bologna, made as a pendant to the earlier one by Niccolo da Bari.

15. G. F. Young: The Medici; Modern Library ed., 1933, chapter xi.

16. The degree to which Michelangelo was inclined to feel external affairs in a purely personal way is reflected in his impetuous, premature flight from his native city to Bologna in 1494, when he merely anticipated the coming expulsion of the Medici and the unrest that was likely to follow.

17. As an example of what I have in mind, I may refer the reader to the account of the Medicean tombs given in his admittedly subjective and emotional little book, "The Art of Michelangelo" by H. H. Powers, pp. 194-203. In all fairness, the reader may be referred to a discussion of Michelangelo in which the influence upon him of Savonarola is greatly belittled. This is Romain Rolland's "Michelangelo" translated by Frederick Street (Bonibooks, 1935, pp. 8-14).

    Later, much later in his life, Michelangelo did make statements to the effect that art should not permit itself to partake of sentiment or to express feeling too strongly, but should remain aloof as if on a pedestal. These observations are recorded by François de Hollande. "Quatre Entretiens sur la Peinture," written in 1548 and published in several editions in several languages.

18. Lionello Venturi: Botticelli, 1937, pp. 23-24.

19. This "looking back" is a dramatic gesture that occurs frequently in the master's *œuvre*, and, for that matter, in late Quattrocento and early Cinquecento Italian art. Thus, in the Sistine ceiling no fewer than seven of the nude figures at the corners of the Genesis panels are at least glancing over one shoulder. The Eve in the Expulsion is also doing so as is too the figure of Jonah. In one of the spandrel pictures, we find Judith carrying the head of Holofernes, but looking back over her shoulder at the headless corpse. In the much later "Last Judgment" we find the action repeated to some degree in the figure of the Madonna.

APPENDIX

1. Professor Offner considers these two paintings to be, not by the master himself, but by an assistant.

2. Attribution to Masaccio himself very seriously questioned by Offner.

3. Attributed to Bernardo Daddi in the New York Historical Society's catalogue.

4. Published by Reinach (Repertoire . . . , vol. 3, p. 441) as by a member of the school of Botticini.

5. Published in the Kleinberger catalogue as by Giovanni Bonsi.

6. Published as by Buffalmacco in the New York Historical Society's catalogue.

Notes

7. Attributed in literature to the school of Agnolo Gaddi.

8. Attributed in literature to Paolo di Giovanni Fei by many authors.

9. Another version of this work by Tiepolo is in the collection of Jacques Seligmann and Co., N. Y.

Literature Cited and Consulted

ADAM, J. 1911
   Naturgefühl in den Schriften des Mittelalters. *Xenien*, 1911, p. 321-341.

AELIANUS, CLAUDIUS (*ca.* 140 A. D.)   1616
   De Natura Animalium, xvii.

ALBERTUS MAGNUS   (1193-1280) *see* KILLERMANN.

ALDROVANDUS, ULYSSES   (1522-1605)   1610-1635
   Ornithologia, hoc est de Avibus Historiæ libri xii. 3 vols.

ALLEN, JOHN ROMILLY   1887
   Early Christian Symbolism in Great Britain and Ireland before the Thirteenth
   Century.

D'ANCONA, PAOLO   1924
   La Miniature Italienne du 10ᵉ au 16ᵉ Siècle.

——   1930-1932
   L'arte italiana. 2 vols.

ANONYMOUS   1923
   Die Zweisprach der Tiere (Dialogus creaturarum). A modern edition of the
   early medieval work.

——   1919
   International Studio, vol. 86, p. 53.

ARISTOPHANES (The Athenian Society Edition, 1912)
   The Eleven Comedies. Vol. 2, The Birds, pp. 81-180.

Literature Cited

ARNDT, WALTHER 1925
>   Die Vögel in der Heilkunde der alten Kulturvolker.
>   *Journal für Ornithologie*, vol. 73, pp. 46-76, 214-246, 475-493.

ART INSTITUTE OF CHICAGO 1933, 1934
>   Catalogue of A Century of Progress Exhibition of Paintings and Sculpture.

AUBER, CHARLES AUGUSTE 1884
>   Histoire et Théorie du Symbolisme Religieux avant et depuis le Christianisme.
>   Vol. 4.

AUBERT, MARCEL 1926
>   La Sculpture française du Moyen Age et de la Renaissance.

BÄCHTOLD-STÄUBLI, HANS 1930-1937
>   Handwörterbuch des Deutchen Aberglaubens, vol. 2, p. 302, and vol. 8, p. 482.

BARBIER DE MONTAULT, XAVIER 1890
>   Traité d'iconographie Chrétienne, vol. 2.

BARING-GOULD, REVEREND S. 1866-1868
>   Curious Myths of the Middle Ages.

BARTES, GUILLAUME DE SALUST DU 1633
>   Divine Weekes and Workes. Translated by Joshua Sylvester.

BARTHOLOMAEUS ANGLICUS (*ca.* 1250) 1492
>   De Proprietatibus Rerum. Book XII.

BATMAN, STEPHEN 1582
>   Batman uppon Bartholome, his Books, De Proprietatibus rerum; trans. from
>   the Latin by John de Treviso.

BEAUDOIRE, THEOPHILE 1902
>   Genèse de la cryptographie apostolique et de l'architecture rituelle du premier
>   au seizième siècle.

BECHSTEIN, JOHANN MATTHAUS 1853
>   Cage and Chamber-Birds. Their Natural History, Habits, Food, Diseases,
>   Management, and Modes of Capture. Translated from the German by H. G.
>   Adams.

Literature Cited

BELON, PIERRE 1555
L'Histoire de la nature des oyseaux, avec leurs descriptions et portraits. Paris. p. 353.

BERCHORIUS, PETRUS 1583
Dictionarii seu Repertorii Moralis. Venice. 2 vols.

BERCKEN, E. VON 1927
Die Malerei der Früh-und Hochrenaissance in Oberitalien.

BERENSON, BERNHARD 1913-14
Catalogue of Paintings in the Collection of John G. Johnson. 3 vols.

—— 1916
Venetian Painting in America; the Fifteenth Century.

—— 1918
Essays in the Study of Sienese Painting.

—— 1927-1931
The Study and Criticism of Italian Art. 3 vols.

—— 1930
Studies of Mediæval Painting.

—— 1930
A Reconstruction of Gualtieri di Giovanni. *International Studio*, vol. 97, December, 1930, pp. 67-71.

—— 1930
Missing Pictures of the Sienese Trecento. Pt. III.
International Studio, vol. 97, November, 1930, pp. 27-32.

—— 1931
Lost Paintings of XV Century Siena, pt. 1.
International Studio, vol. 98, February, 1931, pp. 24-29.

—— 1931
Lost Paintings of XV Century Siena, pt. 2.
International Studio, vol. 98, March 1931, pp. 37-41.

—— 1931
Lost Works of the Last Sienese Masters, pt. 3.
International Studio, vol. 98, April 1931, pp. 17-22.

—— 1931
Quadri Senza Casa. Il Quattrocento Senese II.
Dedalo, April 1931, p. 761.

—— 1932
Quadri Senza Casa. Il Trecento Fiorentino. IV, V, II, III.
Dedalo, vol. 12, pp. 5-34, 173-193, 665-702, 819-853.

—— 1932
Italian Pictures of the Renaissance.

—— 1932
Italian Painters of the Renaissance.

BERNATH, M.   1916
Die Malerei des Mittelalters.

BERTAUX, E.   1904
L'Art dans l'Italie Méridionale.

BIAGI, GUIDO   1909
Men and Manners of Old Florence.

BIESE, ALFRED   1905
Development of Feeling for Nature in the Middle Ages.

BOCHART, SAMUEL   1663
Hierozoicon

BODE, WILHELM   1923
Die Kunst der Frührenaissance in Italien. Propyläen Kunstgeschichte, vol. 8.

—— 1926
Botticelli. Klassiker der Kunst, vol. 30.

Literature Cited

BOMBE, WALTER 1914
 Perugino. Klassiker der Kunst, vol. 25.

BONAVENTURA, SAINT, CARDINAL 1212-1274 (ed. by Adolphe-Charles Peltier) 1864-
 1871 S. r. e. cardinalis s. Bonaventuræ . . . Opera omnia Sixti V . . . jussu
 diligentissime emendata; accedit sancti doctoris vita, una cum diatriba
 historico-chronologico-critica. Editio accurate recognita . . . cura et studio
 Adolpho Carolo Peltier. 15 vols.

BORENIUS, TANCRED 1909
 The Painters of Vicenza, 1480-1550.

—— 1913
 The Venetian School in the Grand-Ducal Collection, Oldenburg.
 Burlington Magazine, vol. 23, pp. 25-35.

—— 1930
 Leonardo's Madonna with the Children at Play. *Burlington Magazine*, vol. 56,
 p. 142.

—— 1930
 Florentine Frescoes.

—— 1931
 Italian Pictures in the Rijksmuseum. Burlington Magazine, vol. 59, pp. 60-75.

BORENIUS, TANCRED and E. W. TRISTRAM 1927
 English Medieval Painting.

BORKHAUSEN, MORIZ BALTHAZAR 1797
 Deutsche Fauna, vol. 1, p. 248.

BRIGANTI, GIULIANO 1938
 Su Giusto di Gand. *La Critica d'Arte*, vol. 3, pp. 104-112.

BRINTON, SELWYN 1898-1904
 The Renaissance in Italian Art. 4 vols.

BRISSON, MATHURIN JACQUES 1760
 Ornithologia sive Synopsis Methodica, vol. 3.

Literature Cited

BRITISH MUSEUM 1923
Reproductions of Illuminated Manuscripts

—— 1914-1926
Schools of Illumination.

BUDINI, CORNELIO 1937
Gli artisti italiani in Ungheria. L'opera del Genio italiano all'estero.

BROWN, ALICE VAN VECHTEN, and WILLIAM RANKIN 1914
A Short History of Italian Painting.

BURCKHARDT, JACOB 1935
The Civilization of the Renaissance in Italy. Translated from the 15th edition.

BURGER, FRITZ, SCHMITZ, HERMAN, and BETH, IGNAZ 1913-1922
Die Deutsche Malerei vom ausgehenden. Mittelalter bis zum Ende der Renaissance.

BUSCAROLI, REZIO 1931
La Pittura romagnola del Quattrocento.

BYVANCK, A. W. 1924
Les Principaux Manuscrits à Peintures de la Bibliothèque Royale des Pays Bas.

CABROL, F., and LECLERQ, H. 1900
Monumenta Ecclesiæ Liturgica

—— 1903
Dictionaire d'Archéologie Chrétienne et de Liturgie.

CAHIER, CHARLES, and MARTIN, ARTHUR 1851
Mélanges d'Archéologie, d'Histoire et de Littérature, vol. 2.

CALVERT, ALBERT F. 1906
Murillo.

CALVI, GIROLAMO 1898
Il Manoscritto H di Leonardo da Vinci, Il "Fiore di Virtù" e L' "Acerba" di Cecco d'Ascoli. *Archivio Storico Lombardo*, vol. 25, fasc. 19, ser. 3, vol. 10, pp. 73-116.

Literature Cited

CAMERARIUS, JOACHIM   1590
Symbolorum et emblematum ex re herbaria desumtorum Centuria una collecta a Joachimo Camerario.

CANDEE, HELEN CHURCHILL   1935
The Tapestry Book

CANTALAMESSA CARBONI, GIACINTO   1897
Le Gallerie Nazionali Italiane, vol. 3.

CARTWRIGHT, JULIA   1901
The Painters of Florence

CARUS, JULIUS VICTOR   1880
Histoire de la zoologie depuis l'antiquité jusqu'au XIXe siecle; tr. par P. O. Hagenmüller et notes par A. Schneider.

CECCO D'ASCOLI (Francesco degli Stabili 1257-1327)   1516
Acerba. (Venice: Marchio Sessa and Piero di Ravani Busono), cap. xvii, third book, leaf 55-56.

CECCHI, EMILIO (transl. by Leonard Penlock)   1931
The Sienese Painters of the Trecento

—— 1937
Giotto.

CHOULANT, JOHANN LUDWIG   1858
Graphische Incunabeln für Naturgeschichte und Medizin. Geschichte und Bibliographie der ersten naturhistorischen und medizinischen Drucke des xv. und xv. Jahrhunderts, welche mit illustrierenden Abbildungen versehen sind.

CIACCIO, LISETTA MOTTA   1910
Gli Affreschi de S. M. di Vezzolano e la Pittura Piemontese del Trecento. L'Arte, vol. 13, pp. 349-351.

CIARDIELLO GALLERIA, FLORENCE   1938
Sale Catalogue, February 14-18, 1938.

Literature Cited

CLARK, KENNETH M. 1939
Leonardo da Vinci.

—— 1941
More details from Pictures in the National Gallery.

Codices Graeci et Latini photographicae depicti. Tom. X Dioscurides. Codex Aniciae Julianae picturis illustratus, nunc Vindobonensis Med. Gr. I. Pars altera. Lugduni Batavorum. 1906.

COLASANTI, A. 1932
Italian Painting of the Quattrocento in the Marches.

COLETTI, LUIGI 1930
Studi sulla pittura del Trecento a Padova. I. Guariento e Semitecolo. Rivista d'Arte, vol. 12, p. 323.

—— 1933
L'Arte di Tomasso da Modena.

COLLINS, ARTHUR H. 1913
Symbolism of Animals and Birds represented in English Church Architecture.

COTT, PERRY B. 1941
The Theodore T. and Mary G. Ellis Collection. *Worcester Art Museum Journal*, vol. 4.

COUDERE, C. 1926.
Les Enluminures des Mss. du Moyen-Age.

CRAWFORD, RAYMOND 1914
The Plague in Literature and Art.

CROWE, J. A., *and* CAVALCASELLE, G. B. 1903-1914
A History of Painting in Italy, edited by L. Douglas and T. Borenius, 6 vols.

[CUBE, JOHANN DE (?)] 1497
Hortus Sanitatis Major.

Literature Cited

CUST, LIONEL 1911
Notes on Pictures in the Royal Collection.

DALTON, O. M. 1911
Byzantine Art and Archaeology.

DAVIES, GERALD S. 1924
Michelangelo. 2nd. ed.

DE LOO, GEORGES H. 1911
Jacques Daret's Nativity of Our Lord. *Burlington Magazine,* vol. 19, pp. 218-220.

DEL VITA, ALESSANDRO 1933
La Pinacoteca d'Arezzo. *Rassegna d'Arte,* vol. 15, pp. 75-88.

DOUGLAS, R. LANGTON 1902
A History of Siena.

DOYE, FRANZ VON SALES 1929
Heilige und Selige der Römisch-Katholischen Kirche. 2 vols.

DRAKE, MAURICE, *and* DRAKE, WILFRED 1916
Saints and their Emblems.

DRUCE, GEORGE C. 1919
The Mediæval Bestiaries and their Influence on Ecclesiastical Decorative Art. *Journ. British Archæological Assoc., n.s.,* vol. 25, pp. 41-82.

DUSSLER, LUITPOLD 1927
Signorelli; Klassiker der Kunst, vol. 34.

DVORAK, MAX 1929
Geschichte der italienischen Kunst im Zeitalter der Renaissance. 3rd edition, vol. 2.

ECHTERMEYER, TH. 1872
Auswahl deutscher Gedichte.

EDER, ROBERT 1890-1891
Mystisch-allegorische Vogelgeschichten und deren Ursprung. *Mittheilungen*

Literature Cited

des Ornithologischen Vereins in Wien, vol. 14, pp. 126-128, 141-143, 191-192, 205-206, 223-225, 244-246, 297-298, 312-314, 324-326; vol. 15, pp. 9-10, 32-33, 54-56, 116-118, 138-141, 169-171, 183-185, 193-195, 224.

EDGELL, GEORGE H. 1932
History of Sienese Painting.

EVANS, ARTHUR HUMBLE 1903
Turner on Birds: A Short and Succinct History of the Principal Birds Noticed by Pliny and Aristotle, First Published by Doctor William Turner, 1544. See esp. pp. 50-53, 40-41.

FABRE, ABEL 1927
Pages d'art chrétien.

FFOULKES, CONSTANCE 1909
Vincenzo Foppa of Brescia.

FIOCCO, G. 1931
Carpaccio.

FORSYTH, WILLIAM H. 1936
Mediæval Statues of the Virgin in Lorraine Related in Type to the Saint-Dié Virgin. *Metropolitan Museum Studies,* vol. 5, pp. 235-258.

FRAZER, J. G. 1900
The Golden Bough, ed. 2, vol. 3, p. 25.

FRIEDLÄNDER, M. J. 1924-1937
Die altniederländische Malerei. 14 vols.

FRY, ROGER 1903
A Picture by Solario. *Burlington Magazine,* vol. 1, p. 353.

GABELENTZ, H. von der 1907
Die kirchliche Kunst im italienischen Mittelalter.

GAMBA, CARLO 1937
Giovanni Bellini.

Literature Cited

GANZMULLER, WILHELM 1914
Das Naturgefühl im Mittelalter.

GARDNER, ARTHUR 1931
Medieval Sculpture in France

GEISBERG, MAX 1924
Reproductions of the work of "The Master E. S."

GESNER, KONRAD 1554
Historia animalium. Book 2, pp. 235-237.

——— 1581
Vogelbuch

GOLDSMITH, ELIZABETH E. 1911
Sacred Symbols in Art

GNOLI, UMBERTO 1923
Pittori e miniatori nell' Umbria.

GOERING, MAX 1937
Italienische Malerei des XVI. Jahrhunderts.

GOLDSCHEIDER, LUDWIG 1939
The Paintings of Michelangelo. (Phaidon Edition)

——— 1940
The Sculptures of Michelangelo. (Phaidon Edition).

GOMBOSI, GYORGY 1937
Palma Vecchio: Klassiker der Kunst, vol. 38.

GOODE, TERESA C. 1933
Gonzalo de Berceo. El Sacrificio de la Misa. A Study of its Symbolism and Sources.

GRIGONI, C. 1936
La Pittura Faentina dalle origini alla metà del cinquecento.

Literature Cited

Grimm, J. 1878
  Deutsche Mythologie, 3 vols.

Gronau, Georg 1930
  Giovanni Bellini: Klassiker der Kunst, vol. 19.

Gubernatis, Angelo de 1872
  Zoological Mythology, 2 vols.

Gurney, John Henry 1921
  Early Annals of Ornithology.

Hagen, Friedrich Heinrich von der 1838
  Minnesinger. Deutsche Liederdichter des zwölften, dreizehnten, und vierzehnten Jahrhunderts. Vols. 2 and 3.

Hamann, Richard 1909
  Die Frührenaissance der italienischen Malerei.

Harting, J. E. 1871
  The Ornithology of Shakespeare.

Hartlaub, G. 1910
  Matteo da Siena.

Hashiro, Yukio 1929
  Sandro Botticelli and the Florentine Renaissance.

Haskins, Charles H. 1927
  Studies in the History of Medical Science, 2d edition.

Hastings, James 1928
  Encyclopædia of Religion and Ethics, 13 vols.

Hauptmann, M. 1936
  Der Tondo. Ursprung, Bedeutung, und Geschichte des italienischen Rund-
  bildes in Relief und Malerei.

Hausenstein, Wilhelm 1928
  Fra Angelico.

Literature Cited

HEIDRICH, ERNST 1909
Die Alt-Deutsche Malerei.

HEITZ, PAUL 1901
Pestblätter des xv. Jahrhunderts.

HERBERT, I. A. 1911
Illuminated Manuscripts.

HESS, HANNS 1924.
Die Naturanschauung der Renaissance in Italien.

HEYWOOD, WILLIAM, *and* LUCY OLCOTT 1903
Guide to Siena, History, and Art.

HILL, GEORGE F. 1930
Drawings by Pisanello.

HIRN, YRJO 1912
The Sacred Shrine. A Study of the Poetry and Art of the Catholic Church.

HOFLER, M. 1893
Volksmedizin und Aberglaube in Oberbayern.

HOLROYD, CHARLES 1911
Michael Angelo, 2d edition.

HOPF, LUDWIG 1888
Thierorakel und Orakelthiere in alter und neuer Zeit.

HOWE, WILLIAM NORTON 1912
Animal Life in Italian Painting.

HOWEY, M. OLDFIELD 1931
The Cat in the Mysteries of Religion and Magic.

HUIZINGA, JOHAN 1903
Van den Vogel Charadrius. *Verhandlingen der Koninklijke Akademie van Vetenschappen te Amsterdam. Afdeeling Letterkunde*, n. s., vol. 5, no. 3.

Literature Cited

HUYSMANS, JORIS KARL   1898
   La Cathédrale, 5th edition.
   Illustrazione Vaticana, vols. 1-6.   1930-1936.

INMAN, T.   1922
   Ancient Pagan and Modern Christian Symbolism.

ISIDORE, BISHOP OF SEVILLE   1472
   Etymologiæ.

JACOBUS DE VARAGINE   1485
   The Golden Legend (translated by William Caxton)

(JAMES, M. R.)   1928
   The Bestiary: being a reproduction in full of the manuscript li. 4.26 in the
   University Library, Cambridge, with supplementary plates from other manuscripts of English origin, and a preliminary study of the Latin bestiary as
   current in England. Edited for the Roxburgh Club by M. R. James.

JAMES, M. R., *and* BERENSON, BERNARD   1926
   Speculum humanæ salvationis — Being a Reproduction of an Italian Manuscript of the Fourteenth Century.

JAMESON, MRS. ANNA BROWNELL MURPHY   1866
   Sacred and Legendary Art.   Vol. 2.

——— 1867
   Legends of the Madonna.   4th edition.

——— n. d.
   Memoirs of the Early Italian Painters.

JOEL, KARL   1926
   Der Ursprung der Naturphilosophie aus dem Geiste der Mystik.

JUNGHAUS, R.   1890
   Ornithologische Erinnerungen aus Italien. *Ornithologische Monatsschrift d.
   deutsch. Vereins z. Schutze der Vogelwelt*, vol. 15, p. 91.

JUSTI, CARL   1909
   Michelangelo. Neue Beiträge zur Erklärung seiner Werke.

[*206*]

Literature Cited

KAIBEL, GEORG 1899
    Poetarum graecorum fragmenta. Vol. 6, fasc. 1. Comicorum graecorum fragmenta.

KARLINGER, HANS 1926
    Die Kunst der Gotik. Propyläen Kunstgeschichte, vol. 7.

KELLER, O. 1913
    Die antike Tierwelt. Vol. 2.

KENNEDY, RUTH W. 1938
    Alessio Baldovinetti.

KILLERMANN, SEB. 1910
    Die Vogelkunde des Albertus Magnus.

KING, GEORGIANA GODDARD 1935
    The Virgin of Humility. *Art Bulletin*, vol. 17, pp. 474-491.

KISSLER, J. H. H. 1925
    The Master of S. Miniato.
    Burlington Magazine, vol. 46, p. 235.

KLEBS, A. C., *and* DROZ, E. 1925
    Remèdes contre la Peste, Facsimilés, Notes et Liste bibliographique des Incunables sur la Peste.

KLEIN, JACOB THEODOR 1750
    Historiae Avium Prodromus cum praefatione de ordine animalium in genera.

KLEINBERGER GALLERIES, NEW YORK 1917
    Loan Exhibition Catalogue.

KLEINBERGER CATALOGUE 1932
    American Art Association Sale No. 4800, No. 38.

KNAPP, FRITZ 1910
    Andrea Mantegna: Klassiker der Kunst, vol. 16.

KOLLOFF, EDUARD 1867
Die Sagenhafte und Symbolische Thiergeschichte des Mittelalters (in Friedrich von Raumer, Historisches Taschenbuch, 4th ser., vol. 8, pp. 177-269).

KONDAKOV, NIKODIM PAVLOVICH 1910
Ikonografia B. M. Sviazi grecheskoi i russkoi ikonopisi s italianski ranniago Vozrozhgeniia.

——— 1927
The Russian Icon (translated by E. H. Minns)

KRAUS, F. X. 1897-1900
Geschichte der Christlichen Kunst. 3 vols.

KUHN, C. L. 1936
A Catalogue of German Paintings of the Middle Ages and Renaissance in American Collections.

KUNSTLE, K. 1928
Ikonographie der Christlichen Kunst.

LACOMBE DE PREZEL, HONORÉ 1756
Dictionnaire iconologique.

LASAREFF, VICTOR 1938
Studies in the Iconography of the Virgin. *Art Bulletin*, vol. 20, pp. 26-65.

LAUCHERT, FRIEDRICH 1889
Geschichte des Physiologus.

LECLERQ, HENRI 1907
Manuel d'archaeologie chrétienne. 2 vols.

LEFRANCOIS-PILLION, LOUISE 1935
Les Statues de la Vierge à l'Enfant dans la sculpture française au XIVe siècle. Gazette des Beaux-Arts, vol. 14, pp. 129-149; 204-223.

LEHMAN, ROBERT 1928
The Lehman collection.

Literature Cited

LEHRS, MAX 1908
Geschichte und Kritischer Katalog des Deutschen, Niederlandischen un
Französischen Kupferstichs in xv. Jahrhundert. 9 vols.

LESMOINE, PAUL ANDRÉ 1931
Gothic Painting in France; 14th and 15th Centuries.

LEVERKUHN, PAUL 1890
Die Legende vom Stieglitz *Ornithologische Monatsschrift d. deutsch.
Verein z.Schutze der Vogelwelt*, vol. 15, p. 278.

LONGHI, ROBERTO 1930
Piero della Francesca (translated by Leonard Peulock)

—— 1934
Officina Ferrarese

LOS ANGELES ART ASSOCIATION 1937
Loan Exhibition of International Art, Catalogue.

LUTZE, Eberhard, and Wiegand, Eberhard 1937
Die Gemälde des 13 bis 16 Jahhunderts. Kataloge des Germanischen Na-
tionalmuseums zu Nürnberg.

MACCURDY, EDWARD 1932
The Mind of Leonardo da Vinci.

MACKOWSKY, HANS 1925
Michelangelo.

—— 1930
The Masters of the "Pesellino Trinity." *Burlington Magazine*, vol. 57, pp.
212-223.

MALE, EMILE 1908
L'art religieux de la fin du moyen âge en France: étude sur l'iconographie du
moyen âge et sur ses sources d'inspiration.

—— 1913
Religious Art in France, XIII Century. A Study in Mediæval Iconography
and its Sources of Inspiration.

—— 1922
L'art religieux du XIIe siècle en France.

MARTIGNY, L'ABBÉ 1865
Dictionnaire des Antiquités Chrétiennes, contenant le résumé de tout ce qui est essentiel de connaître sur les origines chrétiennes jusqu'au moyen âge exclusivement.

MARTIN, HENRY M. R. 1923
La Miniature française du XIIe au XVe Siècle.

MARY THERESA, SISTER, of the Cross Springer 1931
Nature-Imagery in the Works of Saint Ambrose

MATHER, FRANK JEWETT, JR. 1923
A History of Italian Painting.

MATTHIESSEN GALLERY, LONDON 1939
Exhibition of Venetian Paintings in aid of Lord Baldwin's Fund for Refugees.

MAYER, AUGUST L. 1913
Murillo. Klassiker der Kunst.

McCOMB, ARTHUR 1928
Agnolo Bronzino

McKENZIE, KENNETH 1914
Per la storia dei bestiarii italiani. *Giornale storico della letteratura italiana,* vol. 64, p. 358-371.

—— 1912
Concordanza di Petrarca.

MEISS, MILLARD 1936
The Madonna of Humility. *Art Bulletin,* vol. 18, pp. 435-464.

—— 1941
Italian Style in Catalonia. *Journal of the Walters Art Gallery,* vol. 4, p. 45.

Literature Cited

MICHEL, EDOUARD   1939
     Flemish Painting in the 17th Century.

MIGNE, JACQUES PAUL   1844-1855
     Patrologiæ Latinæ cursus completus; tom. xliii, cap. xl, col. 531-534; tom. clxxii, col. 958.

MILLAR, E. G.   1926
     English Manuscript Illuminations from the 10th to the 13th Centuries.

MOLMENTI, POMPEO GHERARDO   1903
     La pittura veneziana.

MOLMENTI, P. G. *and* GUSTAV LUDWIG   1907
     The Life and Works of Vittore Carpaccio (transl. by R. H. H. Cust).

MONGAN, ELIZABETH, *and* SCHNIEWIND, CARL O.   1941
     The First Century of Print-Making, 1400-1500. Art Institute of Chicago.

MONKHOUSE, COSMO (editor)   1907
     Heaton's History of Painting (Mrs. Charles Heaton).

MOREY, CHARLES RUFUS   1942
     Mediæval Art.

—— 1943
     Early Christian Art.

MORRISON, RICHARD C.   1931
     Some Paintings by Girolamo di Benvenuto. *Art in America*, vol. 19, pp. 140-146.

MUNOZ, ANTONIO   1905
     Iconografia della Madonna.

MUNSTER, LANDESMUSEUM DER PROVINZ WESTFALEN   1939
     Meisterwerke Holländischer und Flämischer Malerei aus Westfälischem Privatbesitz. Ausstellung veranstaltet in Gemeinschaft mit der Deutsch-Niederländischen Gesellschaft. August 6-October 22, 1939.

MUNTZ, EUGENE   1882
Raphael.

MURATOFF, PAUL   1935
La Peinture Byzantine.

NAPIER, HENRY EDWARD   1846-1847
Florentine History, 6 vols.

NEAL, J. M. *and* WEBB, BENJAMIN   1847
Du Symbolisme dans les Eglises du moyen âge. Avec une Introduction, des
Additions, et des Notes par M. L'Abbé J. J. Bourassé (pp. 255-402 is an
extended summary of William Durand's "Rationale Divinorum Officiorum,"
which was first printed at Mayence in 1459).

OETTINGER, KARL   1937
Altböhmische Malerei.
Zeitschrift f. Kunstgeschichte, vol. 6, p. 397.

OFFNER, RICHARD   1920
Niccolo di Pietro Gerini; pt. 2. *Art in America*, vol. 9, pp. 233-240.

——— 1927
Studies in Florentine Painting. The Fourteenth Century.

——— 1929
Four Panels, a Fresco, and a Problem. *Burlington Magazine*, vol. 54, pp.
224-245.

——— 1930-1934
A Critical and Historical Corpus of Florentine Painting. Section 3, vols. 1;
2, pt. 1 and 2; 3; 4.

——— 1932
The Works and Style of Francesco di Vannuccio. *Art in America*, vol. 20,
pp. 89-114.

——— 1933
The Mostra del Tesoro di Firenze Sacra, I. *Burlington Magazine*, vol. 73,
pp. 72-84.

Literature Cited

OJETTI, UGO, *and* L. DAMI 1934
 Atlante di storia dell' arte italiana. 2 vols.

OLINA, GIOVANNI PIETRO 1684
 Uccelliera overo discorso della natura et prorieta di diversi Uccelli.

OLPHE-GALLIARD, LEON 1890
 Contributions à la Faune Ornithologique de l'Europe Occidentale. Fasc.
 xxxii.

PANOFSKY, ERWIN 1924
 Die deutsche Plastik des elften bis dreizehnten Jahrhunderts. 2 vols.

—— 1938
 Studies in Iconology.

PAULY, AUGUST F. VON 1894
 Real Encyclopædie der classischen Altertumswissenschaft.
 (Edited by George Wissowa.)

PEREZ Y PANDO, JOAQUIN 1930
 Iconografia Mariana Espanola.

PERKINS, F. MASON 1908
 Spigolature. Rassegna d'Arte Senese, vol. 4, pp. 79-88.

—— 1925
 La pittura alla Mostra d'Arte di Montalcino. Rassegna d'Arte Senese, vol. 18,
 pp. 51-71.

—— 1931
 Pitture Senesi poco conosciute. VI *Diana*, vol. 6, pp. 244-260.

—— 1933
 Due Pitture Senesi inedite: Un quadro Duccesco-Una Pala Lorenzettiana.
 Diana, vol. 8, pp. 115-117.

PETRIE, W. M. Flinders 1914
 Amulets.

PHIPSON, EMMA 1883
    Animal Lore of Shakespeare's Time.

PIERPONT MORGAN LIBRARY 1940
    The Animal Kingdom.

PILLION, L. 1931
    Les Sculptures françaises du XIIIᵉ siècle.

PINDER, W. 1925
    Die Deutsche Plastik des Vierzehnten Jahrhundert.

PINEDO, RAMIRO DE 1930
    El Simbolismo En La Escultura Medieval Espanola (esp. pp. 51-60).

PLINY (translated by John Bostock and H. T. Riley, 1890)
    The Natural History of Pliny. 5 vols.

POLISH OWNED WORKS OF ART 1940
    New York World's Fair. Polish Pavilion.

POPE-HENNESSY, JOHN 1938
    Giovanni di Paolo.

—— 1939
    Sassetta.

POST, CHANDLER RATHFON 1930-1945
    History of Spanish Painting, 8 vols. to date.

POWERS, HARRY H. 1935
    The Art of Michelangelo.

PROCACCI, UGO 1936
    Gherardo Starnina; La critica moderna e il soggiorno dello Starnina en Spagna. *Rivista d'Arte*, vol. 18, p. 77.

PUDELKO, GEORG 1935
    The Minor Masters of the Chiostro Verde. *Art Bulletin*, vol. 17, pp. 71-89.

[*214*]

Literature Cited

QUEPAT, NERÉE (pseudonym for Henri René Paquet) 1873
   Monographie du Chardonneret.

REBER, B. 1900
   Vorsichtsmassregeln gegen die Pest in früheren Jahrhunderten.
   Korespondenzblatt f. Schweizer Aerzte, no. 21.

REINACH, SALOMON 1905
   Répertoire des peintures du moyen âge et de la renaissance. 4 vols.

—— 1924
   Apollo. An illustrated Manual of the History of Art throughout the Ages.
   New edition.

REYMOND, MARCEL 1897
   La Sculpture Florentine.

RICCI, CORRADO 1903
   Pinturicchio.

—— 1907
   La Pinacoteca di Brera.

—— 1910
   Piero della Francesca.

—— 1930
   North Italian Painting of the Cinquecento.

—— 1931
   Correggio.

RICCI, SEYMOUR DI 1910
   New Pictures by Francesco Napoletano.
   Burlington Magazine, vol. 18, p. 24.

RICE, D. T. 1935
   Byzantine Art.

RICE, JOHN PIERPONT 1908
   A critical edition of the Bestiary from the Acerba of Cecco d'Ascoli.

Literature Cited

RICHARDSON, GEORGE   1779
   Iconology, or A Collection of Emblematical Figures, vol. 2.

RICHTER, GEORGE MARTIN   1937
   Giorgio da Castelfranco, called Giorgione.

RICHTER, JEAN PAUL   1883
   The Literary Works of Leonardo da Vinci, vol. 2.

RIGATUSO, LUCIA   1934
   Bartolo di Fredi.   *Diana*, vol. 9, pp. 214-267.

RIPA, CESARE   1709
   Iconologia (English edition; London, B. Motle)

ROLLAND, ROMAIN   1935
   Michelangelo. Translated by Frederick Street.
   Bonibooks, N. Y.

ROSEN, FELIX   1903
   Die Natur in der Kunst. Studien eines Naturforschers zur Geschichte der
   Kunst.

ROSENBERG, ADOLF   1905
   Raffael: Klassiker der Kunst, vol. 1.

ROSS, MARVIN CHAUNCEY   1941
   The Master of the Orléans Triptych. *Journal of Walters Art Gallery*, vol. 4,
   pp. 9-25.

ROTHES, WALTER   1908
   Anfänge . . . der Altumbrischen Malerschulen.

RUSHFORTH, G. M.   1900
   Carlo Crivelli.

SALMI, MARIO   1932
   Masaccio.

SALTER, EMMA GURNEY   1912
   Nature in Italian Art.

Literature Cited

SANDBERG-VAVALÀ, EVELYN   1925
    La Pittura veronese del Trecento e del primo Quattrocento.

———   1929
    Le Croce dipinta italiana e l'iconografia della passione.

———   1934
    L'Iconografia della Madonna col Bambino nelle pittura Italiana del Dugento.

SAUNDERS, O. ELFRIDA   1932
    A History of English Art in the Middle Ages.

SCHARF, ALFRED   1936
    Filippino Lippi.

SCHLESINGER, MAX   1912
    Geschichte des Symbols. Ein Versuch.

SCHMECKEBIER, LAURENCE   1938
    A Handbook of Italian Renaissance Painting.

SCHÖPPLER, HERMANN   1909
    Ein Prager Pestarzneibuch aus dem Jahre 1679. *Janus,* vol. 14, pp. 725-745.

SCHOTTMÜLLER, FRIDA   1924
    Fra Angelico da Fiesole; *Klassiker der Kunst,* vol. 18.

SCHUBRING, PAUL   1923
    Die Kunst der Hochrenaissance in Italien: *Propyläen Kunstgeschichte,* vol. 9.

SEDGWICK, HENRY DWIGHT   1933
    Italy in the Thirteenth Century, 2 vols.

SERRA, LUIGI   1929-1934
    L'Arte nelle Marche, 2 vols.

SEYMOUR, WILLIAM WOOD   1898
    The Cross. In Tradition, History, and Art.

Literature Cited

SIGERIST, HENRY E.   1925
Deutsche medizinische Handschriften aus Schweizer Bibliotheken.
Archiv f. Geschichter der Medizin, vol. 17, p. 239.

SINGER, CHARLES   1917-1921
Studies in the History and Method of Science, 2 vols.

SINIBALDI, G.   1930
La Pittura del Trecento.

SIREN, OSVALD   1906
Dipinti del Trecento in alcuni Musei tedeschi di provincia.
Rassegna d'Arte, vol. 6, pp. 81-87.

——   1914
A Late Gothic Poet of Line.
Burlington Magazine, vol. 25, pp. 15-24.

——   1916
A Descriptive Catalogue of the Pictures in the Javres Collection belonging to Yale University.

——   1917
Giotto and Some of his Followers.

——   1920
Simone Martini et les peintres de son école.

——   1922
Toskanische Maler im 13th Jahrhundert.

——   1924
Three Early Florentine Trecento Pictures.
Burlington Magazine, vol. 45, pp. 285-291.

——   1926
A Madonna by Taddeo Gaddi.
Burlington Magazine, vol. 48, pp. 184-186.

Literature Cited

SIREN, O., AND BROCKWELL, M. W.   1917
Catalogue of a Loan Exhibition of Italian Primitives in Aid of American War Relief. F. Kleinberger Galleries, N. Y.

SKINNER, C. M.   1925
Myths and Legends of Flowers, Trees, Fruits, and Plants. 5th impression.

SPRINGER, ANTON HEINRICH   1884
Physiologus des Leonardo da Vinci. *Berichte über die Verhandlungen der Königlich Sächsischen Gesellschaft der Wissenschaften zu Leipzig, Phil.-Hist. Klasse, vol. 36, p. 244-271.*

SQUINDO SALE   1903
Catalogue.

STADLER, H.   1916-1920
Albertus Magnus: De animalibus libri xxvi. Nach der Cölner Urschrift. Beiträge zur Geschichte der Philosophie des Mittelalters.

STANGE, ALFRED   1934-1936
Deutsche Malerei der Gotik, 2 vols.

STEELE, ROBERT   1893
Medieval lore; an epitome of the science, geography, animal and plant folklore and myths of the middle ages; being classified gleanings from the encyclopedia of Bartholomew Anglicus.

STERLING, CHARLES   1938
La Peinture Française

STIX, ALFRED *and* ERICH V. STROHMER
Die Fürstliche Liechtensteinische Gemäldegalerie in Wien.

STRACK, HERMANN L. *and* BILLERBECK, PAUL   1922
Kommentar zum Neuen Testament aus Talmud und Midrasch. Vol. 1, Das Evangelium nach Matthäus.

STRUTT, EDWARD C.   1906
Fra Filippo Lippi

STRZYGOWSKI, JOSEF   1899
Der Bilderkreis des griechischen Physiologus, des Kosmas Indikopleustes und Oktateuch. (*Byzantinisches Archiv, 2.*)

SUDHOFF, KARL   1923
Pestschriften aus den ersten 150 Jahren nach der Epidemie des "schwartzen Todes" 1348, xv Pesttraktate aus dem östlichen Süddeutschland, Böhmen, und Osterreich in der 2. Hälfte des 15. Jahrhunderts. *Archiv für Geschichte der Medizin*, vol. 14, pp. 103-105.

SWAINSON, CHARLES   1885
Provincial Names and Folk Lore of British Birds.

TAYLOR, HENRY OSBORN   1911
The Mediæval Mind, 2 vols.

——   1920
Thought and Expression in the Sixteenth Century.

TESTI, LAUDADEO   1909
La Storia della Pittura Veneziana. Parte Prima, Le Origini.

THEOBALDUS EPISCOPUS (translated by A. W. Rendell)   1928
Physiologus: Metrical Bestiary. Facsimile of the 1942 Cologne print.

THOMPSON, D'ARCY WENTWORTH   1895
A Glossary of Greek Birds.

THORNDIKE, LYNN   1941
A History of Magic and Experimental Science, vol. 6.

TOESCA, PIETRO   1912
La pittura e la miniatura nella Lombardia.

——   1927
Storia dell' arte italiana, vol. 1.

——   1929
Florentine Painting of the Trecento.

Literature Cited

TOLNAY, CHARLES DE 1943
    The Youth of Michelangelo.

TROCHE, ERNST GÜNTER 1936
    Italienische Malerei des vierzehnten und fünfzehnten Jahrhunderts.

TROLLOPE, THOMAS ADOLPHUS 1865
    History of the Commonwealth of Florence, 4 vols.

TWINING, LOUISA 1852
    Symbols and Emblems of Early and Medieval Christian Art.

TYCHSEN, OLUF GERHARD 1795
    Physiologus Syrus, seu Historia Animalium XXXII in S. S. memoratorum,
    Syriacae . . . edidit, vertit, et illustrat O. G. Tychsen.

VALENTINER, WILHELM REINHOLD 1924
    Studies in Italian Gothic Plastic Art. II. Agostino di Giovanni and Agnolo di
    Ventura.
    Art in America, vol. 13, pp. 3-18.

—— 1930
    Unknown Masterpieces in Public and Private Collections.

—— 1935
    Tino da Camaino: a Sienese Sculptor of the Fourteenth Century.

—— 1938
    Catalogue of an Exhibition of Italian Gothic and Early Renaissance Sculpture.

—— 1938
    The Lost Giovannino of Michelangelo.
    Art Quarterly, vol. 1, p. 37.

VAN DYKE, HENRY 1894
    The Christ Child in Art. A Study of Interpretation.

VAN MARLE, RAIMOND 1929-1937
    The Development of the Italian Schools of Painting. 18 vols.

Literature Cited

VASARI, GIORGIO 1878-1885
Le Vite de piu Eccellente Pittori, con nuove annotazioni e commenti di Gaetano Milanese. 9 vols.

VENTURI, ADOLFO 1900
I quadri di scuola italiana nella Galleria Nazionale di Budapest. *L'Arte*, vol. 3, pp. 185-240.

—— 1900
La Galleria Crespi.

—— 1901-1938
Storia dell'arte italiana. Vols. I-XI.

—— 1902
The Madonna.

—— 1905
La Quadreria Sterbini in Roma. *L'Arte*, vol. 8, pp. 432-440.

—— 1906
La Galleria Sterbini in Roma.

—— 1931
North Italian Painting of the Quattrocento (Emilia).

—— 1931
North Italian Painting of the Quattrocento (Lombardy, Piedmont, Liguria).

VENTURI, LIONELLO 1911
Le origini della pittura veneziana.

—— 1926
La Collezione Gualino.

—— 1931
Pitture italiane in America.

—— 1937
Botticelli.

[*222*]

Literature Cited

VICENZA, MUSEO CIVICO 1912
Catalogue of the Collection.

VINCENT OF BEAUVAIS (1190 ? — 1264) not later than 1478.
Speculum naturale (Press of Adolf Rusch, Strasburg), 2 vols.

VIOLLET-LE-DUC, E. (n. d.)
Dictionnaire raisonné de l'architecture française du XIᵉ au XVIᵉ siècle.
10 vols.

VITZTHUM, GEORG, GRAF 1903
Bernardo Daddi.

—— 1907
Die rheinische Malerei zu Anfang des 14. Jahrhunderts auf ihre Quellen
untersucht.

VITZTHUM G., *and* VOLBACH, W. F. 1924
Die Malerei und Plastik des Mittelalters in Italien.

VLOBERG, M. 1937
La Vierge et l'Enfant dans l'Art Français, vol. 2.

VON HOVORKA, OSKAR, *and* KRONFELD 1909
Vergleichende Volksmedizin, vol. 2.

VON HOVORKA, OSKAR 1915
Geist der Medicin. Analytisce Studien über die Grundideen der Vormedizin,
Urmedizin, Volksmedizin, Zaubermedizin, Berufsmedizin.

(WALKER, JOHN) 1941
National Gallery of Art. Preliminary Catalogue.

WARDLE, WILLIAM L. 1936
Beelzebub (in Encyclopedia Britannica, ed. 14, vol. 3, p. 313).

WEALE, W. H. JAMES 1906
Netherlandish Art at the Guildhall.
Burlington Magazine, vol. 9, pp. 239-244.

—— 1912
The Van Eycks and Their Art.

WEBBER, FREDERICK ROTH 1927
Church Symbolism. An Explanation of the More Important Symbols of the Old and New Testaments, the Primitive, the Mediæval, and the Modern Church.

WEIGELT, CURT H. 1925
Giotto: Klassiker der Kunst, vol. 29.

—— 1928
Uber die "Mütterliche" Madonna in der italienischen Malerei des 13. Jahrhunderts.
Art Studies, vol. 6, pp. 195 ff.

—— 1930
Sienese Painting of the Trecento.

WEISBACH, W. 1901
Francesco Pesellino und die Romantik der Frührenaissance.

WELLMANN, M. 1930
Der Physiologus. Eine religionsgeschichtlich-naturwissenschaftliche Untersuchung.

WILLIAMSON, G. C. 1899
Francesco Raibolini, called Francia.

WILPERT, J. 1903
Le pitture delle catacombe.

WÖLFFLIN, HEINRICH 1913
The Art of the Italian Renaissance.

WOTTON, EDWARD 1552
De differentiis animalium libri decem.

Literature Cited

WRIGHT, THOMAS   1841
    Popular Treatises on Science during the Middle Ages.
    (Includes a translation of "Le Livre des Créatures" by Philippe de Thaun,
    ca 1121; pp. 74-131).

YOUNG, G. F.   1933
    The Medici. Modern Library edition. Chapter xi.

Index

Index

Andrea da Salerno, 101, 166
Andrea del Sarto, 67, 68, 71, 108
Andrew, St., 38, 148, 151, 153, 155
Angel appearing to St. Anne, pl. 10
Angelico, Fra, 30, 67, 68, 69, 77, 108, 142, 177, 182
Angers, Musée Napoléon III, 40, 66, 150
Animal Kingdom (Pierpont Morgan Library), 171
Anna Selbdritt, 49
Anne, St., 24, 38, 49, 139, 141, 155, 161, 174
Annesley-Gore collection, 160
Annunciation, 5, 19, 54, 55, 83
Ansanus, St., 38, 153
Anthony, St., 145
Anthony Abbot, St., 38, 91, 163
Anthony of Egypt, St., 38, 157
Anthony of Padua, St., 38, 100, 166
Anti-plague symbolism, 27, 87, 104
Antonello da Messina, 102
Antonello Palermitano, 167
Antoniazzo Romano, 105, 116, 168, 188, pl. 138
Antonio da Crevalcore, 39, 162
Antonio da Saliba, 167
Antonio Veneziano, 142, pl. 59
Apocalypse, 133
Apocryphal books of Bible, 39
Apolinar Sanchey collection, Madrid, 138
Apollonia, St., 38
Apostle Thomas, 31
Apple, symbol of death, 27, 55, 120
Apricarius, Charadrius, 11
Arezzo, 185
 " Pinacoteca, 44, 150
Aristophanes, 11
Arndt, W., 11, 171
Art Institute, Chicago, XII, 30, 52, 59, 95, 138, 140, 141, 163, 169, 175

Art Institute, Detroit, XII, 14, 74, 152, 183
Art, religious, 4
Ascension Day, 14
Ass, 88
Assisi, San Francesco, 64, 159, 160
Auber, M. l'Abbé C.A., 34, 175, 178
Augsburg, 174
Augsburg, Gemäldegalerie, 101, 166
Augur, disease, 2, 10, 75, 83, 87
Augustine, St., 38, 143, 154
Augustine, St., Expounding the Rules, 85
Austria, 5
Avanzo, 98
Aviform plaything, 25
Avignon, 46
Avila, cathedral, 49
 " school of, 19, 49
Aymard collection, 149

Baal, 27
Baalzebub, 27
Bacchus, 189
Bache collection, IX, 26
Bächtold-Stäubli, Hans, 175, 176, 178
Baldese, Ambrogio de, 141
 " " " Pseudo, 141
Baldovinetti, 67
 " school of, 40, 142
Baldung, Hans, called Grien, 37, 59, 118, 140, pl. 28
Baltimore, Walters Art Gallery, IX, XI, XII, 10, 41, 47, 52, 99, 138, 149, 150, 151, 157, 158, 159, 165
Bambino Vispo, 43, 78, 110
Banchi, 8, 115, pl. 54
Baptism, 33, 34, 73, 121, 131, 134
Baptist, cup of, 121
Baptist, St. John,
 see John the Baptist, St.
Barbara, St.

Index

Index

Index

Index

Index

Girolamo da Santa Croce, 157
Giusto di Menabuoi, 98
Golden oriole, 20
Goldfinch, 1, 2, 5, 7, 8, 9, 14, 16, 17, 18,
    19, 20, 21, 24, 25, 27, 29, 30, 31, 32,
    33, 34, 35, 37, 38, 39, 40, 41, 42, 43,
    44, 45, 55, 65, 66, 68, 73, 74, 75, 76,
    77, 78, 79, 80, 81, 82, 83, 84, 85, 87,
    88, 89, 90, 91, 92, 93, 94, 97, 98, 99,
    100, 102, 104, 169, 170, 172, 174, 175,
    176, 177, 178, 179, 180, 181, 182, 183,
    184, 185, 186, 188, 189
Goldfinch, Bohemian, 58
    ″   as disease augur, 60
    ″   in Dutch art, 56
    ″   entry of into charadrius
        legend, 23
    ″   in Germanic art, 57 ff
    ″   held in hand, 113
    ″   iconographic and stylistic
        details of, 107 ff
    ″   identified with charadrius,
        15
    ″   in Italian art, 62 ff
    ″   list of painting containing
        the, 137 ff
    ″   Michelangelo's treatment
        of, 126 ff
    ″   nest of, 29
    ″   open mouthed attitude of,
        112, 113, 114
    ″   protected patient from
        illness, 20
    ″   relation to other symbols,
        120
    ″   in Russian icons, 60, 61
    ″   and the scroll, 118
    ″   size of, 121 ff
    ″   on a string, 115
    ″   symbol of Death, 9
    ″   ″   ″ Fertility, 28
    ″   ″   ″ Resurrection, 7

Goldfinch, Symbol of Soul, 7
    ″   types of pictures in which it
        occurs, 36 ff
    ″   unattached, 117
    ″   upside down, 110
    ″   variations in coloring, 125
    ″   ″   ″ pose, 113
    ″   ″   ″ proportions,
        123 ff
    ″   white, 116
Golubitskaia, 60
Goldscheider, 129, 189
Gonfalone, anti-plague, 89, 186, pl. 120,
    121
Gonzaga, Francesco, 178
Gonzalo de Berceo, 12, 171
Gonziacus, Cardinal Franciscus, 178
Go-cart, 49
Good and Bad Government, fresco of,
    77
Good Preacher on Earth, 35
Gothic, French, 3, 4
    ″   Italianized, 75
    ″   painting, 46
    ″   sculpture, 59
    ″   tradition, 96
Göttingen, Gallery, 147
Gourd, symbol of Redemption, 120
Gozzoli, Benozzo, 87, 115, 117, 120,
    145, 184, pl. 60, 61
Graffione, 117
Grandi, Ercole, 95, 121, 123, 163
Greece, 60
Greenfinch, 121
Gregorio di Cecco di Lucca, 153
Griggs, Maitland F., collection, 74
Gualtiero di Giovanni, 77, 123, 153
Guariento, 98
Guercino, 93, 94, 162
Guido da Siena, 76
Guidoriccio da Fogliano, 77
Guinea fowl, 104, 121

[236]

Index

Index

Master of Fabriano Altarpiece, 26, 86,
    120, 123, 124, 159, pl. 112
    ″ ″ Horne Triptych, follower of,
    147
    ″ ″ Magdalene, 16, 62, 65, 147,
    173, pl. 33
    ″ ″ Mansi Magdalen, 54, 139
    ″ ″ Marble Madonnas, 183
    ″ ″ Orleans Triptych, 10, 52
    ″ ″ Pratt Madonna, 112, 153,
    pl. 87
    ″ ″ Rucellai Madonna, 19
    ″ ″ St. Cecilia, 147
    ″ ″ St. Cecilia, follower of, 147
    ″ ″ San Martino, 147
    ″ ″ San Miniato, 36, 72, 148
    ″ ″ San Miniato, shop of, 148,
    pl. 68
    ″ ″ San Torpé, 97, 164
    ″ ″ Siena Duomo Sacristy, 153
    ″ ″ Solsona Last Supper, 44
Matthew, St., 38
Matteo di Giovanni, 77, 154, pl. 86
Matteo di Giovanni, studio of, 154
Matteo di Gualdo, 159
Matteo da Viterbo, 46
Mauritshuis, The Hague, 6
Mazzola, Filippo, 106, 120, 163, 168,
    pl. 137
Medea, 189
Medicean Library, 16
Medici, 132, 190
Medici, Don Garcia de', 1, pl. 1
Medieval Spanish architecture, 51
Meditation on the Passion (Carpaccio),
    83, 84, 169
Megenberg, Konrad von, 18, 35, 174,
    178
Meinhard, Mrs. M. H.. collection, 19
Meiss, Millard, 42, 179, 180
Meissner, 12
Meister der Marter der Zehntausend, 59

Meister der Spielkarten, 59
Meister E. S., 59
Melozzo da Forli, 87
Memmi, Lippo, 77, 100, 119, 124, 154
Metropolitan Museum of Art, ix, xii, 37,
    51, 74, 83, 84, 90, 101, 114, 119, 142,
    149, 156, 163, 166
Mice, bringers of disease, 27
Michael, Archangel, 143
Michael, St., 38, 69, 146, 151, 153
Michelangelo, xii, 10, 41, 70, 75, 126 ff,
    179, 183, 188, 189, 190, pls. 139, 140,
    141
Middle Ages, 1, 2, 3, 22, 23, 25, 26, 29,
    31, 42
Milan, 63, 91
    ″ Brera, 20, 91, 100, 161, 163, 166
    ″ Cagnola collection, 152
    ″ Crespi collection, 161, 166
    ″ Museo Civico, 161
    ″ Poldi Pezzoli collection, 43, 161
Milanese art, goldfinch in, 62, 64, 91, 92
Milk of Doctrine, 44
Minor schools of Italy, goldfinch in the
    art of 96 ff
Misericordia Madonna, 44, 89
Missel des évêques de Paris, 2
Mocetto, Girolamo, 158
Modena, goldfinch in the art of, 62-64,
    100
    ″ Pinacoteca Estense, 97, 163
Mongan, Elizabeth, xi, 179, 184
Monica, St., 38
Monkey, 95, 121, 186
Montagna, Bartolommeo, 100, 166
    ″ Benedetto, 100, 166
Montalcino, Museo Diocesano, 151
Monte Sancto di Dio, 176
Montefollonico, S. Sigismondo, 151
Montelupo, Raffaelo di, 183
Montemarciano, Oratory, 43, 69, 146
Montepulciano, Gallery, 37, 153

[*244*]

Index

Index

Index

Index

Index

Index

PLATES

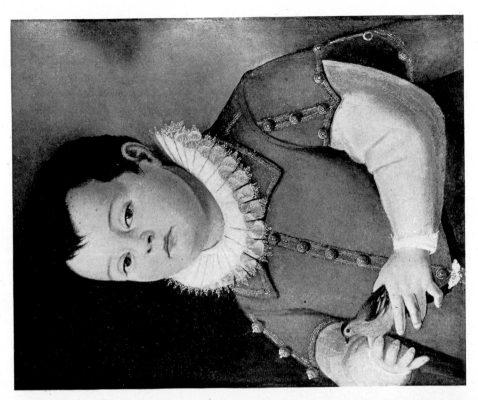

Pl. 2

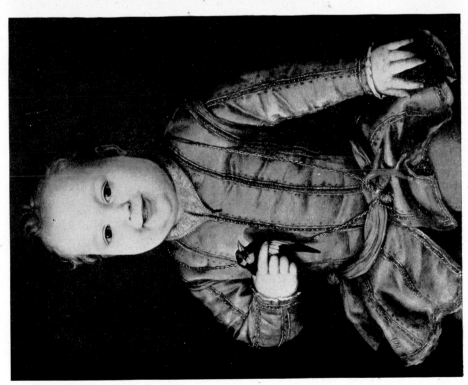

Pl. 1

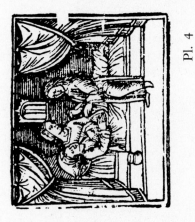

Pl. 4

Pl. 5

Pl. 3

Pl. 7

Pl. 6

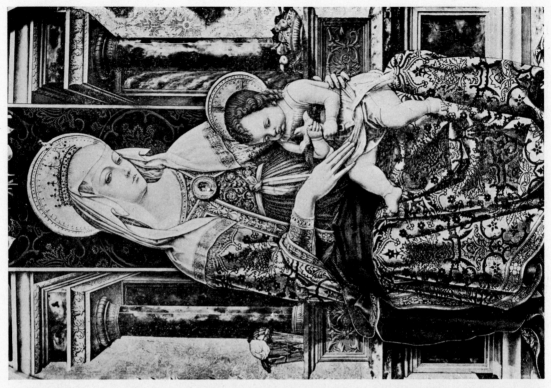

Pl. 9

Pl. 8

Pl. 11

Pl. 10

Pl. 13

Pl. 12

Pl. 15

Pl. 14

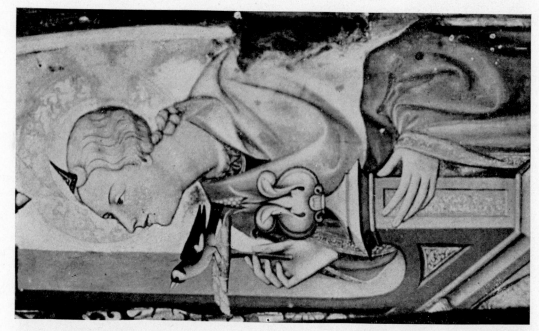

Pl. 16a

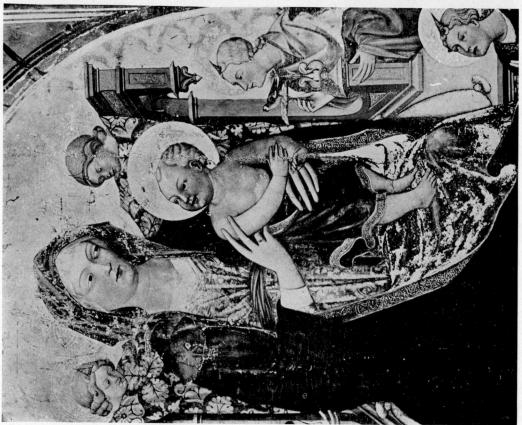

Pl. 16

Pl. 17a

Pl. 17

Pl. 19

Pl. 18

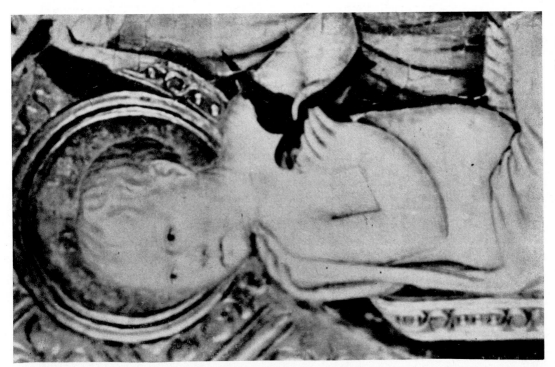

Pl. 20

Pl. 21

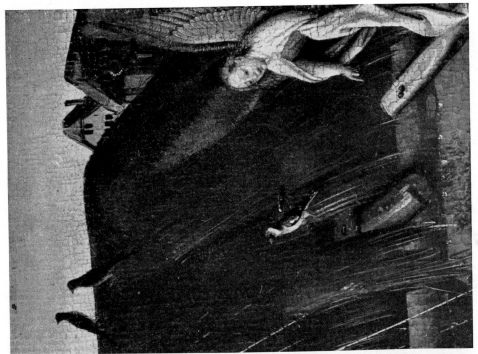

Pl. 22a

Pl. 22

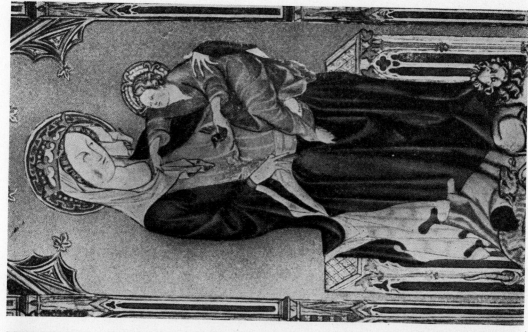

Pl. 24

Pl. 23

Pl. 26

Pl. 25

Pl. 28

Pl. 27

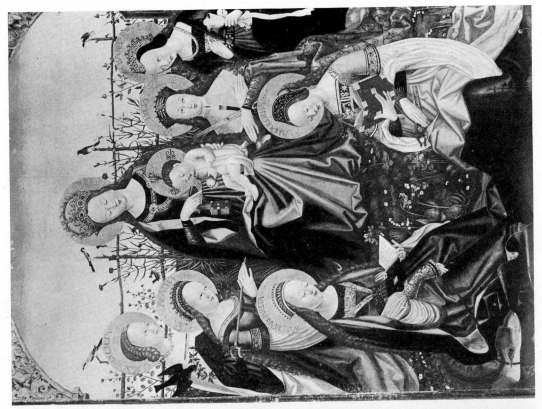

Pl. 30

Pl. 29

Pl. 32

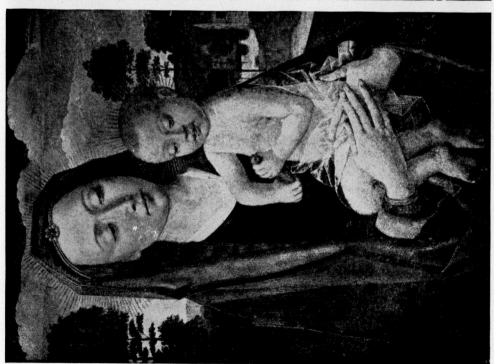

Pl. 31

Pl. 34

Pl. 33

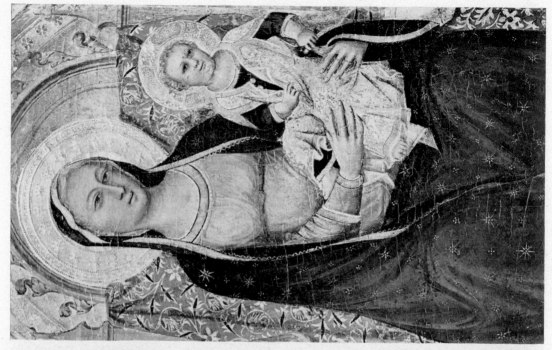

Pl. 36

Pl. 35

Pl. 38

Pl. 37

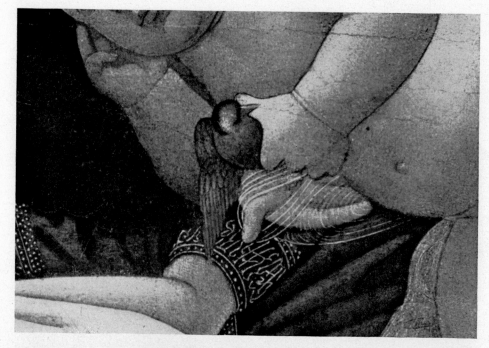

Pl. 40

Pl. 39

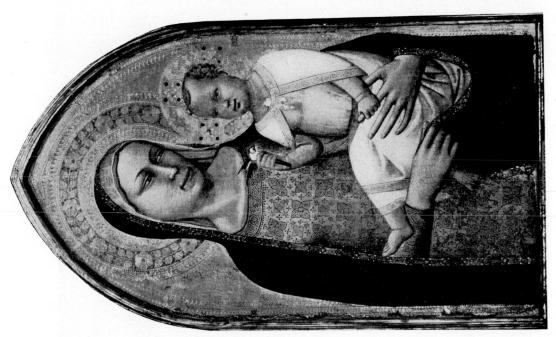

Pl. 41

Pl. 42

Pl. 44

Pl. 43

Pl. 46

Pl. 45

Pl. 48

Pl. 47

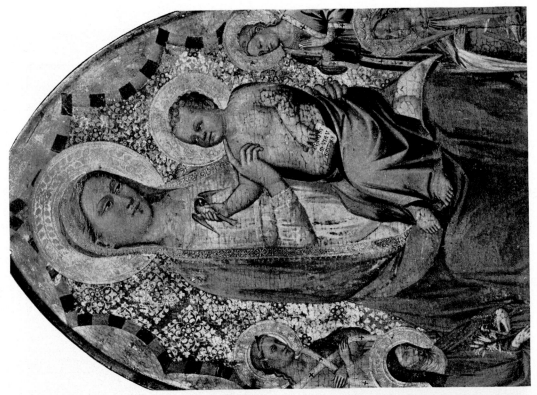

Pl. 50

Pl. 49

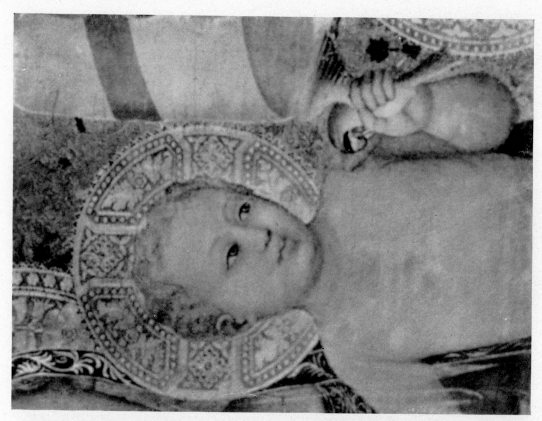

Pl. 51

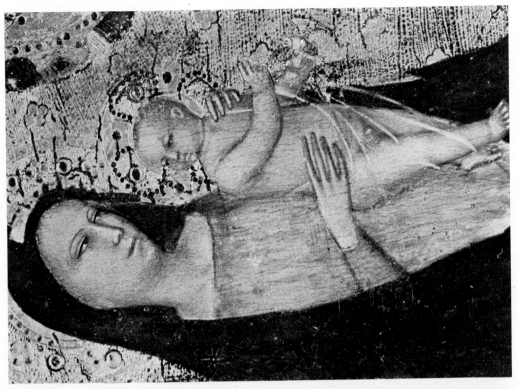

Pl. 53

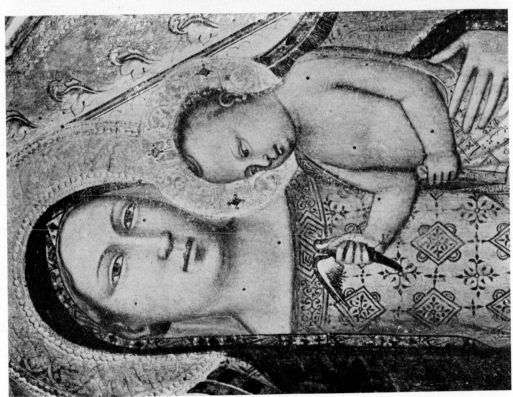

Pl. 52

Pl. 55

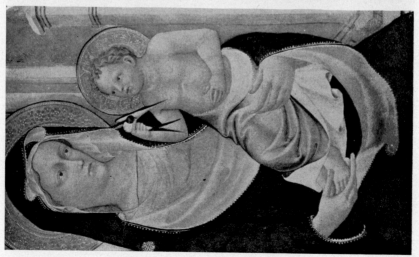

Pl. 54

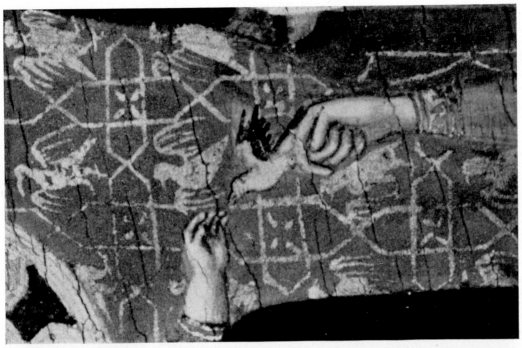

Pl. 56

Pl. 57a

Pl. 57

Pl. 59

Pl. 58

Pl. 61

Pl. 60

Pl. 63

Pl. 62

Pl. 65

Pl. 64

Pl. 66

Pl. 67

Pl. 68

Pl. 69a

Pl. 69

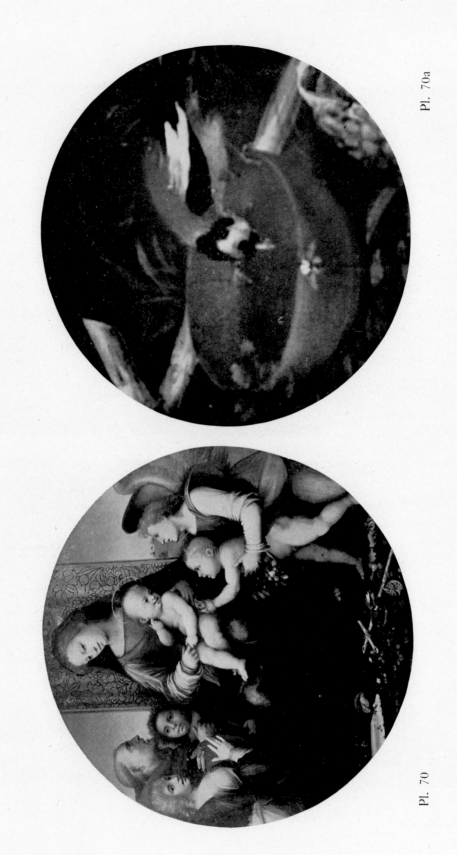

Pl. 70a

Pl. 70

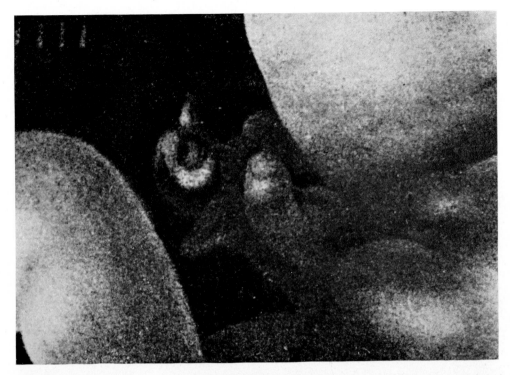

Pl. 71

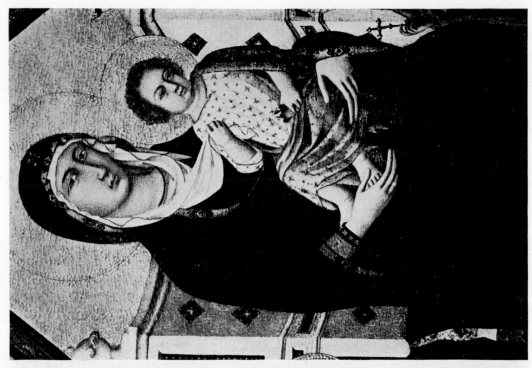

Pl. 73

Pl. 72

Pl. 75

Pl. 74

Pl. 77

Pl. 76

Pl. 79

Pl. 78

Pl. 80a

Pl. 80

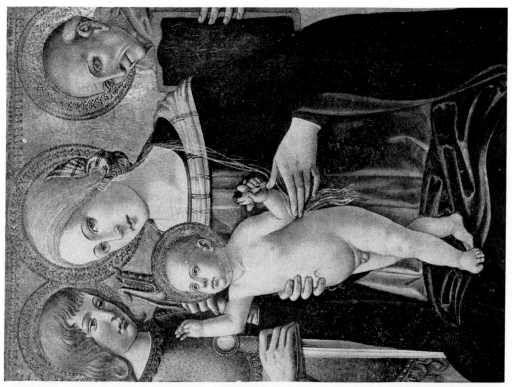

Pl. 82

Pl. 81

Pl. 84

Pl. 83

Pl. 88

Pl. 87

Pl. 90

Pl. 89

Pl. 92

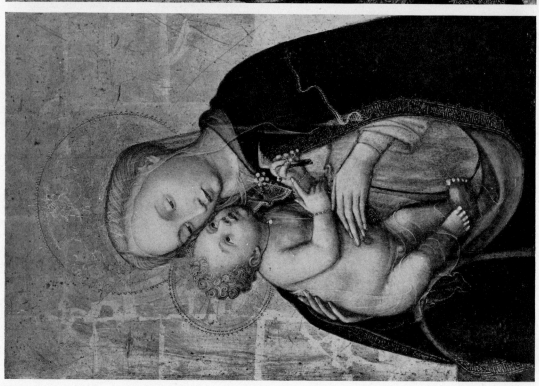

Pl. 91

Pl. 94

Pl. 93

Pl. 96

Pl. 95

Pl. 98

Pl. 97

Pl. 100

Pl. 99

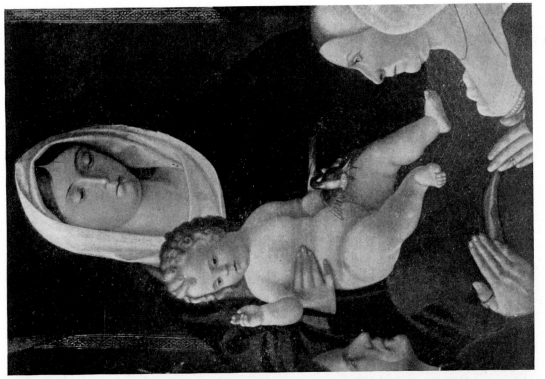

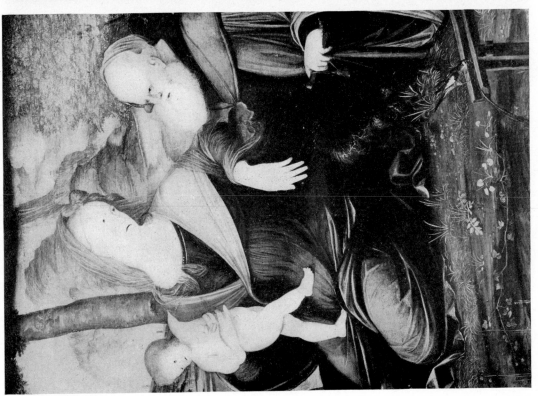

Pl. 102

Pl. 101

Pl. 104

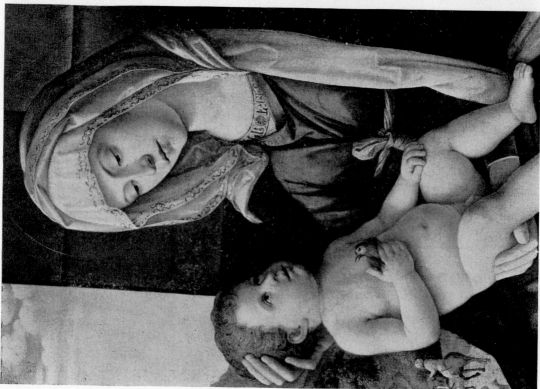

Pl. 103

Pl. 106

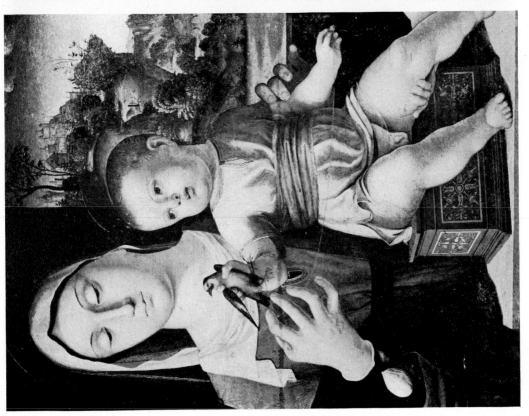

Pl. 105

Pl. 108

Pl. 107

Pl. 110

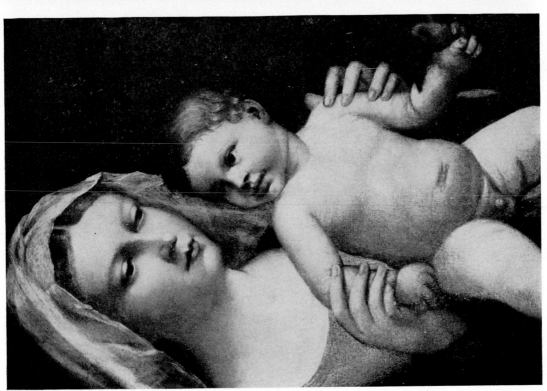

Pl. 109

Pl. 112

Pl. 111

Pl. 114

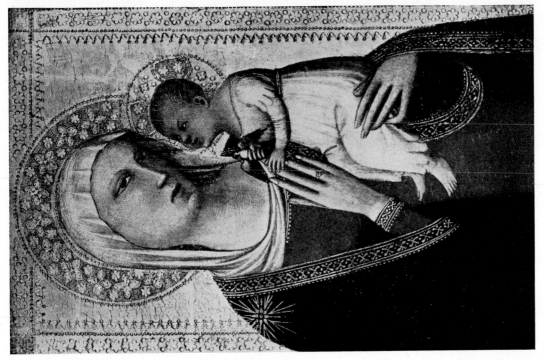

Pl. 113

Pl. 116

Pl. 115

Pl. 118

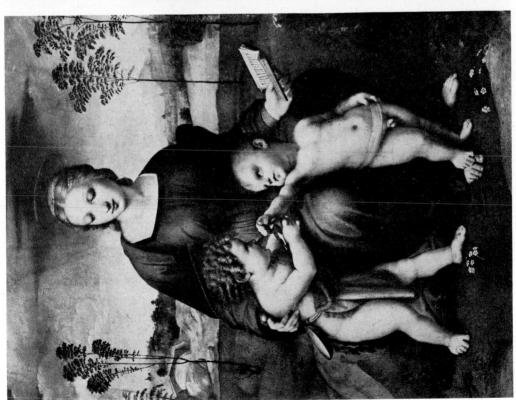

Pl. 117

Pl. 119

Pl. 121

Pl. 120

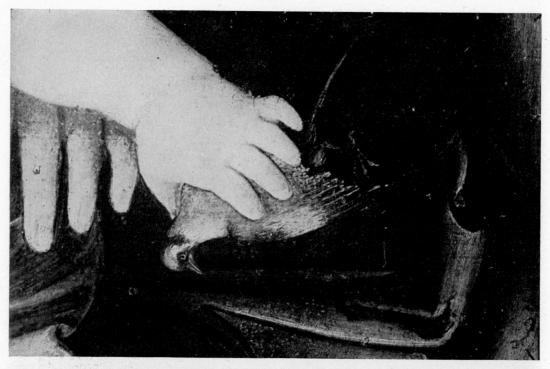

Pl. 122

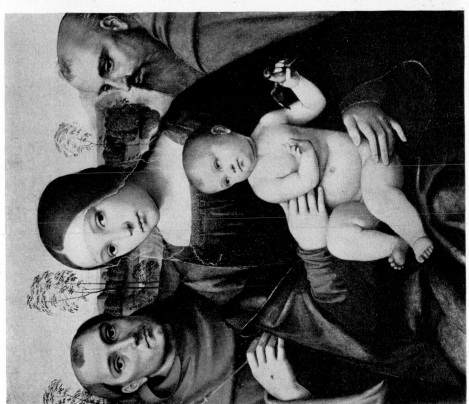

Pl. 124

Pl. 123

Pl. 126

Pl. 125

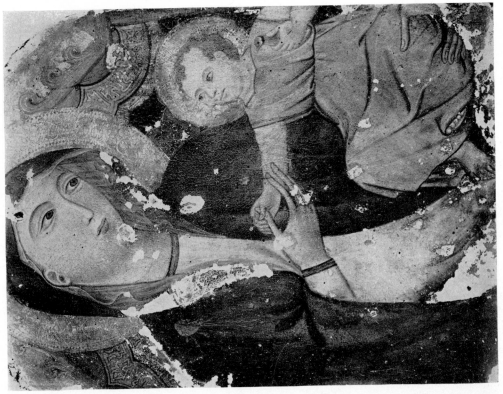

Pl. 128

Pl. 127

Pl. 130

Pl. 129

Pl. 132

Pl. 131

Pl. 133

Pl. 135

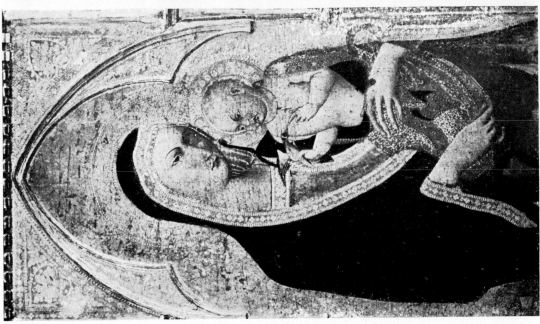

Pl. 134

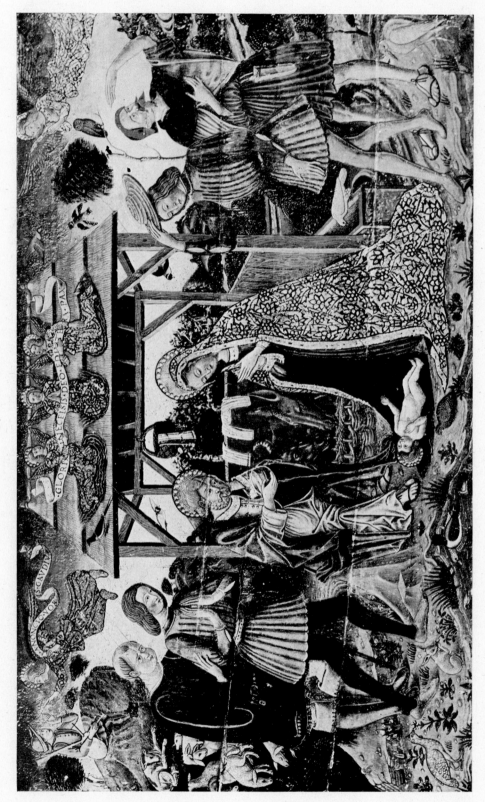

Pl. 136

Pl. 138

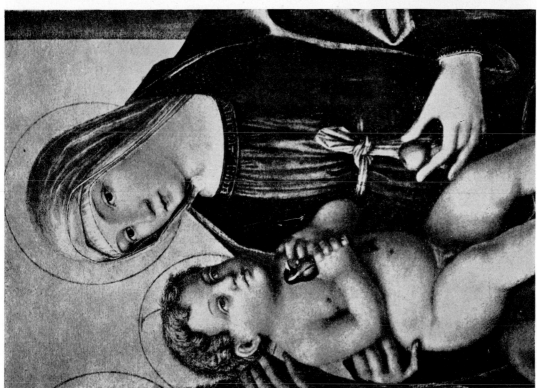

Pl. 137

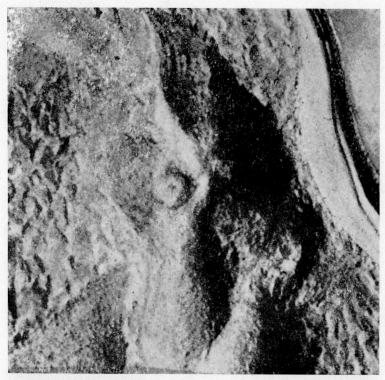

Pl. 139a

Pl. 139

Pl. 141

Pl. 140